The University of the Future

Recent Titles in
Contributions to the Study of Education

The University of the Future

THE YUGOSLAV EXPERIENCE

Miroslav Pečujlić

Translated from the Serbo-Croatian
and Edited by Tanja Lorković

Foreword by John W. Ryan

Contributions to the Study of Education, Number 22

GREENWOOD PRESS
NEW YORK • WESTPORT, CONNECTICUT • LONDON

Library of Congress Cataloging-in-Publication Data

Pečujlić, Miroslav.
  The university of the future.

  (Contributions to the study of education, ISSN
0196-707X ; no. 22)
  Bibliography: p.
  Includes index.
  1. Education, Higher—Yugoslavia—Aims and objectives.
2. Higher education and state—Yugoslavia. 3. Higher
education and state. 4. Educational sociology—Yugoslavia. I. Title. II. Series.
LA1008.P39 1987   378.497   86-31899
ISBN 0-313-25430-3 (lib. bdg. : alk. paper)

Library of Congress Catalog Card Number: 86-31899
ISBN: 0-313-25430-3
ISSN: 0196-707X

First published in 1987

Greenwood Press, Inc.
88 Post Road West, Westport, Connecticut 06881

Printed in the United States of America

The paper used in this book complies with the
Permanent Paper Standard issued by the National
Information Standards Organization (Z39.48-1984).

10 9 8 7 6 5 4 3 2 1

Many thanks to my colleagues Helen Ryan and Robert Felsing, who read the translation and gave me invaluable advice.

—Tanja Lorković

CONTENTS

Contents

FOREWORD

One of the constants of modern and modernizing societies of our time is an emphasis on education and educational issues. This is especially so in developing countries where issues of education touch on a wide range of social, economic, and ideological topics.

This study by Miroslav Pečujlić provides a most interesting case in point. Although focused primarily on the development and consequences of university reform in Yugoslavia, the study ranges widely over topics of social justice, economic development, and ideological perspective. In fact, the work might well be read primarily in the context of how educational organization and policy are quite deliberately shaped to reflect the goals and policies of the cultural and political framework within which they exist.

Education, especially university education, occupies a central place in the ideology of progress in capitalist and socialist worlds, but not because of a congruence of philosophy. Instead, capitalists and socialists both see a world driven by science-based phenomena characterized by an ideologically neutral physical universe. While the uses of science and knowledge can be manipulated and controlled in accord with ideology, the basic knowledge itself belongs equally to socialist and capitalist worlds.

Interesting are the quasi-universal constants that emerge from this analysis of Yugoslav higher education. In spite of a vocabulary specially suited to a socialist environment, the discussion of the major issues in Yugoslav higher education might have been presented at an American academic gathering, albeit couched in somewhat different terminology.

For example, Pečujlić offers a complex discussion of the role higher education plays in the maintenance of economic advantage, the continuation of elites, and the creation of self-perpetuating managerial classes. He discusses the flaws in meritocratic systems where tests of skill may give advantage to those whose parents have wealth and opportunity. He demonstrates that university education has often been more accessible to the children of the elite than to the children of less advantageously placed parents. He shows how the growth of technocracy has dramatically shifted the focus of privilege and advantage from land and property to education and the credentials and skills provided by higher education.

This analysis would surprise no American student of higher education, although the experience of the United States has been much different from that described in Pečujlic's analysis. Because of the fluidity of class and opportunity in the United States and also of the tremendous national investment in higher education institutions of all types that were begun in the nineteenth century and have been greatly expanded since the Second World War, many problems of access to higher education have been solved in this country. To be sure, not every school is equally accessible to all Americans, privilege and wealth still provide advantages to those who attempt to attend elite private institutions, but few nations in modern times have provided the range of educational opportunity to its citizens or achieved the high participation rate in higher education that the United States has.

In spite of this progress, in the United States and in much of the rest of the developed world, critics of higher education in the decades of the 1960s and 1970s focused on issues of access for minority groups, women, and other segments of the population regarded as disadvantaged. Programs to adapt the system of higher education to the needs of these special groups proliferated in the developed countries of the West. In the United States the goals of open admissions, affirmative action, student power, and the free university dominated the campaign. These challenges to American higher education in the 1960s and 1970s often involved an intense debate over those issues of equity, equality, and purpose that inform Pečujlić's work, and in the western industrialized countries, the discussion sometimes became heated and the action violent.

What lessons from the American experience, then, have relevance for Yugoslav initiatives? One consequence of the ferment in American higher education has been the realization that radical changes in the academy often have unintended results. Open admission and student involvement in educational design can, if not carefully implemented, lead to a serious reduction in the quality of education, even if also leading to improvement in access and reduction in the influence of privilege. Because the achievement of social goals and the achievement of scientific competence do not always follow the same paths to success, the pursuit of one can often impede the advancement of the other. If, in the effort to widen the base of university education, admission standards or graduation requirements decline, the quality of the institution's instruction may also decline unless special, expensive, and complex programs of remediation can be instituted.

The experience of American educational reform in the 1960s and 1970s demonstrated that the achievement of social goals and equity in higher education requires a massive investment in new facilities, techniques of instruction, and designs for excellence. Simply opening the doors of the university to new constituencies inadequately prepared for advanced study produces only the illusion of democratization, for the knowledge needed to succeed in science and technology requires background preparation and skills acquired only with some difficulty over the entire period of education from primary school through the university.

Indicative of the difficulty of higher education reform is Pečujlić's discussion of the "brain drain" and the derivative nature of transferred technology in the developing world. Here, of course, lies the great dilemma of higher education. By definition, developing countries have limited resources to fulfill the needs of their societies. Education, the sine qua non of a technologically advanced society, proves expensive, and rarely do the resources of a developing country extend far enough to provide world-class higher education to all of its citizens. However, if a developing country chooses to limit the numbers of citizens who can participate, it can afford better higher education, at the cost of creating or perpetuating intellectual and scientific elites and without any assurance that the educational system can produce or the nation can retain sufficient people with world-class skills.

Some developing countries attempt to shortcut the difficulties of constructing homegrown higher educational facilities by sending their advanced students overseas to the developed world to acquire needed skills. This is a strategy not emphasized in Pečujlić's work. Nonetheless, such a strategy, if implemented carefully and intelligently, can help a developing country jump forward rapidly, for it recognizes that the most difficult part of educational modernization is not acquiring modern facilities or up-to-date laboratories, but training the people who can use them to create, teach, and research.

In short, Pečujlić's work provides a most useful perspective for the English-speaking audience. It demonstrates the strengths and weaknesses of international educational statistics and clearly indicates the universality of higher education problems, whatever the ideological perspective of the analyst.

Such comparative analyses of education illustrate the complexity of cross-cultural comparisons; it often proves impossible to extract the university from its cultural and social context, to compare universities in the United States and Yugoslavia, for example, as if they belonged to essentially the same species. While the knowledge and science studied in these institutions are equivalent, their institutional connections to their societies could not be more different. Every university student body is a product of a school system from primary through secondary education that determines many of the characteristics of the university student. Issues of privilege, access, and preparation, while most easily seen at the university, can rarely be solved without changes in the entire school system.

Similarly, cross-cultural comparisons of institutional structures must take the complexity of these structures into account. To speak of American higher education as if a statistical average could encompass its variety and complexity for comparative purposes is to render the data presented meaningless. Generalizations that fit the experience of Harvard, Yale, or Columbia may have little relevance to the great public universities of America, and even less utility on reflecting the reality of small colleges or the community college system. Thus, cross-national comparisons of higher education must proceed with caution, lest the important comparative lessons be lost in the inadequacies of the data.

To outline the difficulties of comparative analysis, however, is to commend Pečujlić's discussion for raising many important issues, presenting useful case studies drawn from the Yugoslav experience, and advancing our understanding of the prospects and challenges of higher education development and reform. For this work, we all stand in Dr. Pečujlić's debt.

John W. Ryan
President
Indiana University

ACKNOWLEDGMENTS

I wish to express my greatest gratitude to the faculty and student participants of the many symposia devoted to the reform of the university, and to the various colleagues with whom I directly collaborated, namely, the prorectors, deans and student-deans of the University of Belgrade, the secretary of the University Committee, the president of the University Assembly and the presidents of the Youth Organization and trade unions.

I am especially grateful to the many participants of the symposia for raising so many fundamental questions regarding the reform of the university. More than fifty participants from the colleges of the social sciences, engineering, medicine, the natural sciences and mathematics, the bioengineering sciences, and the university institutes entered into fruitful discussions. These participants included the deans of the colleges, the secretary of the University Committee and the secretaries of the college conferences, the League of Communists, the student-deans, the members of the University Conference of the League of Socialist Youth, and the prorectors and rector of the University of Belgrade. My gratitude goes also to the participants of the Symposium of the League of Communists of the universities devoted to the self-managing transformation of higher education; to the participants of the Symposium on the Main Orientations of the Reform (January 1978) in which delegates from all colleges and delegates from the University Assembly took part; to the participants of the symposium devoted to the forms of the connections between the colleges, the economy, and social services in which the deans of colleges and the president of the City Conference of the League of Communists of Belgrade took part; to the participants of the Symposium of the Assembly of the University devoted to student participation in self-management; to the participants of the symposium devoted to the self-management of students in which the student assistant deans, the members of the University Conference of the League of Socialist Youth, the members of the editorial boards of the newspapers *Student* and *Vidici* took part; and to the participants of the symposium with representatives from the Chamber of Commerce of Belgrade concerning possible connections between the colleges and branch associations in the economy.

I am grateful to the rectors of the University of Niš and the University of Kragujevac, and to the members of the working group for the development of the preliminary draft of the document for the Commission for the Reform of Higher Education of the Assembly of the Socialist Republic of Serbia.

Many thanks to my friends who have read parts of the manuscript and have offered many valuable suggestions, and particularly to Professor Zoran Vidaković.

This work and others cited in the bibliography offer suggestions for practical measures and ideas regarding the reform of the university that have been expressed by my predecessors, the faculty, and students. Such are credited when they appear. We are not starting from untilled ground.

Miroslav Pečujlić

Part I

The Socio-Economic Basis of Education

1

THE UNIVERSITY
AND THE NEW REALITY

We live so submerged in the present that often we don't see how much our own era has changed within a single generation.

The condition in which higher education finds itself is not a simple extension of prior practice; the problems of today are essentially new. The universities are at a great historical crossroads, and we must begin to understand that they were not made for the world of today. The explosion of science and education is introducing us to a new epoch in the history of education. The university finds itself stretched between its traditional structure, which is directed at a small number of intellectually elite, and the demands of the legions of youth who are knocking at its doors. Once peaceful oases of knowledge, removed from the tempestuous mainstream of life, universities have become the decisive battlefield for social classes whose primary concern is the future of their children and the nature of the society in which they and their children will live. The storms that swept like hurricanes through the universities in the heart of the West and Far East have shown that higher education is becoming one of the decisive arenas for the clash of the mighty forces of our time—a violent aspiration for equality and the renewal of rigid class differences in a new form. What we are faced with today is not the necessity to correct details but the necessity to enact profound changes in order to face the alternatives that will encroach on the

Translator's explanatory comments appear in brackets within the text and in notes differentiated from those of the author.

fundamentals of the educational process. We are faced with the inevitability of a long-term period of social change, which is not only triggered by political demands, or a series of irrationalities, but by more profound causes, by the facts of new realities, by the demands of the era in which we live.

What are these new forces that have entered into our lives?

First, the laws of growth manifest themselves in a new light. The basis of forces of production has been largely altered. Already today and more so in the near future, development will increasingly depend on science and its application. Science is becoming the key factor in the development of civilization. At the same rate by which labor is removed from direct production, the sciences and their application become a much more powerful, productive force. They pervade the whole production process, become the basic impetus for progress, and, finally, the decisive factor in the increase of productive forces.

We should remind ourselves that we are the contemporaries of 90 percent of all scientists who ever lived, that in the last forty years there were as many scientific discoveries registered as there had been throughout all prior civilization. Society has come to a turning point where the patterns of the growth of forces of production are seen in a new light. The classical industrial revolution created as its educational basis an elementary school model that satisfied the needs of a simple labor force for factory production. Social development found its impetus in the intellectual forces of a relatively small number of people. The technical revolution that is now taking place is linked to a cultural revolution of unprecedented proportions. Radovan Richta describes this tendency as follows:[1]

	Classical Mechanization	Complete Automation
	Percentage of Labor Force	*Percentage of Labor Force*
Unskilled labor	15	—
Semiskilled labor	20	—
Skilled labor	60	—
High school education	4	60
College education	1	34
Postgraduate education	—	6

Once science has become the driving force of progress, education will assume the greatest significance. In the future, societies with the best educational systems will have the status previously given to those richest in resources or most highly mechanized.

Knowledge will assume the most strategic position among the numerous factors that lead to the increase of productivity; the influence of knowledge on the productivity of labor runs from 30 to 50 percent. The increase in the level of education of workers in the era of the scientific and technical revolution is more important for economic development than is the amount of capital investment.[2]

Edward Denison reports that in the United States of America from 1909 to 1929 the national income had been growing at the rate of 2.8 percent, and of that, 42.9 percent was attributed to a more highly educated work force. During the period of 1929 to 1957 the national income grew at the rate of 2.9 percent, and of that, education was given credit for 69 percent.[3] Research on the factors that influence the increase of national income was conducted in the United States of America, the Union of Soviet Socialist Republics, Great Britain, France, the Ivory Coast, the United Arab Republic, Denmark, Chile, and the Philippines. The results indicate that only one part in the increase of national income (20 to 40 percent) is a result of new investment, while 60 to 80 percent is due to education.[4] Stanislav Strumilin has proven in his studies that elementary education makes it possible for a worker to increase his efficiency and income by 79 percent, with a high school education by 235 percent, and with higher education by 320 percent. The expenses of a worker's education "pay off"; they are paid back to society within 1.5 years of the worker's employment.[5] Strumilin also states that 27 percent of the Union of Soviet Socialist Republics' national income is created by virtue of its investment in education.[6] Some results of research conducted in Yugoslavia on the influence of education on worker productivity have shown that education is a great factor in the increase of productivity.[7]

Secondly, we are living in an era of higher education for the masses, an epoch of the greatest cultural revolution of our time. The following facts show an X-ray picture of the stormy explosion of education:[8]

—In 1973 the world educational complex (without China and Vietnam) comprised a gigantic army of 532 million students, one fourth of the total world population.

—Within only two decades (1950-1970), there was a leap from 38 to 113 million students in high schools.

—This explosion was the most extreme, however, in higher education. Here is an image of the rhythm by which its turtle's crawl has changed into a horse's gallop:

1950   6.6 million students (3 percent of the population between the ages of 20-24)

1960   11 million students

1970   26 million students

1980   60 million students

1990   115 milion students (if the current trend continues; 24 percent of the population between the ages of 20-24)

—The number of teachers is rising dizzily; from 564,000 in 1950 to nearly 4 million in 1980.

The statistics reveal one surprising correspondence: within twenty-five years the number of students at universities will reach the number of high school students. This same correspondence can be extended to university professors whose number today equals the number of high school teachers twenty-five years ago.

In Yugoslav society there was a giant leap forward from 16,970 university students in 1937, to 424,000 in 1978; the number of students has increased 23-fold, and the number of professors 16-fold. On the eve of World War II, there were only 26 institutions of higher education in Yugoslavia; by 1978 there were 19 universities and 336 faculties, academies and other advanced institutions. In number of students, Yugoslavia has risen to the upper ranks of the European scale.

THE CONTRADICTIONS OF THE EDUCATIONAL "BOOM"

The educational "boom" is a gigantic driving force of technological and cultural development, but it also contains the seeds of dangerous contradictions.

First on the list of crises is the decline of educational quality in so massive an enterprise. Mass education does not have in itself to be poorer in quality. But any democratization of education invites a decline in intellectual standards. One of the key goals of the reform of the university is to prevent this decline. In changed "quantitative" circumstances, an effort on the part of schools to offer the same high quality presents a very delicate and difficult task.

Part of the problem is inefficiency: in West Germany, only 60 percent of the students accepted in the first year of university actually finish their studies. The same is true of Belgium. In France, the percentage is 57 percent; in Italy, 63 percent; and in Holland, 58 percent. Many students complete their studies after many years, and the number of those who never finish is high—somewhere between 20 and 30 percent.[9]

The manner of study becomes a serious problem too: the protracted separation of youth from work and real life has grown into pathological proportions. The university becomes "an escape" from production and labor. Particularly in the developing countries it is the consistent practice to educate too many students in the humanities and law and not enough in natural and technical disciplines. For instance, it is an unfortunate paradox that the agricultural countries have the weakest schools of agriculture.

There are increasingly limited job opportunities for students, and the more and more painful discrepancy between the aspiration to study and the inability to find employment is reaching dramatic proportions. The schools are becoming "gigantic containers" for the young, who appear to be unneeded.

This whole array of problems, that superficially appears as a series of "internal" irrationalities within the university, reflects the much deeper irrationalities of society. This we shall discuss later. At present we wish to state the following facts:

Universities find themselves stretched between a traditional structure created for, and directed at, a small number of the intellectual elite and the contemporary epoch of mass higher education, with an ever increasing number of young as well as adults who are knocking at their doors. Is it possible for higher education to keep its traditional structure (which essentially hasn't changed since its beginning) in an epoch of mass higher education? Is there a substantial difference between the institutions of higher education that had six million students yesterday and those that will have 100 million tomorrow? What can be preserved from the traditional organization and methods, and what has to be replaced to suit better the aspirations of human beings and the needs of society? What are the objectives of a university education? Who will be allowed to study? What should one study, and how does one do so? Is the university also a scientific or research center? Is the university an institution that is taking care only of community needs, or is it also fulfilling personal aspirations? How does one solve the relationships between quality and quantity under the existing conditions of mass education? All these themes together with the even more fundamental problem of the role of the university in keeping or changing a class society are proclaiming the crisis and the new horizons of education.

The time has passed when higher education is considered a luxury rather than a social necessity. The growth of higher education is inevitable—the universities will become the basis of mass education in the near future. It would be impossible and wrong to curb admission to the universities. Placing limits on enrollment would not be the correct solution to the problem because the acquisition of higher education is an expression of democratic aspirations—the intent to minimize social differences. All-encompassing higher education is not only a social issue, but a means by which all productive forces of a society could be engaged. The bare facts reveal that the world's most advanced industrial powers have the greatest degree of highly trained manpower. Top-level science can only be developed if there is a broad base from which to choose. Here are the percentages of young (18-25) that are entering institutions of higher education: in the United States of America, 49 percent;[10] in East Germany, 33 percent; in Japan, 26 percent; in the Union of Soviet Socialist Republics, 23 percent. These differences in percentages are even more noticeable if we observe the gaps in world proportions:[11]

U.S.A.	40.9%
U.S.S.R.	26.0
Sweden	18.2
Japan	17.1
France	15.9

Bulgaria	15.9
Argentina	15.2
Poland	14.9
Czechoslovakia	14.5
Yugoslavia	13.5
Romania	11.3
Italy	9.7
Peru	8.6
West Germany	8.4
Hungary	7.6
Spain	7.3
Mexico	4.4
Iran	3.5
Tunisia	2.5
Indonesia	2.1
Libya	0.9

The gap is charged with contradictions of volcanic proportions—it is 1:500.

In 1972 the money spent for education worldwide was $223,000,000,000—or 5.7 percent of the gross income. (In 1960 the percentage was 3.9.) Out of that 223 billion dollars, 207 (or 92 percent) was spent on education in developed countries, and only 16 billion dollars (or 7.7 percent) in developing countries. Consequently, the developed countries with one-third of the total population and one-quarter of the young have spent ten times more for education than the developing countries. This huge gap continues to expand. Yet even the Third World has been gradually affected by the mass expansion of education.

We should try to understand the causes of this great educational expansion and begin to develop new perspectives, new paths that will offer the possibility of more productive solutions. The emergence of mass education results both from the action of several powerful present day forces and from those of a future that has already begun.

Higher education is the most fluid of all collective activities. Its aspirants exhibit many different individual ambitions and social needs. These demands are very difficult to satisfy while at the same time maintaining peace. Because of this problem, it is impossible to limit substantially or precisely plan or establish a continuum from higher education to immediate employment. But what is possible and even indispensable is to provide more direction, to establish a better balance between the goals of education and those of social welfare.

Although individual educational institutions have their relatively independent histories as well as their own dynamics, their turbulent development is a consistent expression of similar social forces. A study of the nature of the demands on higher education reveals that higher education attempts to satisfy many different functions—it is a civilizing, productive, and social activity all in one. At the same time this complex entity contains a range of interacting contradictions; like Pandora's box it is overflowing with difficulties and hopes.

FUNCTION OF CIVILIZATION

Modern civilization is characterized by a more developed consciousness of the value of knowledge and culture—goods that are increasingly more esteemed per se. The education of a person becomes an important part of his inner life; it becomes indispensable to the development of a free and versatile personality. The desire for spiritual growth, for the transcendance of one's limitations, for a richer inner life, for an understanding of the world and the ability to participate in it—these desires have become a driving force of our time. Refined culture that provides social prestige and spiritual satisfaction has magnetic power.

The desire for education becomes a basic personal need of contemporary humans. It has its own source, its independent orbit, that isn't solely dependent on technological and social demands. This concentrated urge expresses the point of development that the human race has reached—the homo sapiens of the end of the twentieth century. It is an expression of the historical and anthropological evolution of the basic attributes of man as a generic, natural-historical, cultural being. It is an expression of the need to develop one's own faculties, to become a full member of the race, to live the life of contemporary humankind.

This desire is the result of a great cultural revolution of our epoch that took place practically unseen. It is a result of the evolution of Gutenberg's Galaxy within which our lives are taking place: the development of the press, radio, television, electronic information systems, universal city culture, notwithstanding the serious limitations and pathological distortions of mass culture. A new world was formed by people, a new cradle where, from infancy on, one participates in the life of the world, where every day one also experiences a microcosm of the planet, where one is fed on new cultural juices.

This radical change is becoming more obvious with each generation. Of course, there will be people without these aspirations—there will always be spiritual dwarfs as there are physical ones. But the human multitude is the bearer of this aspiration. The need for education becomes almost instinctive. Yet at the same time, it is a new kind of rationality that aims at the development of one's talents, that manifests the demand for equal participation in contemporary life. It is a rare individual who accepts lower class status—a modern pariah closed in the ghetto of ignorance will fight to cross the cultural barrier that will free him from inferiority.

Class differences are more difficult to endure not only because of material inequity but also because the development of culture is making these differences unacceptable. For thousands of years, people accepted class inequality almost as a natural phenomenon. But this structure has been shaken, the predetermination of divine descent, the biological reasons for upper classes ("the blue blood") have been done away with—this sort of discrimination is barely acceptable to the young. As society is freeing itself from material privation and as mass culture is growing, unprecedented egalitarian aspirations are taking place. "I am not inferior, I am not a person of less value although I am poor—I want to have the education that others have, or if it is not available to me, my children will get it."

This feeling touches the depth of a person's soul; it hits harder than does any discomfort from material disparity. And this feeling is the real progress of civilization and culture; this is the fruit of a plant that has bloomed for a long time. A big wave of new human needs has risen and this wave cannot be repressed. Concessions have been made, but it is still not well understood how irrepressible this force is. It is an administrative error to imagine that one can program a slowdown of this vital force. The force will not submit itself exclusively to the demands of technology and politics, it has a life of its own as well.

Although this great human aspiration sometimes gets twisted and deviates into a fight for prestige or competition for positions, for social success, still education contains great revolutionary potential. Human faculties are becoming the most revolutionary productive force of our time, a force that cannot be controlled by the Procrustean methods of profiteering logic or the sterilizing bureaucratic organization of labor. Technology can easily be adjusted to function within the old world of the division of labor. But it is more difficult to do the same with human talents. The societies that do not accept that fact will go through a period of great disorganization and shock.

PRODUCTIVE FUNCTION

Mass expansion of higher education is a component of the scientific and technological revolution; it is needed to provide the expert cadres for a modern industrial society. This productive function of education conflicts with an economy based on the profiteering usage of cheap labor. It also has its battles with the bureaucratic organization of work that more easily manipulates and rules the less educated. Both systems devalue education, preserve incompetence, and perpetuate the unemployment of educated people. Inadequacies within the economic system and the ossified hierarchical division of labor, together with existing material difficulties all combine to promote unemployment among the educated. There is a surplus of creativity that society does not know how to use. At the university this contradiction is sharpened. The university is causing society harm. It becomes a place where the employment difficulties of the young are post-poned rather than solved.

There is an additional method of invalidating the expert cadre. Side by side with the flourishing of the scientific-technological revolution two contrary developments are taking place: the level of education of the active working force is being raised, and there is a contrary tendency to lessen its value.

One development is a general elevation of the cultural and educational level of the employed as a result of the hidden needs of production in the epoch of technological civilization. The working process becomes a mechanism as complex as the finest watch, develops into a complex entity in which all individual processes depend on each other and are connected by invisible links. If one part stops, the whole system is paralyzed. The system functions because of the perfect cooperation of all individual positions. The whole depends on each individual—this is a principle of modern, complex technology.

Such real interdependence demands a broader insight, a broader base of knowledge and a greater competence from each individual. A higher and higher level of professionalism of a *collective worker* (that is, of a working body in its entirety) is needed. An understanding of the technological process must be broader than the mere knowledge of the narrowest job or of a few partial work operations. This aspect of production is not obvious as long as the system functions smoothly. The moment something goes wrong, it is necessary to understand all parts of the whole in order to be able swiftly to establish and, by collective activities, to eliminate the cause of disturbance and reactivate the production process. For this process are necessary a sound level of expertise, the ability to communicate at a professional level, and an understanding of the technological processes and the ways that they are activated. In critical situations it is not enough only to know which button to press. A real need is, therefore, a higher culture, greater expertise, and a much broader understanding of the whole by all the participants. They must be able to operate in ever more complex technological processes. From this need stems the strong trend for raising the level of education, the trend for mass higher education.

But the main goal of economics is profit and not the development of faculties. And herein is contained the action of the contrary trend. Capitalism and bureaucracy are exploiting those broader faculties and expertise, but they are paying only for the one narrow segment that relates to the immediate work place. They are paying less although they are using much more; they are paying wages only for the immediate task. Productivity, which is the result of the linkage of individual operations and knowledge—the result of collective expertise—is being seized as a free gift. The worker's knowledge and abilities are used but he is left unacknowledged and underpaid.

The growing body of human talent and the commensurate phenomenon of inadequate pay for this talent is a fact of our time. Mass higher education has reduced the price of the labor force. People have been constrained to accept this situation under the economic coercion of unemployment and the tough competition of the labor market. Mass higher education is needed for the management of the new productive forces that people have created. But the recognition of just a fraction of these achievements and subsequent inadequate pay for them are the answers of capitalism and bureaucracy. Surplus value is being drained from workers and converted into instruments for the accumulation of someone else's wealth. Society as a whole contributes to the expense of education, but the products of this underpaid expertise are seized gratis by the proprietors/ruling class. The dequalification of the professional labor force becomes a new form of drainage of surplus value.

The economic coercion that forces people to accept the fact that they are less able than their potential would have them be, that they utilize fewer qualifications than they have, is a form of human disablement. In this, one can already discern a phenomenon (which will be discussed later in detail)— that of a glaring contradiction between human capabilities and their reduction to mere goods. This phenomenon is identified through the realm of economics, but higher education is taking an active part in its formation.

The real driving force and logic by which the scientific-technological revolution is growing is still not a free evolution of either the potential that the new forces of production carry within themselves or the revolutionary potential that is surpassing the limits of all former assaults of civilization. By their essential characteristics, these forces belong neither to the technocratic systems of the bourgeoisie nor to bureaucratic socialism—both having too narrow a framework for their full capacity and their human usage. This is a limited scientific-technological revolution that is set in motion by the narrow goals of the maximization of surplus value and bureaucratic power.

SOCIAL FUNCTION

In addition to technological necessity, there are other forces that influence the fast growth of higher education. Higher education finds itself exposed to the conflicting interests of different social groups. The university is no longer a secure haven for the education of the children of the wealthy. It cannot bar from its classrooms the children of the less privileged classes. Education is seen as a remedy that can alleviate the suffering caused by the divisions of society—the remedy that can lead to social equality. What used to be a privilege is now looked upon as a right of all citizens. If one does not go to school, his social status is lower.

The fight for democratic reforms within education has produced many fruits; it has lessened cultural barriers and reduced social segregation in many countries. Yet equality in education cannot be gained only through changes in the existing school systems. There is also an opposing trend that transforms higher education into a new, large mechanism that maintains social inequalities and provides the basis for stratification. Inequality is maintained through education. The right to education leads to economic privilege and power, to high social status. A chance to enter well-paid and highly prestigious professions depends more and more on education. Education becomes the most important inheritance that one can bequeath to children. Education takes the form of "cultural capital," a particular form of private property that is a substitute for actual inheritance. It becomes the transmission of power and privilege. Because of these motives, large numbers take part in the race for education. They are overcoming the hurdles that in many countries still prevent the masses from achieving higher education.

The forceful spread of the new forces of science and mass education is anything but a linear development of peace and harmony. On the contrary, the development of science and education is a profoundly contradictory and explosive process in which several powerful social forces clash. The destiny of education, and of many aspects of society as well, depend on the outcome of this clash. We shall discuss this construct of fighting forces later. For the sake of illustration, there is a large discrepancy between the productive and social functions of higher education. Production—based both on the profiteering motive and the maintenance of hierarchical power but not on the development of human needs and abilities—and social needs dramatically clash with each other. The social function contributes more towards mass higher education than does the profiteering motive that is trying to limit it. This contradiction is one of the hidden causes of unrest at institutions of higher education and consequently within society as a whole, of the unemployment of the young intelligentsia, and of the trend to employ the young in jobs for which they need fewer qualifications than they actually have.

The combination of the rapid growth of the number of students and many contradictory social functions are challenging the traditional, closed form of the university. The crisis is universal—from the highly developed countries to those of the Third World. It is not temporary because the university does not exist in a vacuum. Its inner irrationalities signify the deep contradictions of contemporary society, they are an aspect of the crisis of civilization. The university will either be able to form new perspectives or it will add to the explosive danger. This is where a real issue is. Because the contradictions of higher education have such deep roots, they will not be mastered easily or swiftly.

2

THE CRISIS OF
THE TRADITIONAL UNIVERSITY

Science and higher education are the decisive driving forces of technological and societal development.[1] The university, once an enclave isolated from powerful social movements, a second-class superstructure, now becomes a decisive battlefield for the conflict of powerful contemporary trends. The character and direction in which the university will develop, and not merely quantitatively, are portentous elements in the development of society. Decisions between such important alternatives as private ownership or nationalization, self-governing socialism or bureaucratic collectivism, depend on them. The type of society that will be formed depends to a great extent on what kind of education and what quality of science are chosen to be developed. Science, the organization of knowledge, is the most powerful force in the development of civilization in society; it is able either to direct us to modernity or oppress us through technological colonization and thus delay authentic self-development.[2] Education offers the hope for a democratic society; it can dispel class differences from generation to generation; it can lead towards a community of free producers.

Nevertheless, science can be used as a tool to preserve the old civilization; it can administer a transfusion of fresh blood into its worn-out forms. By using the human work force as hired labor in the service of profit or bureaucratic power (which means a monopoly of privileges for one group and deprivation for the others), this outmoded structure can acquire a new front. Higher education has become a great historical arena where social classes battle for the future of their sons and daughters. The hopes for a better future depend on that extraordinary power, the availability of education for all. Struggles about the kind of education to be achieved are vital to the struggle for a different world. Two great events that swept two different parts of the planet—the radical student upheavals of 1968 in the heart of the Western world, and enigmatic events in the Far East, the Great Proletarian Cultural Revolution in China—are living testimony to the battles waging around the citadel of the university.

The social functions of science and education should be taken into more account when attempting any reforms of the university. This vital aspect of the university leads to questions: what kind of university and what kind of society do we desire? The two questions are closely connected, for they are offering a choice among possible futures.

The university is at a turning point of historical importance, a line between technocratic reform and the possibility of a genuinely socialist university.

This great crossroad, this duality of possible future, is caused by the twofold character of contemporary science.[3] The general public has a split, seemingly "schizoid," attitude toward science and technology, an attitude where images of heaven and hell, fear and hope, complete social pessimism and naive optimism unite. This attitude expresses a basic intuitive truth: this same power than can free humanity, that can create a society in which it is possible to meet human needs, can oppress the whole of mankind. This twofold potential of science expresses the two faces of the general dialectic of contemporary civilization. These two images of science—its use and abuse—will be analyzed.

TWO FACES OF SCIENCE

One of the finest creations of civilization is the convergence of higher education and science, and along with that, the university as a place where knowledge is created and transmitted. The university is the center of a gigantic accumulation of erudition, of the development of intellectual ability, of universal cognition, of the search for truth—all this is a record of civilization. But, because of all these qualities, the university is often captive to the conservative cry: "The tradition of all the dead generations weights like a nightmare on the brain of the living."[4] From this derives the university's other aspect—pedagogical conservatism, resistance to innovation, bookish knowledge too far removed from actuality.

The tree of knowledge and the tree of life appear to belong to different worlds. Higher education is the masterpiece of civilization made up of class societies. What has the potential of universal knowledge and promoting values is transformed into a monopoly of the elite; it tends to form the young within the narrow demands of a given system without attempting to cross its borders. The universal value of knowledge and this narrow configuration are joined like Siamese twins. But the university has also been the expression of one other great cultural aspiration—from antiquity through the Renaissance—an aspiration not exclusively connected to the ruling class. That is the universal development of culture that conquered all limitations and did not permit higher education to become the trophy of a small circle of the elite. Modern science has grown from the spiritual ground that always had a twofold image, a "double life," and it is forcing the contradictions of the two sides to the breaking point.

Humans have conquered gigantic new production powers that have brought us to the threshold of a new world. Scientific and technical achievements unknown to earlier epochs have entered our lives. In the last 50,000 years of human existence, there were about 800 life units (generations) with an average lifetime of approximately sixty years. Six hundred and fifty of these life units were lived in caves; only during the last seventy was it possible to have some communication between the generations; only during the last seven has the printed word been known; within the last two, the electrical motor has been utilized, and the majority of today's products have been developed within the last life unit. Atomic energy, automation, and cybernetics bring new possibilities that will completely change our traditional life and work.

Each production method has its own principles and driving force. In the limited production of artisans, the quantity and quality of workers were decisive; in classical industrial production the structure became more diffuse through the employment of capital and a larger work force.[5] Society has reached a point of change where the forces of production are formed differently. In the future, production will depend more on science and its application than simply on the quantity of invested work and the quantity of means of production. Science becomes a decisive factor in the growth of civilization. The laws of growth of the forces of production and particularly the relationship between science and immediate production have altered. This change shows that when certain limits were imposed on forces of production and accumulated capital, it was more profitable to concentrate all means of production on direct production. When the limitations are removed, the situation takes a radical turn. During early industrialization the quantity of means invested in any expansion of a network of factories was the measurement of economic growth. In earlier periods science followed industry, but now has caught up with and is already leading it. In the new technical epoch, scientific work, equipped with cybernetics, will become the predominant and prescriptive form of human work. Marx, who understood the basic laws of the development of this civilization, had foreseen it.

But as heavy industry develops, the creation of real wealth depends less on labour time and on the quantity of labour utilized. . . . It depends rather on the general state of science and on technological progress. . . . In this transformation, what appears as the mainstay of production and wealth is neither the immediate labour performed by the worker (. . . since it is transformed more and more into a supervisory and regulating activity . . .) nor the time that he works—but the appropriation by man of his own general productive force, his understanding of nature and the mastery of it; in a word, the development of the social individual. The theft of others' labour time upon which wealth depends today seems to be a miserable basis compared with this newly developed foundation. . . . The surplus labour of the masses has ceased to be a condition for the development of wealth in general. . . . It is no longer a question of reducing the necessary labour time in order to create surplus labour, but of reducing the necessary labour of society to a minimum. The counterpart of this reduction is that all members of society can develop their education in the arts, sciences, etc., thanks to the free time and means available to all.[6]

The tendency is obvious: the more industrially developed a country is, the more her economic potential and social progress depends on scientific potential, or in other words, on human ability. Science as a force of production radically differs from the traditional industrial force of production; its development entirely depends upon, and is more directly connected to, the growth of human faculties. The industrial utilization of workers as mere attendants of machines has as its foundation the simple reproduction of labor and does not provide the incentive necessary for the growth of human abilities. Only under the regimen of a scientific-technical revolution will humans and their abilities become the most effective force of production. The powerful automated machines have the excellent ability to reduce human work, to make it more productive, to provide a life that is unconstrained and more worthy of man. They make it possible to attack a fatal division between the intellectual and physical, management and labor. Routine work can be taken over by machines—in the plants and in the offices—while human activity is transferred to the realm of research, design, control and management—a realm of creativity.

Scientific work and automation undermine the foundations of the traditional oligarchic work organization.[7] Rather than a series of partial functions, production becomes a system of rotation, exchange of functions, a possibility for alteration and collective execution. Cooperation abolishes the division of work into settled, partial and isolated operations; a collective execution of tasks is introduced, along with group responsibility and collective decision making. Many observers of these changes point out that management without the active cooperation of all participants is helpless. A smooth functioning of large automated units depends on the motivation of its workers; otherwise entire production cycles can be brought to a halt. The complexity of new technology makes former relations—giving orders and merely executing these orders—outmoded. Such relations are not suited to the new technology. Autonomy of a work group, a new type of voluntary cooperation, is an essential requirement of the organization of work. Many a researcher has already concluded that industrial organization is characterized by one strong tendency—it is becoming increasingly less bureaucratic. It is less the type of organization with a rigid hierarchical structure and more an organization where the democratic authority of the entire working group is responsible for basic decision making.

The complexity of new technology renders the relationship of "orders— and their mere execution" inadequate to the task of setting in motion the modern forces of production. The creative work that engages all intellectual potential cannot accept coercion; its inner trait is personal autonomy. Participation in the controls and decision making in a work situation, cooperation, workers' control—all forms of self-management—are the slogans of our time, a part of the whole of societal change. Self-management ceases to be only a political or moral appeal.

Thanks to the new powers of production, humanity has for the first time been able to realize its ancient dream of freeing itself from the yoke of privation, of closing the gap between the rich and the poor. While the yearly gross national income for the entire world during the era of the first industrial revolution was only about four billion dollars, and at the beginning of the twentieth century about 380 billion; today it amounts to 6,000 billion dollars.

But with foreboding predictability, the new sources of productive power, contrary to their great liberating potential, can become equally destructive for nature and humanity; they can be misused in order to oppress people and whole communities.

Societal development, much as the ancient god Janus, is showing its other face. Nearly 40 to 50 percent of all scientists are working on discoveries and the application of means to destroy a world whose peace is sustained by the constant threat of war. The abyss between the rich and the poor, this striking contradiction of our time, has increased form 1:3 to 1:90. The greatest absurdity of our time is created: the development of underdevelopment. In order to keep its inhuman wealth, the developed center dictates the productive, economic, and social structure of the periphery. This contemporary practice of oppression differs from the past: a new phase of dependent development is taking place. From outward dependence, which is maintained by political coercion, comes an inner, organic dependence. This inner subordination is done through technological subjugation, patterns of work organization and consumption that finally filter down to the periphery. The transfer of technology has two different faces. On one side, there is a transfer of knowledge, an emergence into a contemporaneousness. At the same time, science and technology are the most powerful means of oppression and technological colonialism. There is a strong trend to divide the world into zones with several centers of intellectual expertise[8] and technical innovation while the rest of the population is victimized and remains at the bottom of the pyramid. The victimized are only allowed to imitate the activities of the innovators, and their role is one of routine execution of work. In the dependent countries, a special type of intelligentsia is formed—a satellitic intelligentsia—one that acquires neither the ability nor the will to create. Without interest and ideals, this intelligentsia's objective is the mere acceptance of foreign practices and their transplantation, even though they may not satisfy the needs and the peculiarities of the particular nation to which they are applied. This situation is exacerbated by the alarming "brain drain," the emigration of scientific and professional cadres. By this means the poorer countries become an auxiliary reservoir for the most developed world centers.

To illustrate, below are a few facts about the frightening gap within the world of education, a disparity charged with social dynamite. While in industrial countries all children of school age attend school, in economically backward countries 90 percent of all children do not. As a result, the number of illiterates in the world (of which there are presently more than 700 million) increases annually by 20 to 25 million. In Europe and America, there are two-and-a-half times more students than are in the rest of the entire world. In North America, one student in eight attends some institution of higher education; in Europe, the relationship is 1:20; in Asia, 1:38; in Arab countries, 1:45; in Latin America, 1:49; in Africa, 1:90. An additional fact underlies the situation. The Common Market countries produce 101,000 graduates of higher education yearly, while the United States of America provides 450,000; the population of the United States of America is only ten million more than that of the Common Market countries. In the Soviet Union, 331,000 people are acquiring higher education (out of a population of 223 million). This means that the production of cadres with higher education in the Common Market countries—although the number of inhabitants is practically the same—is barely one-fourth of that produced by the United States of America—and one-third of Soviet production.

Oppression is accomplished through cultural and scientific hegemony, through the enslavement of consciousness, by maintaining patterns of production, technological and industrial development, patterns of consumption and types of urbanization. These patterns or models are presented as the only possible, sustaining forms, as destiny herself; a different world is impossible to imagine. Enslavement of one's own intellectual creativity is the enslavement of one's own future.

It is very important to understand that science and technology are not negative forces in and of themselves. They are not demonic powers endowed with their own ominous vitality that will enslave humans unless they halt their development. Today, life without a scientific component would be untenable—it would be like a man without a backbone to hold up his frame. It is of decisive importance to become cognizant of the structure of social powers, types of social organization, or, in other words, who will determine whether science and technology will have a humanistic, liberating role, or whether it will be transformed into a weapon for domination.

What are these social powers, these protagonists, who can control these alternatives? In attempting to give name to the weapon, one cannot start by criticizing science and technology by themselves. They do not originate in a vacuum but in a social arena, within the bourgeois civilizaton or within bureaucratic socialism, that both deeply penetrate and affix a strong seal that ultimately sterilizes any liberating potentials for science and technology.

The double function of production—one that is characterized by the creation of goods and the other whose exclusive goal is the multiplication of capital and acquisition of power—is profoundly deforming the forces of production as well as scientific research. These patterns of development manifest themselves again during the period of early, heavy-handed socialism, in societies where the forces of production were not developed. In their attempt to enter into contemporaneousness, they adopt many preexisting patterns of industrialization and urbanization, such as the conspicuous consumption of the developed bourgeois societies, although these molds only serve to renew the social division between those who rule and those who are ruled.

UNION OF POWER AND KNOWLEDGE

Science, so deformed and repressively used, is no longer neutral. It is becoming an agent that molds human relationships into a particular shape; it is becoming one of the cornerstones of society's hierarchial structure. It is becoming an essential participant in the technocratic reorganization of contemporary neocapitalism by: (a) assisting in the formation of the central management grouping; (b) cementing the union of management with the new middle classes; (c) transforming knowledge into new forms of power, and thus creating a basis for the reproduction of the new structure of class (hierarchical) relationships that is more relevant to the society called "postindustrial" by Daniel Bell, and "technotronic" by Zbigniew Brzezinski.

The ruling upper classes are a social organism of two closely intertwined groupings. One grouping consists of large owners, mandators of united capital, and heirs of the previous generation's magnates. With them are joined the top professional managers, a new business elite, carefully selected and educated, who have the ability to install a system that produces capital by applying contemporary technology and science within a complex social and technical organization. These two groupings have radically altered the Western system. The technostructure retains power in the hands of the owners of the means of production rather than delivering it to the experts, scientists and organizers who take part in the collective decision making. The unification of owners and experts allows the capitalists to have at their disposal all information needed for knowledgeable management. Technocracy develops when the attributes of the magnates—property, the desire to rule, the intuition and traditonal education of the upper classes—are no longer adequate. Our technological epoch is asking for managerial skills, optimal programming and systematic regulations, is asking for cadres who will be able to control and keep in check the legions of technicians and experts who in turn directly supervise the mass of workers. Similar tendencies are found in the social structure of bureaucratic collectivism.

Technocracy is creating new difficulties whose solution has a far-reaching influence on the education boom, or more specifically, its social role. The central owner/manager grouping is a small minority of the population. To create a stable, acceptable, and legitimate social system, it has to attract a broad assemblage of the middle class to its side. This must be done in order to form a class coalition, cementing the unity of the ruling class block that is buying the loyalty and interests of the middle classes. Above all, this effort must attract a new complex team, who will take middle but important positions in the gigantic mega-machine, members with expertise in the management of big cybernetic systems, in technology and science, advertising and consumption, and in the psychology of behavior. A broadly based hierarchy of functions is not created as much by the needs of technology as by the conscious striving to separate this big social organism from workers by promoting prestige and status differences, and tying such benefits to the interests of profit and the ruling class. This system forms the manpower motivated to run production and maintain power over people, to carry on simultaneous reproduction of production and sustain hierarchical relations in production.

The bulk of the middle class is no longer the petty bourgeoisie and small proprietors, two groups who are rapidly disappearing from the social scene. This is a new middle class: legions of employers, experts, professionals, intellectuals—the world of white-collar workers. For the most part, they are not owners and their social status is based on the sale of their intellectual capital. Education offers the opportunity for more economic privilege and higher social status. Cultural capital becomes the most important inheritance that one can bequeath to one's children, the capital that can secure for the educated a command over another's work, that can create the modern work aristocracy. An academic degree becomes the modern equivalent of the right to manage. The conservative sociologist Helmut Schelsky states that "there is a general aspiration toward a better professional education, as a substitute for the bourgeois aspirations for property."[9] This system consciously opens a new and apparently broad spectrum for social advancement, one that appears to offer equal possibilities in the distribution of privileged positions. At the same time, the system tries to neutralize the radical demands of the masses and the dissatisfaction of the declassed petty bourgeoisie by opening a new and attractive field for action. The transformation of the petty bourgeoisie into degreed academicians is the attempt to constrain politically these subclasses, for without the prospect of future privileged existence, they could effect a dangerous political explosion. The delicate balance that is essential in maintaining a stable relationship between the labor market and the system becomes an essential concern of the university as well.

But the education boom provoked by these forces carries within itself the portent of a twofold controversy that is capable of corroding social unity.

In the first place, promises for advancement, aroused aspiratons for the privileges that a degree was to bring about, and the myth of equal opportunity all clash with the realities of the system. The tip of the hierarchical pyramid is just that, and access to the limited area at the top does not necessarily depend on educational success or intellectual ability. The status that education used to give is not commensurate with the massive increase of the size of the educated classes. There is still social mobility, but this mobility covers a short distance path in social space. Research has shown that only 3 to 4 percent of all workers' and peasants' children rise to the ranks of industrial leaders. On this upward path, there are many more barriers today than there were in the past. Admission to the upper levels of the corporate hierarchy is less and less acquired through longevity in the firm. Increasingly, admission requires high educational qualifications that are more easily achieved by the children of the upper classes.

In the second place, the world of work and management of the highly professional middle classes is itself torn by the opposing forces. It has two components: technical expertise and hierarchical function. The managers perpetuate capitalistic and bureaucratic hierarchical power over work, and the relationship between them and the workers is one of inequality. The managers command. Still, this situation cannot change the basic fact that the managers, too, are exploited by, and forced to sell their intellectual working power to, the owners. This aspect of the professional's life is further provoked by the inherent need to acquire more education. The majority of graduates know that their technical qualifications will be outdated within an average time of five years, and that their degrees are not much more valuable than were the manual qualifications of the past. They do not offer much prospect of escaping the workers' destiny. The work conditions of employees and intelligentsia, in one regard, are becoming increasingly similar to the work conditions of assembly-line production. Unemployment and job insecurity—widespread among engineers, professors and technicians—are symptomatic of the change. Merely a sudden change in production will brutally toss the aged and surplus cadres out into the streets—a rude awakening to the adverse risks of their employability, a presentiment that they will become the intellectual proletariat of technological society.

This is the basis for the formation of the technocratic coalition of the ruling class and the new professional middle classes. But there is also a basis for the alliance[10] of the working classes and highly educated experts for whom the destiny of the intellectual proletariat is in store. To clarify this point, one must understand that there is a difference between the experts (technicians) and technocracy, which, rather than being the power of experts (science), is actually the power of reorganized capital and bureaucracy over the huge majority of intelligentsia and workers. It is a power that equally strangles the industrial workers and the creative potentials of the majority of the intelligentsia.

This whole vital complex of circumstances leads to the radicalization of the young intelligentsia and experts. One result of this is the crisis now faced by the traditional university, and another, the deep contradictions within society. The discontents are encroaching on education and are questioning the whole meaning and content of contemporary culture; they are attacking its bourgeois ideological content. At the same time, they criticize the repressive authoritarian pedagogy, which, under the guise of transferring objective knowledge, educates for obedience and conformity. This criticism extends to the whole societal structure built on complicated bureaucratic (technocratic) hierarchies. One becomes cognizant of the fact that it is one and the same repressive structure dominating the young intelligentsia and workers, and that it has power over all manifestations of life, from economics and politics to all of culture. This system inhibits the creativity of individuals and groups in all sections of society. The antitechnocratic movement, although only in its infancy, has as its ideal more equality; it is opposed to the university (learning) because it views it as factor in the reproduction of class relationships. The sophisticated antitechnocrats demand participation and self-management; the less sophisticated lose themselves in anarchistic spontaneity.

INCUBATORS OF THE ELITE AND FACTORIES OF THE INTELLECTUAL PROLETARIAT

A widespread ideological myth has developed around the meritocracy of education. The main reason for the myth is to create the illusion that the system is good, healthy, and that if one fails in his endeavors, it is exclusively the result of personal inability. We are made to believe that if one fails to better himself, it is solely his own fault. A well-socialized person assumes all culpability for all failures. It is now assumed that the destiny of one man is not dependent on an existing social system but only on his individual abilities, though, in reality, the case is almost the opposite. Personal failure is singly attributed to inability or the lack of willpower to seize the unlimited possibilities that are equally available to all capable and energetic people. This meritocratic myth is masking the reality of social process. I must stress that I am not denying the values of personal competence, motivation, energy and talents. To the contrary! But it is obvious that the selection process is influenced by many social circumstances that greatly deter, or, on the contrary, facilitate the academic success of people solely by merit of their social station. It is important not to mistake the mask for the face—the reservoir of human potential is broader than it presently appears. But the myth will linger for a long time, as myths are wont to do. Instead of collective action that aims at transcending the modern caste divisions of technological society, this myth directs human energy toward cut-throat competition. Education becomes a rivalry between the children of workers and those of the middle classes; it is an Archimedean lever that artificially ranks individuals to their various levels within the social structure. The monopoly of knowledge, the uneven distribution of cultural capital, tends to become the basis of social stratification in the industrial technocratic society. I will discuss only two mechanisms through which this process occurs: (a) the stratification of the university—separation of the elite institutions from those that serve the masses; and (b) the social selection that is taking place through the invisible allocation of cultural capital.

The visible, easily recognized form of intervention by which the university promotes the stratification of people into their future roles is apparent in the sharp divisions among the universities themselves. On the one side are a few elite universities, the incubators of the future ruling intellectual elite (Cambridge, Oxford, Harvard, Princeton, polytechnical schools of higher education, and others). The degrees from these centers, protected as they are from the masses by the barrier of expensive fees, open the door that leads to the upper rungs of the social ladder. On the other side is a galaxy of universities that are producers of mass, routine, intellectual work power, the intellectual proletariat. The differences between the two types of education in content and pedagogy are unbridgeable.

The nature and quantity of education given to a child is closely connected with his parents' rank in the work hierarchy. Children with parents of lower status are sent to the schools where the emphasis is on a type of behavior appropriate to the social activity of the parents: submission and inability to work without directives. Sons and daughters of those who occupy positions of authority within the work hierarchy are usually educated in "enlightened" institutions where there is an emphasis on the development of "independent work."[11]

"The principle of correspondence"—concordance between the authoritarian relationships in pedagogy and the hierarchical structure of production—is a key element in the continuation of the hierarchical structure within society. The function of education is to prepare young people for their future economic fate in production—either to rule or be ruled. On one side there are schools that increasingly resemble the stiff, faceless organization of an office or the uniformity of assembly-line production. On the other side, one can earn a universal, top-grade education whose intent is not obedience and discipline, but rather an education that opens the individual to wide cultural perspectives. The pedagogy of these schools is not petty or

stereotypical; it centers around the personality. The individual characteristics of the student are carefully nurtured, his character is formed, and
his creative abilities developed. The personality is of course formed within
the confines of the social and cultural horizons of the ruling class, through
its values and long-term, historical goals.

Every mature ruling group has to face the problem of how to preserve
and develop human quality, how to realize its leadership, not only through
force but also through a spiritual hegemony, by the ability to find creative
solutions to the problems of living. Each developed class system of any
duration sooner or later comes to a point where its members undergo a
crisis of personality, a decline of their spiritual abilities, and this
deterioration leads to a crisis within the system. This crisis occurs not only
because the human reservoir from which the elite are drawn is too narrow,
but also because of the spiritual laziness of ruling groups that are attracted
more to the trappings of power than to intellectual ability.

The formation of elite intellectual centers is one answer to this challenge.
An example is the perfection of the Mandarin system in old China, where a
path to state functions led through a system of rigorous examinations and
discriminating learning of classical texts. Another model is the masterful
Jesuit formation of personality as a conservative answer to the cultural
revolution of the Renaissance, an answer that assumes the values of the new
order but at the same time discharges them of all radical content. Yet
another method is described by the famous philosopher Bertrand Russell in
his book *Education and the Social Order*. Russell graphically explains the
subtle process of the formation of the conscience and character of one ruling
elite. The member of the elite in the process of education

learns to wear an armour and to seem callous; in his school life, he aims at power
and glory to the exclusion of all other objects. . . . Instinctively, he looks about for
opportunities of similar enjoyments in later life: he desires people to govern, people
to whom he will seem a god-like being. So he goes to live among uncivilized people,
or at least people whom he believes to be uncivilized: he becomes an empire builder,
an outpost of culture, a man whose mission it is to bring Western enlightenment into
dark places. . . . he is kind and gracious, upright and hard working, stoical about
loneliness and discomfort, which are no worse than what he endured in his first years
at school. . . . My compatriots might be red-faced, hard-drinking, spending their
working hours in exploitation and their leisure in sport and bridge, wholly ignorant
of Occidental culture, and not even aware that any Oriental culture exists. Yet in
contact with men who knew not only what was worth knowing in their own civilization, but far more than most public school men of the civilization of the West, these
ignorant boors would preserve the insolence of military conquerors, content to let
their superiority be proved by the guns of their warships.[12]

The differences between the authoritarian pedagogy aimed at the routine
work power and a free one that is practiced on the limited number of elite

students at the modern technocratic university is subtly illustrated in Andre Gorz's text:

Higher education in nearly all capitalist countries has two totally different branches: higher education of the "humanistic" and liberal type (the traditional university), and the schools for technicians and engineers. While the first is more liberal and informal, the second imposes strict, military-like discipline. The mission of the universities is to transmit knowledge and create individuals who are able to use it independently. The schools for technicians and engineers, in addition to transmitting and applying knowledge, strive to train each individual in such a manner that he can immediately be absorbed into the hierarchical and authoritarian system of the factory, laboratory or bureaucracy. The students of the first institutions acquire the critical intelligence that makes it possible for them to work independently as professionals, researchers, entrepreneurs or teachers. Their degree does not channel them into a specific profession, but rather, a choice can be made after a period of wandering. In contrast, the second type of schooling produces students who are trained for a precisely determined occupation, for a definite position within a social hierarchy and the division of labor. There are two reasons for choosing this particular type of education and occupation. Firstly, the social background of these students does not offer them the chance to become other than hired labor; and secondly they have neither the time nor money to risk a period of unemployment upon completion of their schooling. They are trying to "socially raise themselves" and they are seeking a paid job that will put them "above" the laborer or simple office clerk; but their choice will forever prevent them from attaining the managerial positions reserved for the oligarchy. The nature of their ambition is such that it can be realized only within the established order, so they must accept its gradation of values, must not aim too high and must have respect for the powerful. And these schools form just such a consciousness. . . . The students are taught special skills that are immediately applicable; they are trained to define the means for the realization of predetermined goals, and they must never question those goals (only questions about their realizations are allowed). These schools offer to their students a typically subordinate "culture," one that is reduced to the effective materialization of given means.[13]

Ekard Kancov describes German schools in the same manner and goes on to define the consequences of such pedagogy. In his description, the students almost exclusively learn by rote, and develop the ability to quickly assimilate fragmentary knowledge; as a result, they cannot absorb anything that is outside of their specialized knowledge; they are unable to study independently; they are completely devoid of the critical approach to their own specialization; they lack thoughts, and are without the ability to make independent decisions. This type of education causes an individual to behave the way the company expects him to behave . . . in effect the individual becomes: uncritical, stereotyped, a noncom of production, and easily adapted to execute the orders of the higher officers of production.

A DIVISION OF "CULTURAL CAPITAL" AND SELECTION

A second essential element in an individual's success is the social factor of selection, the role that *cultural capital* plays, a fact proven by many researchers. In spite of the unquestionable democratization of education, of the acceptance by the universities of children from poorer and subordinate classes, the members of the upper classes are numerously more represented than are the children of workers, peasants, and clerks. In fact, if one were able to make a choice, it would be more important to opt for parents within the privileged class than for potential ability.

During the recent decades, the working class has been the majority of the population of developed countries (40 to 60 percent). The students that originate from workers' families represent only 5 to 25 percent of the total number of students. The students that are descendants of the poorer classes have fewer chances to enter the university than do the students from the privileged strata. These chances are 28 times fewer in France, 26 times fewer in Holland, 12 times fewer in West Germany, 5 times so in Great Britain, 5 times so in Sweden, and 3.5 times so in Yugoslavia. We are, then, far from a world in which the factor of intellectual ability will determine the development of personality and quality of education.[14] Research in France has shown that only 1 percent of the sons of farm workers enter the university, while 70 percent of the students are the sons of businessmen. In the United States of America, half of all middle class children enter the university, while only one out of every twelve working class children attain higher education.

All data from the OECD [Organization for Economic Cooperation and Development] study indicate that, in spite of the expansion of education, the representative percentage of students from the lower classes has not changed much. In spite of democratization, in spite of more opportunity to attain degrees of higher education, the tendency of self regeneration of social groups is very strong. The doors to the universities are somewhat more open to children from working families, but at the same time there have been no changes within the hierarchy of class positions, thus preserving the nucleus of the old system with renewed vigor. In high school, workers' children predominantly prepare themselves for manual labor, while employers', managers' and other professionals' children prepare for intellectual occupations. In higher education, workers' and farmers' children are oriented toward trade schools, while the children of professionals and managers go to the university. The expenses of a university system are paid by society as a whole, but middle and higher income groups proportionally enjoy more of its benefits.

Education becomes a form of *cultural capital*, a special form of private property that supersedes family inheritance. Research has shown that as a rule, the children from nonmanual classes are more successful in school than are those of the working classes. This success is the result of both material conditions and cultural ambiance. Better nutrition, more privacy, the availability of textbooks and other school supplies, a large home library and media equipment (a record player, tape recorder, radio, television, etc.), and the opportunity to use free time for study and rest (children from workers' families spend the majority of their free time working in their fathers' shops or out in the fields)—all these are true advantages. More highly educated parents better prepare their children for school. It is enough merely to mention the help they offer with homework!

Pierre Bourdieu and Jean Claude Passeron have observed that children from the privileged classes have the advantage of a "language capital," or in other words, they possess a sophisticated vocabulary essential to higher education.[15] However, the failure of the working classes cannot be blamed exclusively on the lack of material circumstances, for these can be overcome by strong willpower and ability; failure is more the lack of motivation, an ideology of acceptance. That a person is predetermined to do manual work is a belief that seems to be systematically formed. The family environment and cultural ambiance, verbal fluency, expensive training, the spiritual abilities required and evaluated at the selection process, the fact that the teachers belong to the same subculture—all these factors when combined weigh heavily in the selection and the measurement of success. Even when the selection process (tests, examinations) tries to be objective, those classes with inherited cultural capital fare much better. The invisibility of cultural capital does not diminish its strength any more than the invisibility of gravitation makes it less powerful. Academic success depends not only on natural abilities and talents, but also on the distribution of cultural capital and a will to invest in the academic market. Research done by the Institute for Education of SR Slovenia (*Zavod za šolstvo S.R. Slovenije*) shows that the number of pupils who failed and had to reattend the same grade level had increased threefold when comparing the children of farmers with those of salaried employees. Or, research done in the Socialist Federative Republic of Yugoslavia shows that there are ten times more *A* students among children whose parents both have a university education.

The investment in their childrens' careers, and thus their success, is considered by parents to be a crucial factor in the transfer of the families' privileges. An academic degree becomes a primary personal goal and failure to attain one turns into a family tragedy:

A strange metamorphosis is happening in August and at the beginning of September. Tested and respected people, engineers and professors, intelligent and proud, people who lived through war and a difficult period of reconstruction all of a sudden lose their human dignity. They are transformed into humble, contrite petitioners who block the hallways, wait in front of the doors of deans, rectors, ministers; who bombard with telephone calls their well connected friends; and who, on their knees, implore, "Accept my son or daughter to the university!" Not a single possibility is left unexplored in this search for connections; they even take to bribes, they smear the reputation of many important people. But what matters more than their bribery is their ability to pay for special and expensive private lessons, to procure tutors, or to save their children from obligatory work in order to ready themselves for the next year's entrance examinations. Shocking results were found—90 percent of successful candidates accepted by the university had expensive private lessons and tutors and even bragged abut it. The more expensive the tutor, the more prestige the student enjoys. It means that our system of free education, equally available to all is violated by "Rubles"; it has turned into a competition among tutors with fattened billfolds.[16]

This account published in *Komsomolskaya pravda* vividly describes the underside of selecton and at the same time points at similar symptoms in the socialist countries.

A selection process that is influenced by elements other than the candidates' abilities produces various effects. Because of more difficult entrance requirements and of the greater difficulty of achieving in higher education, the youth from the lower classes drop out of school in higher percentages than do the youth from other milieus. As research done in France shows: if, for instance, one assumes 100 to be the number of students from each social class in the first grade of high school, the students that graduate will be distributed as follows: 86 will belong to the highest social classes, 55 to the middle classes, and only 21 (out of 100 in the first grade) will be working-class children.

Analysis has singled out two factors that decisively influence selection: natural abilities and an unequal distribution of cultural capital—material and cultural advantages that different classes either enjoy or are deprived of. However, in this analysis we must introduce still one more element as being essential: the social conditioning that produces the very concept of "success" or "intelligence," the relationship between the evaluation of intellectual abilities and the class structure of society.[17] This evaluation is not made on the basis of criteria that are independent of the structure of society. To the contrary, the prime mover in this delicate process is the existing sociocultural model that reigns in any given period or place and serves as a scale for the evaluation of people. And this model too is socially determined, particularly by the fact that evaluation of intellectual abilities, of intelligence, has become an essential function in society. Education has become a decisive factor in the competition between the middle- and working-class children for the attainment of social success. It is a very complicated operation though. This evaluation process plays the role of arbiter only within the confines of the educational system as students are promoted or discarded in their quest for higher and higher levels. However, in managerial positions within corporations and institutions, there is a turning point at which relationships change. What matters depends on other determinants, and not so much on academic success. What matters is the social status of the family, the strength of family connections, property. The types of abilities that are required at this level very often have nothing to do with talent.

Samuel Bowles has proven empirically that there is not a strict correlation between academic success and high standing in the managerial hierarchy. Education is a kind of general prerequisite, an elimination tournament. The university (except for the small number of very elite ones) is producing a reservoir of potential candidates for the middle positions and the future intellectual proletariat. The measurement of intelligence becomes a powerful weapon in this competition. It offers both indication of and legitimacy to social stratification and at the same time controls social mobility: the ones that are acceptable to the middle classes are allowed to enter new ranks, i.e., they take part in upward mobility.[18]

The definition of intelligence has not been created by the whole of society. Rather, it is determined by the spiritual and cultural perspectives of the dominant classes. The stronger social groups define its very notion— what intelligence is, what intellectual abilities are—they identify its distinctive traits, ways of thinking and behaving that are esteemed. Many of these traits are so defined that they correspond to those faculties that are endemic to the members of the dominant class, the very ones that are acquired only through the distinctive subculture of the middle and upper classes. Quite obviously, this does not mean that there is not intelligence of a different nature—it means that from one broad spectrum there are certain types of behavior and thinking, and, as a result, certain abilities that are selected as the pronounced manifestation of intelligence. Alternative definitions of intelligence are granted less importance if not totally ignored.

Sir Francis Galton is one of the first scholars to introduce the concept of the measurement of mental abilities. He was a relative of Charles Darwin and an aristocrat. His work *Hereditary Genius* contains a sampling of 997 eminent personalities. The sampling does not include industrial, business, and banking leaders because they did not belong to the aristocracy, i.e., the upper classes. According to Galton, "eminency" could be found only within the limits of certain practices—aristocratic practices. His study faithfully reflected the views of his class regarding true eminency.[19] One French dictionary from the first part of the nineteenth century gives the following definition of a worker: "A worker is a person who performs a mechanical task in which there is no need for the usage of intelligence."[20]

The evaluation of intelligence and intellectual ability is done by teachers who for the most part represent the intelligentsia of the middle and upper classes but not the working class. The classical Spearman's test of general intelligence, in addition to measuring abilities in such subjects as Latin, Greek, and mathematics, attaches great importance to the teacher's general impression of the student's abilities. The general impression created by the student is the result of a very subtle process; many factors and personal affinities influence it even subconsciously. Very often a rating of "good and able" is granted only to those personalities whose characteristics and behavior correspond to the teacher's idea of what a good and able child should be. Furthermore, concepts change. What one generation considers to be absolutely objective, exact criteria for the measurement of intelligence is rejected by the next as being a one-sided illusion. Precious empirical material could be gotten from greater attention to research in psychology, social psychology, and the theoretical basis of tests and measurements, as well as in the expansion of new research fields within psychology itself. All of this could provide us with a better understanding of the very concept of evaluation of abilities—intelligence—and the ways in which social conditioning affects that evaluation.

The different forms of selection also have one hidden function. They create among the minority an elite awareness, and they assure the majority that their inability to succeed should be blamed wholly on personal inadequacy. The system has an inherent tendency to produce a small number of "technicians of social success" and a great number of social "rejects," "children of failure," the ones who are predestined to social defeat. The nature of the selection process has yet another social function: as long as there is a great number of open positions waiting to be filled with manual, unskilled labor, the schools have to keep producing enough "failures" whose only choice is to accept these jobs. To insure the continuance of hierarchical social relations, a definite number of young has to be convinced by the objective process of school selection that they are only capable of performing unskilled work. They have to be persuaded that their failure at school is exclusively the result of their personal and social inferiority: "They lack a gift for learning." And conversely, the ones who succeed at school have to be convinced that their good grades are exclusively a consequence of their natural "talents," and that better grades lead to social privileges.

What we are talking about is a methodological division of the classes into clearly defined and separate entities. In this manner the social system becomes an instrument of social hierarchy. Education is permeated with a spirit of cutthroat competition: at the very outset it is clear that the success of one group is based on the failure of the other. Those who will fail are forced into lower positions. The school system does not often favor "the most gifted ones" but rather it rewards the most ambitious, the ones who, out of desire to climb socially know best how to adapt themselves to the hierarchical character of the educational institution, an institution of which the future relationships in production are but a projection.

A CRITICISM OF MERITOCRACY

We have arrived at an obstacle which will continue to challenge our best resources for a long time. We are face to face with one of the most persistent prejudices: as soon as we determine different abilities, they must be hierarchically classified as *higher* and *lower* in order to form a foundation for essentially different social classes. Once a superior position has been won, it leads to proprietary claims and their bequeathment. This is a key problem in determining the nature of future society, or in other words, a key problem with socialism. What kind of society do we wish to develop? Class differences can be carried over into the future—their general characteristics extended in a new fashion and supported by new explanations. The axis of the reproduction of class relationships has shifted: it is no longer centered on just property or political power; it has also incorporated knowledge (education), different abilities that alter a person's standing.

The new concept of the scientific basis of inequality finds particular support from two modern theories: *sociobiology*[21] and the ideology of *meritocracy* of Daniel Bell.[22] Both concepts state that essentially different abilities are inborn, hereditary, that they are only an epiphenomenon of the genes (DNA), and, therefore, that the transfer of abilities is merely chemical. Their only principles are (1) that the ego wills itself to survive, and (2) that the fittest will survive; and from these, hierarchy necessarily results.

DNA is a true mover of the universe, an originator of all human behavior; economy, morals, religion, sex, jealousy, conflicts, friendships—all are just the epiphenomena of DNA. All living beings are merely an outer shell in which genes reside, the real bearers of ability. This concept dictates that a social order of inequality is actually a biological order. Changes in the social structure will never succeed in altering any genetic structure. Revolutions are useless: all should revert to their natural social position. The social order is determined by DNA. There is no longer any need for politics to answer to egalitarian utopia; science (genetic fatalism) has already given its negative answer. "Academic education which has selection as its goal, does not have to teach knowledge; it only has to identify (code) the kind of genes one has."[23] But if this notion contains even some truth, this truth is not essential to humans as a generic species. The development of human abilities is sociocultural and not primarily animal. The genetic program that controls survival is too moderate to regulate all culture. Man is distinguished from the other species by his culture and work, and this is primarily because the genetic apparatus does not work alone in insuring survival. Each new culture is a new creative process, a genetic program is always the reproduction of the same. Without creative renewal with each generation, there is no human species.

Similar concepts are the base for the ideology of meritocratic selection: success and ability bring the elite to the fore of society, a working team that is uniquely prepared to organize society on the basis of optimal technological rules. The meritocrats argue that although the elite who combine knowledge and direction have a privileged position, the fruits of their activities—an abundance of everything—will be used by everyone. People will be satisfied because their needs will be amply gratified; the inactive masses are made happy by the deeds of the ablest. Only a selected few are really individuals of significance. The human multitudes remain gray, assembly-line production, rolled off the same conveyer belt. The elite, a managerial machine, are in apposition to the mass inability of people.

I will cite a few ideas from the work *The Coming of Post-Industrial Society* by Daniel Bell, who is the most influential representative of the ideology of meritocracy.

"The decisive division in contemporary society is not between the ones who own the means of production and some nondifferentiated 'proletariat' but rather, it is between the ones who have decision-making powers and the ones who do not have that power."[24] In Western society the dominating system was one of ownership, but that system has been disappearing in the last decades. Currently, says Bell, there are in the West three systems in the area of social relationships, all of which overlap: the system of ownership, one that is losing its importance; the system of political institutions and organizations; and the system based on knowledge and qualifications; the last one has gained in significance. The university has become

an arbiter of class stature. . . . it has gained a near monopoly in creating the future stratification of society. On this basis new social relationships and new structures spring up. At the nucleus of the new structures are experts, divided into three classes: a creative elite of scientists, specialists, administrators and organizers; a middle class of engineers and professors; a proletariat of technicians, of younger service personnel and assistants.[25]

Finally, the fourth class is manual labor. The layers of social stratification are defined by a social status based on the hierarchy of knowledge. What is essential in Bell's scheme of social structure is the relationship between the social stratum, which is based on knowledge, and the different areas of social activity. There is no room for a bourgeoisie in Bell's scheme. As a whole, the middle class is absorbed into other social groups. Without the bourgeoisie, and with such an interpretation of the working class, the antagonisms of the opposing forces of bourgeois and proletariat disappear. Bell's image of the "post-industrial society" is one in which the intelligentsia, with all creative and organizing abilities, dominate society. "It could be said," writes Bell, "that the present scientific class, its character and organization . . . contains within itself the configuration of future society."[26] Bell's theory rests on more than the disappearance of past class differences; in addition, he points out the necessity and legitimacy of the new class divisions with "the class of experts—meritocracy" playing the leading role.[27]

I will advance only one counterargument to Bell's theory, and then propose a different concept of human abilities, a different way of looking at an individual—specifically, what he is and what he might become. The evaluation of success and an elevated position in the hierarchical pyramid

are not proof that superior knowledge and intelligence determined the selection. Because the selection process occurs within a particular system, it can
also award mediocrity. Conformists, presumptuous and overbearing
people, obedient executors with limited abilities, get selected also, while the
talents of creative, original innovators are very often squelched. Many
managers have been limited, unscrupulous, and mediocre. The hierarchi-
cal/prestigious system of selection and measurement of abilities deforms; it
allows one kind of ability to filter through and blocks the others. It projects
a distorted image of human potential. It is a strange and mysterious game
that the system plays with human abilities, their evaluation, recognition
and remuneration. The entirety of it is deeply contradictory; it sorts through
the abundance of true abilities and selects only one narrow segment for
recognition.

The whole of human abilities has been reduced to labor power—goods.
Goods stand as the only measurement of human ability within the capitalistic and bureaucratic selection process while on the contrary, throughout
the development of all civilization, a producer is enriched by new abilities
and aspirations. What I am talking about is the possibility of enhancing the
creative powers of all humans. But capitalism harnesses this new force with
uncannily dehumanized instruments that create and maintain someone
else's wealth. On the other side, the bureaucratic system of selection
primarily aims to maintain and renew bureaucratic power. The selectees
know how to conform to the hierarchy. Within capitalism, the abilities of a
small number of individuals well adapted to the needs of the reproduction
of the system, are artificially magnified, given much more value than their
real potential deserves. (The whole system of social roles in functionalistic
sociology is a theoretical explanation of this practical need.)

Labor power, the very heart of any class system, is an elusive and mysti-
fying phenomenon. The whole operation has a twofold goal: the first,
economical, and, with that, the ideological. Its purpose is to get more value
for less, to exploit more talent and knowledge than is paid for. It justifies
itself ideologically by giving legitimacy to the class division of people. Its
individuals must be consciously reconciled to the differentiation between what
they really are and what the system recognizes that they are; they must
accept the capitalistic/bureaucratic exploitation of one's abilities. There is a
need for a great demystification of human ability, one that will unveil all
existing prejudices in order to judge the horizons of human power
objectively.

Working power—this socially accepted measurement of human ability—is,
however, not the whole of human potential. The obvious evidence of
ability does not suffice; beyond this there are also real abilities that the
system both exploits and underpays, as we have previously discussed. And
there is further potential that is even more suppressed—latent abilities that
can be developed only through revolutionary practice. Class selection,
although tending to limit human power, will never completely halt the

development of human aspirations, abilities, and potentials. From this emerges the greatest social upheaval, the intense and irreconcilable contrariety of the modern world, the widening gap between the development of human needs, ability, and power, and the efforts to limit, inhibit, and enslave them. This contradiction, a driving force from the Renaissance to modern time, has become more and more tumultuous, more and more irreconcilable. People believe that a better life is possible, a fuller one that can be achieved by developing their own creative powers. With increasing volume they refuse their status as Lilliputians in an artificial world that is directed for them by the great movers of the world scene—Capitalism, Bureaucracy, and Technocracy.

The idea that hierarchical ranking is indispensable and eternal when dealing with natural abilities is problematic. For human abilities are infinitely diversified and elusive. There is a great wealth of different talents that are unique; there are many different qualities that cannot be hierarchically measured. However, it is hardly possible to determine the importance of any ability, since different operations require completely different talents. Imagination, a gift of inventors, is a marvelous talent, but is it less important than the ability to contradict prevalent opinion and predict danger with strength and wisdom and thus mobilize the public? The abilities to predict with accuracy, to reflect realistically, to work with both energy and patience—such different human qualities cannot be ranked on any scale. The richness of different qualities is such that there are no objective measures. The differences are only that there are a variety of abilities; they are of equal weight and they do not warrant class differentiation.

We cannot even guess at all human talents that lie dormant. More people than we imagine carry within themselves potentials that stay enslaved if not completely sterile, while they could be developed into creative and productive energy for all humankind. It is a matter then of the development of collective abilities and powers, ones that inspire whole generations by actions and deeds. We have to aspire to a social milieu in which every man is important and self-reliant, has not only his own physiognomy, but also his distinct qualities. Everyone carries within himself his own unique abilities that should be encouraged and respected. From our own experiences, from the times of great collective actions and enterprises, comradeship, and solidarity, we know that there is the possibility of achieving such a life. If a mass of people cannot develop the potentials that exist within themselves, but are suppressed—all of us, the whole of society, are the losers.

The fundamental equality of different human talents does not mean uniformity, but an infinite broadening of the horizons of human abilities.

Unacceptable also is another central idea, the idea of people being happy because they benefit from the deeds of the elite whose creativity provides abundance and promotes progress. Such paternalism conflicts with everyone's authentic need for autonomous action, with the need for the creative development of one's own personality, one's own abilities. It is inadequate that some create and work, and that others be cared for and provided with the results of some top-level activity. This concept of needs derives from a class society, from a repressive structure of needs that has stifled personal autonomy. If only the leaders were to act and the rest merely enjoy the benefits of their creativity, all abilities of society would gradually disappear. Only by the development of these abilities, rather than by the continued reliance on tired blood, will the stream of new life flow again in the arteries; each new generation will be a new detachment of builders of the future.

Let us conclude. Hard facts persistently point to the realization that success at school and the current methods of selection are not exclusively the results of natural talents, abilities, and energy, but are also the results of many important social and cultural factors. I am not denying the importance of culture nor am I arguing that the evaluation of knowledge and success be discarded nor even diminished because of its social origin. Rather, I wish to say that different natural abilities, special talents and different creative gifts must not be negated. To ignore all precedence would be destructive, it would not assist in developing the spiritual abilities of more and more people, it would not be a way to "let a hundred flowers blossom." Events and the failure of the Chinese Cultural Revolution show with crystal clarity that such action leads to a dead end. But it is of crucial importance to sharpen our senses to the problem, to face it with open eyes, without hypocrisy, with fewer class prejudices—to have an honest relationship with it. We have to find a way to cut across these two bad extremes: the degradation of knowledge, and deterioration of standards, or, on the contrary, the transformation of knowledge and cultural capital into the means for reproducing class structures and an inhuman existence. We have to provide a possibility for everyone to develop his own abilities. "Everyone who has the germ of a Raphael should be able to become Raphael."[28] We have to broaden, not limit, the reservoir of the spiritual abilities of society. The great mission of liberating pedagogy is not to form ready-made, ordinary abilities, but rather to strive for an individualized approach that stimulates each ability and talent.

We have to admit to the lie that two-thirds of the youth who come from the working class and peasant milieus are incapable of higher education, and also that all of our children—the children of salaried employees, professors, politicians, managers, experts—have achieved the highest education only because of their natural giftedness, only because they were the ablest ones. We have to understand and admit the relative importance of school grades; we cannot merely, because of the differences in the third decimal of an individual's score (3.500 means rejection, while 3.501 means acceptance) condemn people at an early age to remain in the same castes till the end of their lives. For the differences between a young man who enters the factory and the one who enters the university are not only the differences between the two occupations, but also they are the differences between the two worlds, the two classes. Transition from one to the other is obstructed with such barriers that they are overcome only in exceptional cases, and it requires efforts that destroy the best years of one's life. Instead of that, we should open a normal path of continuous development, one which provides professional improvement and ascent on the ladder of education. And all this must be done not only for the exceptional but also for all who are motivated, who have willpower and show results. The significance of all this is the theme that I shall develop later. Thus far I have only described and generally criticized the meritocratic understanding of selection.

ACADEMIC MARKET

Technocracy has made a deep and far-reaching impression on the structure of, and social relations within, the university, both of which elements had remained unchanged for centuries. A brilliant and lively description of these events is given in Robert Nisbet's book *The Degradation of the Academic Dogma*. The inner structure of the classical university is a union, with several very special and different groups living in coexistence. The nucleus of social relations is a deeply rooted system of hierarchy that historically has originated from our aristocratic, feudal-corporate inheritance. The hierarchical structure among older and younger teachers and assistants is a form of authoritarian gerontocracy. Students are subjected to this relationship, being under both the power of the administration of the university and that of teachers without the right of participation. This power completely deprives them of active participation in decision-making processes regarding pedagogy, studies, examinations, programs, and grades. A storm of revolt and a demand for participation—as a reaction to this situation—rumbled through the West. The qualities of youth—energy, bravery, the search for novelty—are not fundamental to advancement or participation in powerful councils. This is not to say that the academic community is hostile to the qualities of youth. Rather, youth's energies are appreciated only when expressed in the right places, such as the classroom, library, and laboratory, but never in the centers of power where decisions are made. What counts in decision making, so the notion goes, is the wisdom and experience of the elders—very valuable qualities indeed, but not the only ones.

Democratization within the university is another vital element that acts as a certain counterbalance to the powerful hierarchy and lives in coexistence with it. The teachers' collective enjoys a limited form of self-government. The deans, "the managers" of colleges, were only the first among their peers (*primus inter pares*), a concept quite different from one of total and unchangeable power. The scientific and pedagogical reputation of leading personalities in the university setting has rested upon the authority of their knowledge. The status of professor has offered a special kind of job security, which could be jeopardized only if the pedagogical mission was flagrantly violated. In addition to some access to participation, this special kind of autonomy allows teachers the freedom to think critically, an essential element of creativity.

In the classical academic community a powerful spirit of corporate solidarity governs, together with feelings of honor and respect that membership in such community brings about. The devotion to one's profession, a mission of scientific/pedagogical work, strict demands on oneself, intellectual standards for one's own work are prevalent. The need for truth, thirst for new knowledge, for its value—knowledge for knowledge's sake and its transfer—this is the central mission and cohesive power of the academic community. But this solidarity, which is by its nature and historical origins guild-like, meets up with the academic tendency to live in an ivory tower, and what results is an elitistic consciousness, the feeling of superiority towards the rest of society. And from this feeling results a closed off atmosphere, its members isolated and only dealing indirectly with the society from which it comes. The university does not participate in developing scientific solutions to great social problems, it only educates experts who will do so once they enter public life.

The technocracy that we have described has cut through these inner relationships and has caused radical changes, but its effects are extremely one-sided. The pendulum has swung to the other extreme. The positive values contained within the university have become degraded. The foundation of this degradation is a big economic transaction. Capital penetrated into the system and knowledge and science were transformed into goods. With an extraordinary gift for observation, Nisbet describes this deep change in the social relationships and atmosphere, the degradation of intellectual values and the emergence of a whole new brand of people. What Nisbet has not seen clearly enough is the broader social context within which all this takes place. The university and science are transformed into an operation, an adjunct to big corporations and government.

Beginning in the 1940s an immense amount of money began to flow into the more distinguished American universities . . . the dollar volume would be difficult to state exactly. Without any question . . . many billions have been involved. . . .

I firmly believe that direct grants from governments and foundations to individual members of university faculties, or to small company-like groups of faculty members, for the purpose of creating institutes, centers, bureaus, and other essentially capitalistic enterprises within the academic community to be the single most powerful agent of change that we can find in the university's long history. For the first time in Western history, professors and scholars were thrust into the unwanted position of entrepreneurs in incessant search for new sources of capital, of new revenue, and, taking the word in its larger sense, of profits. Where for centuries the forces of commerce, trade, and industrialization outside the university had registered little if any impact upon the academic community beyond perhaps a certain tightening of forces within, the new capitalism, *academic capitalism*, is a force that arose within the university and that has had as its most eager supporters the members of the professoriat.

I am not suggesting that there is, or should be, any natural disaffinity between the university and wealth. Much less do I imply that members of the academic community should take vows of poverty any more than of celibacy. There is no reason why the academic aristocracy should not be, in the good society, as wealthy as any landed aristocracy.[29]

As we see by this quote, the conversion of knowledge and degrees into goods has deeply changed the structure and atmosphere of the university; new social groups with new social roles have been formed, and the university has adopted a new purpose and status. The conversion of knowledge into goods has adversely affected human relations; the feeling of cooperation and solidarity has given way to fragmentation and atomization, and all relationships are reduced to the infallible instinct of self-interest, the prime motivation being only who, how, and how much can be made.

Suddenly great differences developed between those universities that were rich and those that were poor, the differences completely unrelated to the intellectual values of the institution. All depended on greater managerial skills and a ruthless ability to tap the sources of money.

One notable case in point is the participation of eminent professors in the richly funded and ill-reputed Pentagon project "Camelot." A purpose of the project was to develop effective sociopsychological techniques to combat the progressive revolutionary movements of Latin America. With such activity as this we must recognize that we have arrived at the point of the degradation of scientific authority and intellectual standards. A new breed of people has emerged, ones who are placed at the head of educational/ scientific institutions, a type of professional entrepreneur, with an inexhaustible energy for meetings and administration. More and more time is given to conferences and organization, and less and less to students. Universities are under the firm hold of a proliferating administration that, by its very nature, demands increasing dependency as bureaucracy expands and work becomes more formalized. Deans are no longer the most prestigious scientists and pedagogues, but individuals with managerial skills who know how to find new sources of financing. The ability to conduct financial transactions and to administer—the profile of a businessman, not an intellectual—is what will count in selection of deans. Students can no longer view the university as an intellectual community; a business corporation led by managers has taken its place.[30]

A civilization based on the principles of profit, power and prestige has deeply permeated positivistic science; it has altered its professional mentality and manner of creating scientists, in short, the whole technocratic scientific subculture. There is a strong tendency to create a form of science and knowledge that can be evil—one used for the purpose of domination. "Established science has become a church with its own dogma, hierarchy and heresies. It has its popes, cardinals, and the power to excommunicate. This power was felt by some scientists who dared to disturb the reigning scientific orthodoxy and for that they were nailed to the pillory."[31]

The very criteria for deciding what will be scientific cognition and what will not points to the unbridgeable gap between professional expertise and national culture, experience and consciousness. This identification process is a tool for creating experts who are merely narrow specialists (*fachidioten*). The fragmentation and disintegration of knowledge is retained because it has a very useful social function. A specialist's mind can be contained within a very limited contemplative frame. He is directed to take care of one small part of the social machine, and a broad, all-embracing view of society is hidden from him. He is formed into a one dimensional man who cannot think in terms of social values and the social consequences of his work, a man who washes his hands of all of it. There is an opinion that modern science, by every definition, has to be value-neutral, "deaf" and "indifferent" to human worries and daily struggles. The ethic and ideology of the puritan ruling class has tried to create an unfeeling science, a carbon copy of the capitalist businessman or bureaucratic power-wielder.

We must realize that a change in reality should necessitate a change in the patterns of scientific cognition. Science cannot afford, without serious risk, the luxury of value-neutral position or indifference. The dramatic evolution of the productive power of science, powers which are at the same time destructive, has led to such necessity. If scientists consider only technical efficiency, and for greater profits, the cheapest means of dumping industrial wastes, and are totally indifferent to the pollution that endangers human life; if urbanization is developed without any considertation for the destruction of nature; if the researchers in modern agricultural laboratories lack concern about soil fertility, about human nutrition, and the essential nutritive qualities of food; if economists plan savings primarily through the extensive exploitation of human labor power; if new chemical and bacteriological compounds are discovered, but there is no thought given to the possibility of harmful applications—then we have to question the value of our efforts.

If science does not develop sensitivity to human needs, if it does not search for solutions that are at the same time rational and humane, then science will become one link in the chain of antihuman practice.

I will quote from Einstein to underline what I have said:

A man of science is in a way proud because his work, and the work of men like him, although indirectly, has totally changed the economic life of mankind. But at the same time he is also depressed because the results of his work have brought about such an acute threat to the existence of humanity, because the products of his work . . . delivered the concentration of economic and with it political power into the hands of small minorities, on whose manipulations the destiny of more and more amorphous masses become completely dependent. He is so humiliated that he even helps, when ordered, to perfect the means for the annihilation of humankind. . . . Is it necessary for a scientist to suffer such humiliations? Did he not, in his exclusively intellectual aspirations, forget about his responsibilities and dignity?[32]

Contemporary technocratic attitudes have created a deep gap between science and the human purpose for which science was engaged. This gap is responsible for a massive loss of scientific energy, for resignation and personal tragedy, the personification of which are the giants of atomic science who, as if they played a role in a classical drama, renounce their own work. This gap brings about a huge loss of energy and talent, and lessens the ideals and motivation that are necessary in scientific endeavor.

The scientists are at the same time both the privileged and the victims of the technocratic form of science; the intellectuals become themselves objects and victims of the hierarchy and division of labor. The type of knowledge that they have at their disposal individually or collectively is at the same time a subordinate knowledge stigmatized by the social relations in current existence. "Each of us alone, and all of us together know much more than do our predecessors. But all this knowledge at our disposal has not given us greater autonomy, independence and freedom."[33]

These same feelings are expressed by the students who criticize ideological content and the manner in which knowledge is being used. How can economists talk seriously about the rational usage of goods in a world screaming with the contrast between the wealth of the highly developed countries and the poverty of the Third World? How can a young physicist ignore the ideological crisis that has shaken the very basis of contemporary physics? How can he persuade himself that his research is useful to humanity in an era that makes atomic bombs? How can he avoid questions about responsibility, when the leading atomic scientists question the very function of science and its role in society? How can students of social psychology close their eyes to the professional roles assigned to them: to be servants to the sacred interest of profit, helpers in draining the working power of laborers, or to be launchers of yet another completely useless product to the marketplace? Industrial sociology is above all interested in adapting man to the machine, rather than the contrary. It never asks how to make work more adapted to man. . . . The political sociologist Stouffer[34] has suggested a method of improving morale within the American army without ever asking the basic question, What in general is the role of the army in contemporary society? The practical organization of capitalism creates many contradictions and the different branches of sociology are expected to remove them without ever asking questions about the character of the system. One need only look at the terminology that is employed: hierarchy, adaptation, social control, equilibrium in order to realize the purpose of the endeavor.[35]

REVOLUTIONARY POTENTIAL OF KNOWLEDGE

The picture of science we have thus far painted is not complete, but it describes only one tendency, one side of scientific activity. It is incomplete because science, although stigmatized by the milieu in which it has been created, never becomes completely integrated into the system. Scientific activity, that is to say, work that produces knowledge—just as any other work—has its own, inalienable autonomy. Science can be put to the service of some predetermined goals; it can develop in certain directions, at the expense of all others. It can be so directed that it answers the questions asked by the power-wielders and shuns all others. It is impossible, however, to stop scientists from asking themselves questions that differ from new assignments. In addition they always have the opportunity to choose differing methods of posing and solving the same problems given to them by the power-wielders.

The very act of revolutionizing productive power and knowledge creates aspirations within the new culture, aspirations that cannot be confined within a bourgeois ideology that is monolithic and unyielding. New ideas open ways to new horizons and a new critical consciousness about society, regardless of how much the ideology attempts to force this consciousness into technocratic molds. It is impossible to transfer higher education without at the same time transmitting a germ of critical conscience, impossible to educate and still completely stifle its members from speaking the truth about the way in which society functions.

Critical cognition, although perhaps restricted, is nevertheless developed regarding one's way of life, production, cities, and education. It carries within itself potential dangers to the bourgeois manner of production. It expresses the new needs and aspirations of people who are forcing their way through the cracks of the reigning realm of science; they are breaking through its floodgates. Streams of progressive ideas flood into the technocratic shrine of science. These ideas incorporate the desire for an alternative university, one that will bring about more equality in society.

But the scientists, influenced by these progressive ideas and their own noble motives, find that the new possibilities are suppressed whenever possible. Thus, they become acquainted with the ideological and cultural arbiters to whom they are subordinated; they become aware that the orientation and content of scientific activity could be different, but if one wishes to make these differences become reality, it becomes obvious that one has to change society as well. The scientists realize that they both belong and do not belong to the powers of social change.

There are similar stirrings in the world of work as well as in the world of science. It is felt that the time has come when it is possible to live differently, to have a life with more meaning, dignity and freedom. Aspirations for a different quality of personal and social existence are at work. Alternative technology, the organization of work and management free of bureaucratic restriction, property that truly belongs to society, cities more fit for mankind, medicine and psychiatry that are more humane, a pedagogical revolution that offers more space for the creative growth of personality, the engagement of a new world order—a myriad of new alternatives already bombard the nucleus of the old civilization. A new day sets in motion all aspirations, while the night attempts to destroy even the possibility of any. The development of the progress of science and education is not one of subdued calm, but rather, it is a turbulent current of conflicts and contradictions. Higher education and cultural content cannot be attributed solely to class domination. The conservative (technocratic) conscience and the revolutionary spirit meet head on within the institution of education.

A great change in civilization will not, however, be created solely through the efforts of technological seers, exclusively the result of an intellectual construct moved by its own mysterious imperatives. It will be a great social and cultural process whereby the potentials attained by man will be put to the service of other goals, aims and values, to a different quality of human life. From this new collective practice, from the new horizons of civilization, a new technology, a new source of energy, great anticipations and experiments will be born. This is not to say that technology will be rejected, but the new order will not simply adopt ready-made prefabricated elements. This will be a great transformation of all creations of civilization. From this great search, the new scientific-technological basis of the new civilization will be born. A sharper demarcation between the repressive and humanistic usage of science and technology will be drawn. To make technological growth work at the same time for the progress of humanity we do not need obstruction, but rather a new direction, a connection with the broad cultural horizons of a more humane society.

ENGAGEMENT AND FREEDOM TO CREATE

The intelligentsia is deeply engaged in a quest for the social and humanistic purpose of science. It is not a privileged class, nor is it the servant of politics. It is not a fellow-traveler of social movements but an equal, a key participant in social changes, a builder of the new world within all segments of civilization. Intellectual creators aiming at social changes express collective aspirations and practice.

Scientific theory is not an involuntary by-product of this movement; rather, it is the reasoned result of aspirations and collective practice. A translation of demands from the social to the scientific zone can be done only by the scientists themselves. This relationship is truly dialectical; it is intense and productive. A scientific cognition, in order to fulfill its function, requires creativity, and thus must have independence. Even though this creativity must be integrated with the practical, it should never be subordinated to the pragmatism of politics.

Scientific research does not receive its concepts from the person who is giving orders, does not coordinate its explanations, its conclusions with his requests. It does not administer truth according to the commands of the owner, or the ruler. A thought is not true because it is useful, but it is useful because it is true. The integration of knowledge and goals cannot be realized by allowing one segment (political/economic) to direct another segment (scientific) in their thinking and explaining. Scientific cognition is an *active participant of the movement* that aspires to a different state of human existence and must not be submitted for arbitration to any other form of practice. The researchers themselves participate in the definition of goals and the analysis of their justifiability. The definition itself is an important component of cognition, of the formation of awareness of different possibilities and alternative solutions. Only in this manner can the proverbial Scylla and Charybdis be avoided; the degeneration of science into mere apologetics or indifferent objectivism.

True spirit cannot tolerate any external coercion; it cannot exist if its results are adjusted to reflect the will of any other power. But true spirit is always found in the social segment; it is an essential ingredient of all class movements and not at all remote to any social activity. Real critical thought is never propaganda, but neither is it merely some ephemeral idea. This complex situation is described by Max Horkheimer.

Relatively independent theoretical thinking goes with the development of a class as a necessary critical element to enhance progress. If critical theory consisted only of the formulations of the momentary feelings and notions of one class, it could not be considered to be an intellectual aspect of the historical process of emancipation, but only an interpretation of what exists. Likewise the same is true of a scientist who would decide to subscribe only to the ideas of one part of the class, party or leadership. A dialogue between the progressive elements of the class and the individuals who criticize should be understood as necessary reciprocity. There is the constant possibility of tension between the theoreticians and the class to which their thinking pertains. The uniting force of those social powers which work for freedom is at the same time a disuniting element. . . . Without the possibility of such conflict there would be no need for theory.[36]

Individual quality along with goal-oriented theory and research together inform the creation of a more just human condition. To this ideal one should be loyal.

3

SOCIALISM AND EDUCATION

Higher education in socialist countries, its development and destiny, is organically united to all aspects of the revolutionary process. It is also a living compromise, a hybrid between the new enthusiasm for changes and the corresponding pressure to return to the traditional bourgeois pedagogical principles. It has become a powerful lever of democratization by lessening social differences, but at the same time it acts as an instrument to renew the same class differences in new robes. In spite of this, education has sprung forward in a manner worthy of Prometheus.

Democratization of education, the broad welcome by the universities to the children of workers, peasants, and salaried employees, is a major achievement of social revolution. The educational aspirations of the masses, awakened by the social changes and demands of a new system, are combined to form a powerful force. The progress made in the realm of education in socialist countries is substantially greater than the concurrent progress in the material sphere, and it has surpassed many societies that are considerably better in technological development. Education is a means of conquering the contemporaneity, an investment in human capital, the development of human resources for the future. The secret to great industrial development of these societies is to educate legions of young professionals.

The U.S.S.R. is at the very top of the scale in the number of students per capita, and is considerably higher than societies with a national income several times greater. In the U.S.S.R., the number of students per 100,000 inhabitants is nearly 2,000; compared with England where it is 1258; in France, 1880; in Switzerland, 980. Yugoslavia is at the very top of the European scale. Fidel Castro once said: "This whole island (Cuba) is transformed into a big school."[1] The great innovation is not only in the massive increase of educated people; it is not only quantitative growth that has occurred. Great changes reach down to the very roots of the old school. Audacious pedagogical innovations instituted in the U.S.S.R. during the 1920s shook the very foundation of the inherited authoritarian, repressive pedagogy, its bookish concerns, and its methods of acquiring knowledge. The new experiments brought forth a liberating pedagogy and greatly broadened the polytechnical education of its citizens. That the initiatives of the 1920's are still valid today is due to a variety of reasons: the ideas were audacious; the content of knowledge and methods of acquiring it were innovative; the pedagogy practiced related more closely to the real world and better served to develop creative abilities. Another important trend, though very difficult in practice, is to create an organic whole of studies and productive work, and this effort has become a great ideal of socialist education.

Education, although independent of material growth, still shares a common destiny with the revolution and plays a main role in all its events. The temporary obstructions of the revolution, restoration of the old forms of life, bureaucratic counterrevolutions and technocratic reorganizations, hit education hard, and retreats occur. The events that have hold of education are a sign of changes in the historical climate.

The fate of pedagogical orientation during the ups and downs of the Russian revolution is exceedingly instructive. Concurrent with the bureaucratic counterrevolution, with the conservative restoration of the bourgeois style of work and management in industry, with the vigorous breakthrough of Stalinism, there was a restoration in education. The conservative line in Russia did not want the workers and peasants to receive a general education. Strict discipline and obedience were the desired qualities; the bureaucratic leadership had no use for workers who were educated well enough to control production and govern factories. Leaders only wanted a great number of technicians trained for narrow specialties and complete submission. This tendency has gained in strength; curricula have reduced polytechnical education to unconnected specialized techniques nad have exchanged productive work with temporary excursions to factories. To the thesis that "a baker does not have to know geometrical axioms," Nadezhda Krupskaya has responded that workers should be the conscious builders of socialism and not mere executors of the orders from above:

Polytechnical education has as its goal the general study of modern technology, its main achievements and foundations. Society cannot simply adapt the capitalist methods of increasing productivity. A professional science should not be allowed to cripple mentally a person by forcing him into a narrow specialization at an early age; it should not limit anyone's horizons—but it should help all aspects of his whole development. Professional education has to prepare people to be not only mere executors, mechanical workers—it also has to prepare them to become the owners of industry—so that they are incorporated into the creation of socialism.[2]

In vain, Krupskaya warned:

Do we want to reproduce the old division of labor, do we want to train workers to be only narrowly specialized, workers who know only their own particular working operations and who are therefore permanently tied down, or do we want to create the experts envisioned by Marx and Lenin? A worker/producer is not someone who merely executes orders. Today he might execute, but tomorrow he can be an innovator, and beyond tomorrow he can become one of the important organizers in a factory.[3]

But at the time when Krupskaya was speaking, the social scene was already prepared for a reversion to the old patterns.

SPHINX IN THE EAST: THE CULTURAL REVOLUTION IN CHINA

The Chinese Cultural Revolution has been the most dramatic encounter between the old and the new, between the two orientations oscillating from the one extreme to the other. We shall not be able to research its broader social meaning, its manifold content, its violent streams and counterstreams that have swept through the society like hurricanes, its swings to the extremes of right and left. We will only be able to touch upon all of these. But I want to describe the fundamental dilemmas that the cultural revolution has exposed, dilemmas that are unique in their severity.

A Great Proletarian Cultural Revolution has attacked the two most profound roots of the class division of society, practices that still have not changed, even with the abolition of private property and the takeover of all powers by the state. Over and over the green shoots of class division spring up from these roots and continue to thrive in socialist society. They are, on the one side, bureaucratic hierarchy, connected with the division of intellectual and physical work, the division between the ones that rule and ones that are ruled, and, on the other side, the old consciousness, culture and ideology.

The Cultural Revolution has pronounced battle on the rule of the ossified bureaucratic hierarchy, which was formed from the files of the state and party functionaries, and which has become increasingly detached from both the masses and productive work. Bureaucracy commanded the workers to become masters of technical knowledge, to work copiously and to behave like obedient cogs. Among the actions taken were to drastically reduce the number of administrative personnel by sending the ruling cadres to the villages, and to send the engineers and technicians to work on the assembly line, in order to be "reeducated" by workers. The Cultural Revolution aspired to create a new spirit directed against rewards of privilege and wealth to those people who work in public functions.

Mao Zedong's fear of the renewal of all-powerful bureaucracy from the new sources of the "red functionaries" is understood only if one remembers the old sources—the tradition of the Chinese bureaucratic collectivism. A history of several thousand years of life in a fixed "Asiatic mode of production" with an all-encompassing state bureaucracy that imposed itself on all aspects of Chinese society and sucked its vital juices—this history left a heavy weight that greatly oppressed Chinese society. A thousand-year-old bureaucratic tradition was fertile soil for the growth of a new bureaucracy.

The "mandarin system" played a central role in the formation of the bureaucratic machinery, a thin layer of elite intellectuals who became the brain of the ruling class. The path to state functions led through the monopoly of education and rigorous examinations administered to a very few. The concept that a master is also a powerful bureaucrat is so deeply rooted in the conscience of the Chinese that even the name for the supreme deity was "divine bureaucrat" (*tianguan*). Chinese society was threatened by a repetition of the old story—by the renewal of a restricted ruling class recruited form the educated, who graduated from the universities opened to the children of the ruling classes, of the new bureaucracy. Bureaucratic hierarchy in production and society can be preserved only if expertness is secured as a privilege and if the chosen ones retain a monopoly over knowledge and authority. The notion that the ones who possess knowledge should by the very nature of things also possess power and privileges was, therefore, attacked the most violently. The idea that the knowledgeable ones are only a small minority, and that they will always exist as a minority was denied. The nearly pathological separation of school from life was identified as a grave problem. It was demanded that there be an integration of studies and work as a practical means for the elimination of the abyss between intellectual and physical activities. However, the immaturity of this concept made work look like a form of punishment that one must endure in order to obtain the right to enter school. Instead of leading to the intellectualization of work, it proceeded to degrade it. It devaluated intellectual activity by reducing it to the physical. Thus, one serious problem was identified, but it was not wisely solved. To the contrary!

Another aim of the Cultural Revolution was to attain a new consciousness and culture, one which abolished the old world outlook of the bourgeois ideology. For the domination of the Old World was maintained by the aid of the cultural hegemony of the predominant ideas that enslaved the consciousness. The struggle for a new culture has its specific characteristics that cannot be understood without reconstructing the historical position of this giant from the East. This empire, the oldest and most ponderous in the world, is giant in size, but with little strength, and has for centuries been oppressed by smaller but strong modern Western nations. Their science, culture, and technology brought the genuine Chinese civilization to near extinction, and its cultural and national identity was almost obliterated. Later the same process took place under the Stalinist hegemony. The provocation was enormous.

China had to build not only a modern economy but also had to choose its own direction of development, its own character, its own community able to combine the best values of its own civilization along with foreign ones. Only in this way could it overcome the danger of adopting the crudely imposed foreign realities as their own. In this way a demand for a new culture had become the building block for generations of Chinese reformers and revolutionaries. After the armed struggle subsided, this demand was acutely felt and became a component of great social change. It was a demand for new directions in order to facilitate material changes as well as transform personalities.

Revolution in society and in man is inseparable. A transition from private to collective ownership requires a deep change within the old consciousness, a change of habit and motives. It requires the creation of new moral codes. Only in this fashion can proletarian power be consolidated. A change in the government or the use of terror can touch the human flesh, but it will never reach the soul. Mao has defined the Cultural Revolution as a political revolution in the realm of consciousness, as an ethical transformation that reaches to the bottom depths of the human essence. This revolution stressed willpower, conscience, and action far more than impersonal economic patterns and powers.

A broad campaign against the "four olds"—old ideas, old culture, old customs, old habits—had inaugurated struggle between "the public and private world outlook that tears apart the soul of each individual."[4] It made known the dangers of human egoism, greed and selfishness to the revolution. This struggle is a continuation of the tradition that stresses the need for a morality that will limit the human desire for personal gain, and strengthen in our consciences the power of common interests and public good (*gong*). The struggle aims at the destruction of bourgeois egoism and offers in its place collectivism, a collective spirit, and the creation of the "four new."

Do not strive for personal success or gain; do nothing for yourself but always work for others; be completely devoted to the revolution and the people, with a whole heart serve the people of China and the world. The opposites of this are the principles of extreme individualism: think only about yourself, take care only of yourself, desire success, profit and power, reputation and fame; forget about the millions of Chinese people and billions of other people in the world.[5]

The absolute supremacy of the communal over the personal as a basic pre-supposition to the survival of society is the same basic thought of both Confucius and Mao Zedong.

These general ideas were strictly applied to education where they had far-reaching consequences for the universities and largely dictated what type of personality the university had to create during the educational process. The ideas were expressed in the contrasting notions of "red" as a world outlook of the proletarian class, as well as of the "experts," that being the inherited bourgeois world outlook. The stress each faction placed on differing values altered according to the changes in prevalent opinion. One extreme denied that there was any danger in allowing the monopoly of powers to be placed in the hands of knowledge and inherited culture, thus advocating a renewed class stratification. Another called for the exclusive importance of ideology, for the correct political attitude, and has demonstrated a contempt for knowledge and professional competence. What exacerbated this dilemma even more was the general notion that political opinion must be placed above knowledge—"putting politics in command" was the prevalent slogan. To a certain degree, Mao tried to keep a balance between the two components: the social orientation of science, the pursuits in which it should be engaged, and the role of knowledge and expertness. Mao's creation, "the red expert," although overstated for European taste, is witness to the fact that the national development of China has come to the point where Western science and culture can be organically integrated, and altered for the needs of the Chinese socialist society, without obliterating its own identity ("strengthening the nation through foreign borrowing").

This principle, however, never took hold. Far more influential were the extremes that led to the complete degradation and destruction of the achievements of civilization.

Even without any further examination of all this, there were important lessons to be learned. The Cultural Revolution has posed several funda-mental and unavoidable questions. It made us acutely aware of several essential aspects of education, knowledge and culture that have hitherto received no attention in European socialist thought and practice. And it is at this point that its lasting importance stands.

However, the very manner in which the questions were formulated, in which the dilemmas arose, was such that it did not lead to wise solutions (synthesis), but to a choice between the two worst extremes: either the development of science as a tool for social betterment, or the re-creation of it as a system to maintain expertness; either the encouragement of personal interests or of public ones; either the approval of individualism or a com-plete submergence into collectivism. All part of the same problem is the inability to choose universal values and cognitions, from a whole system in which knowledge has become an instrument of social stratification.

None of this occurred by mere chance. This divided world did not achieve a synthesis of the progressive advances of Western and Eastern cultures. Unfortunately, only by this means could the universal wealth of the world be enjoyed by all mankind, each culture enriching the other with its own authentic and unique abilities, by its Promethean searches for forms of life worthy of man. Only through such a synthesis could there develop a solidarity, a collective spirit rather than a bureaucratic maze. Only thus could there flourish an autonomous, independent personality imbued with desires for public good—all this being the aim of liberating pedagogy.

Mao felt the dangers of all-powerful bureaucracy and the restoration of capital in the new society; he was sensitive to serious dilemmas in the development of the new society. But he failed to formulate either a mature or competent strategy nor was he able to build social powers equal to the undertaking—the most difficult social movement ever attempted. It is of no real significance that even though he had true greatness, he also had great limitations ("genius of the radical peasantry"). He was losing the power to curb horrendous extremes, and a gigantic wave of bureaucratic repression swept the country. Its perpetrators inflicted a new form of despotism— voluntarism and forced indoctrination—assuming that the society and people could be bent to their will. The propaganda was that "another great chaos" was proclaimed as a goal, where what was required was a delicate operation that would divide the universal values from the conservative cultural heritage, and as a result, only great destruction has occurred. Nothing new was created. In practice the result at the universities was the discontinuation of classes and examinations. Participation in ideological confrontations and propaganda replaced professional education. The development of science and education was halted for a decade and had to begin again from unbroken ground. And more than that. These mechanized, surgical cuts repressed themes that are real problems, questions that need to be asked. By its extremes, the cultural revolution has caused the pendulum to swing to the other extreme, to revert to archaic practices.

AN HISTORICAL LESSON

Through the great social battles over education, the primary lesson has crystallized. The development of education and science does not unfold directly, but rather in a complicated and deeply contradictory manner. This great accomplishment of civilization becomes a *spiritus movens* of development and the emancipation of people and communities. At the same time it also contains possibilities for misuse; it can be transformed into an instrument of oppression for a renewal of class relations. What, by its very potential, could and should be a universal right can become a privilege for the elite. Deep transformations, new aims and goals, an inner critical cleansing, the formation of the new constitutive principles of science, the creation of not repressive but liberating pedagogy—these are the themes that appear in our time.

This immense spiritual operation, an epochal cultural revolution of our era, cannot be executed through mechanized surgical intervention. One cannot simply abolish the universities with the slogan: "Down with the schools." The university has to preserve, adapt, and develop the great values of civilization and cognitions that intensify our understanding of nature and society. It has to ennoble them and enrich them with socialist culture. These values should not be degraded into a vulgarized, democratized knowledge. A duty of the contemporary university is to hand over the keys of the cultural treasury to the class of producers, to give to the ever broader circle of children from plebeian classes, to whom higher education has become available, at least as many qualities as were given to the bourgeois children.

Our relation toward inherited culture inevitably contains the general patterns of the socialist revolution. All material by which a new society will be built is constricted from the achievements of the bourgeois society, but they are transformed and altered through the revolution. Just as it is impossible to discard the facts of state, power, the market, techniques of organization, it is impossible to discard intellectual achievement. It is necessary to revolutionize and alter these achievements and put them to the service of the new human purposes. With regard to the human spirit, such great critical reinterpretation is unavoidable in the socialist revolution.

Each retreat from this endeavor results in a great penalty. As in the laws of physics, one great extreme provokes another. The extreme that rejected knowledge, science, and culture provided a transition to another—a reversion to the old school, a strengthening of the disposition for technocratic reform.

The university in the socialist countries finds itself at a historic crossroads. Higher education has opened itself up to the new social classes. But at the same time those patterns of the traditional university, though currently experiencing crises, have been retained or restored.

Two possibilities are available to higher education; the outcome is as yet unsolved. One is a technocratic modernization that would limit the new aspirations and needs to fulfill only the demands of so-called hard reality. Actually, this is a poorly conceived notion because in the long term such measures would not solve the fundamental problems facing education, but instead, would accumulate even harder contradictions. The economic crisis produces a serious contradiction in our concept of the purpose of education. It forces on us one answer that offers an apparent rationalization of education, that is of administrative limitations, of restrictions and stoppage of growth—cutting the number of students, freezing the number of faculty, eliminating systematic scientific work, transforming the university into some kind of high school. The necessity to economize is central to this rationalization. But if such measures only limit and do not open up other possibilities such as an increase in motivation, quality, job-sharing programs, and continuing education, they cannot realize a true rationalization and avoid an accumulation of new and more severe contradictions.

The restriction of education is part of a broader tendency to devaluate and diminish the role of professional work. It is expressed by this notion: "Why do we need so many educated people, why do we need such an accumulation of highly qualified cadres?" It is an orientation toward the devaluation of labor power, toward a mass usage of less-qualified and cheaper "labor power" that is retained longer than necessary. It contains a considerably greater proportion of unskilled labor than it does professional work. The bureaucratic approach to labor power and the manner it is used is that the many groupings of unskilled and poorly paid labor exist longer than necessary because they are easier to manage. The vital and necessary steps that would shorten this stage are not taken. The traditional use of a man as simple unskilled labor, however, limits the development of the forces of production and, consequently, wastes human capacities.

There are similar pressures at work in the international division of labor. The developed countries work to perpetrate the technological oppression of the less developed countries, for they provide cheap and less-skilled routine working power. Subsequently, science is put under the power of the technocratic executives of those industrial corporations that have money and power. Pedagogical principles that maintain this balance are srengthened. They work to produce a minority of future managers and a majority of obedient intellectual working power, one which is being prepared to accept the future hierarchical relationship.

The second possibility facing education today involves radical long-term changes that have a distinct socialist nature. The fundamental socialist principle is that it is not possible to develop productive forces if people, who are the originators of such forces, remain less qualified while technology becomes more developed. This statement is an inaccurate understanding of the production forces of our time, one that reflects the narrow horizons of the old structures. It is necessary to turn in another direction: one must look to one's own scientific creativity based on the comparative advantages of one's country in the world economy. This direction makes possible ever-increasing participation in more qualified and more productive work, work which realizes a great common income when placed against expenses. This is a healthier principle than the principle of profit, for profit limits the creative "usage" of intellectual powers. It raises the level of work, as well as the qualifications of workers, leads to a new culture of work and a new quality of life, one that already knocks at the door of the future. This perspective of development does not freeze and stagnate higher education, but rather, it opens up possibilities for essentially new forms and methods of rationalization that rise above mere technocratic reform.

A PLEA FOR THE SOCIALIST UNIVERSITY

One special trait of the socialist university is its core. It is a nucleus from whence all the other traits arise. In a time of social change, higher education is the exemplary expression of socialist democratic aspirations; it is an entity that opposes the class division of society. The type of society in which we want to live depends to a great extent on the kind of education and science we want to develop, the type of personality we want to groom.

This is not only a plea for socialist education; it is also an enjoinder to improve the quality of the present system of mass education. But the real meaning of human quality, the quality of the developed socialist university, will be the subject of my remaining discussion.

There must be also a decisive commitment toward a greater role for the young in society, a generation without whose active participation, talent and knowledge, imagination and sensitivity toward the future, the society will remain static. And precisely in this respect a decisive role is played by the organic intelligentsia of the class of the producers, a historically new power bloc. This is the education of the people's intelligentsia in whom is united a critical spirit, passion for cognition, knowledge and truth and the finest sensitivity to human needs, and to the improvement of living conditions of the producers.

I quote from Einstein, who in his work "Why Socialism?" expresses this idea:

It is not enough to educate a man only for a profession. In this way, though he will become a type of useful machine, he will not be a complete personality. It is essential that he knows what is important to strive for. He must learn how to understand what moves people to understand their ideas and illusions, their sufferings and battles.[6]

This concept is of decisive importance. The intelligentsia must undertake great revolutionary innovations within professions and seek a different social orientation in all areas of life. It has to become the bearer of intellectual, cultural, and moral transformations within its own professions. For, the instigation of social indifference and professional narcissism and competition at the great intellectual "Vanity Fair" is a subtle mechanism for intellectuality's misuse to asocial purposes. Scientists must understand that they are not the earthly sons of technological deities, but real members of humanity. Once this is understood, scientists will be able to prevent science from being used for would-be Hiroshimas.

The organic intelligentsia is radically different from the traditional, satellitic intelligentsia who imitates, but does not have the power to think originally and cannot develop its own creativity. At the top level, the creators touch upon the outer limits of international science, but their activity is firmly based on individual national cultures and needs. Only through the efforts of the organic intelligentsia can we both avoid technological and economic oppression and retain and develop our own identity, our own form of socialism.

Science, however, can have such a character only if it is inspired by the new human needs of its time and its own society. It can succeed only if it is courageously and audaciously engaged in a deeper and deeper endeavor to achieve a socialist content within culture, in brave innovations within all professions, in socio-cultural alternatives that aspire to a different quality of existence—social and personal. With such an endeavor, society will arise gradually but surely from the limitations that subordinate production and consumption, city life, and human relationships, to the fundamental goals of egoistic profit and bureaucratic power. These are the socio-cultural alternatives to neo-capitalism and bureaucratic socialism as well as to formalized self-government where instead of a truly new quality of human relationships, there exists only a facade, an institutional network. Intelligentsia dedicates its knowledge and talent, finds a meaning and fullness of its own in its search for truth and true change in all areas of human existence.

I will enumerate only a few characteristics of such a creative, liberating, emancipating usage of science. It leads to the gradual diminishment, rather than increase, of essential social differences, differences that threaten the very existence and development of large segments of the population, whole social groups, countries and regions. Such technological development is more conducive to the working masses than to the privileged few or to individual countries. We are faced with a need for new patterns of industrial growth, for a transfer of technology that enables independent development and progress free of oppression; for one which will not deepen the cultural and economic abyss between societies.

This mode of development calls for each individual's strength; it requires greater creative participation in all forms of technological development: in the growth of cities, in food and raw material production, in work organization. Simultaneously it furnishes access to the entire world, thus enriching individual experience with its most valuable ideas. This is the nondestructive path of modernization, one which does not destroy the cultural achievements and advances in production accomplished by the original civilization, in its attempt to create new conditions for the work and life of its population. This path does not lead to enormous masses of pauperized and uprooted agrarian populations. This form of technological development retains the progressive tradition of culture and production and transforms it into a starting point for a great mobilization of human energy, for a pattern of development that corresponds to each population's needs.

Modern industry has grown in the developed countries that were rich with capital and wanting of labor—a type of development, therefore, that cannot be simply copied by the less developed societies. The politics of development have to insure that the opportunities for work be developed in the regions where people live, where they can fall back on their many local resources and where life is less expensive, rather than depending only on the metropolitan centers to which people must emigrate. Gandhi once said that the poorer countries must not rely exclusively upon mass production, but rather upon the production of the masses.[7] Modern, automated, serialized production (particularly in the branches that evidence applications for the future) must be combined with the local resources, initiatives and talents. In addition, there must be a great exploitation of each area's own raw materials and these materials must be manufactured rather than exported. Application of technology in agriculture must offer a greater possibility of combining traditional methods and existing experience with contemporary production forces. Such modernization does not lead to such devastations as the destruction of the soil, the decline of fertility and food quality, the increased threat of hunger, biological degradation, and the increased dependence on the more developed world centers.

The alternatives offered extend into the area of urbanization, our collective life conditions. There should be a city that develops according to human needs, not according to the profit/bureaucratic principles that alienate individuals and convert a city into a modern maze. The alternatives also extend into the realm of medicine and biology, where they serve to create authentic improvements for human life and health. Essential to a worthwhile future is more research into the relationship between the manner of work, working hours, the conditions of urban life and their influences on the human body, lifespan, and health.

The university, through its colleges, acts as the protagonist of such scientific research; it becomes an observation post overlooking the worldwide development of science, but each university incorporates its own originality and seeks to serve the needs of its own society. This is the transformation of colleges into collective scientific research centers. A university of this nature is characterized by the creation of a new pedagogy that unites two great traditions—free spirit and the broad horizons of humanistic culture. It is a pedagogy that is not petty, that opens up space for the creative growth of personality, that does not generate conformism, but develops a critical and independent spirit. Only through such pedagogy can there be formed actively participating personalities, ones which are not merely blind receivers and imitators of foreign practices; rather, they are the builders of a new existence that is crucial to development. For our ability to develop our own creativity will be greatly influenced by both the manner by which the future experts are introduced into the profession, and how much of their curricula has represented the golden spirit of research.

That scientific creativity reach full flourish, that there be increased participation in professional work, increased employment of the younger generations, a better proportion between the development of education and the fulfillment of social needs, a fuller merging of education and work, and a decrease in the gap between intellectual and physical work—all these are not possible without simultaneous changes deep within the social structure. Society must have a firm grip on the very basis of production—the working hours of employees. The time has come to change the division of labor and the purpose of production.[8] We must attempt to understand why we work, what kind of work we do, how we work, and even down to what schedule we work.

CRISIS AND THE TRANSFORMATION OF WORK

To sum up, it pays to produce what is beneficial to everyone; the goal is not in creating privileges and hierarchy. Production must center on goods that are of better quality, more durable.

We are at the beginning of an era when the shortening of the workday is inevitable. More work for machines and less for people would enhance both the wider employment of the young and the professional improvement of those who are already employed. It could lead to a gradual redistribution of the total working time of the producers, part of which could be used for education. Gradually more and more workers and producers would be affected, and thus, in the not too distant future, everyone will be able both to work and educate himself.

Another element in this scheme is that there be an orientation toward deeper changes in the social division of labor, toward overcoming the hierarchical or bureaucratic organization of labor, neither of which are open to expertness and knowledge, but rather stimulate conformism and mediocrity, dry up talent, originality, and innovation. Both maintain a predatory mentality—a battle for the small number of positions offering status and prestige at the top of the hierarchical pyramid. All these are factors that discourage the engagement of knowledge, that leave little room for the expression of those professional and creative potentials that are increasingly available in our more highly educated population. It is necessary to free much more room for such initiatives; both the character and manner of work must be changed.

Therefore, instead of the perpetual practice of dividing working operations into smaller and smaller units, instead of assigning entire lifetimes to only one partial working operation, we must seek a program of more collective decision making, for more expression of initiative, innovation and creativity. It is necessary to diminish the administrative hierarchies, for in fact, they are not as much called for by the necessities of technology, as by the need to have control and power over labor, and by the need to maintain the division between intellectual and physical labor. The work process can increasingly become organically connected to continuing education, to the constant acquisition of knowledge and development of abilities. There is no need for the masses to be sentenced to life terms of unskilled working operations that subordinate. Shorter working hours would enable each worker to continuously enrich his practical and theoretical knowledge. A better entity is made with the union of factory and school, productive work and the acquisition of knowledge.

All these elements are different aspects of one and the same goal. A goal of utmost importance is to diminish the more and more dangerous abyss between intellectual and physical work. The psychology of competition for status and prestige, of contempt for all forms of manual labor, is not automatically lessened with material growth and the increase of riches in society; to the contrary, it is amplified. It is indispensable to strongly stimulate early entry into the work force and at the same time offer wide accessibility to all levels of education to those who are already employed. The very nature of a young man who goes to work compared with the one who continues his education is such that there results nearly insurmountable class differences, ones that bind throughout the whole of life. The enhanced possibility to continue one's education to its highest level beyond the initial work situation would diminish the social inequalities that are created through education. For everyone could participate in production and still have enough freedom to seek education, life, and the fulfillment of his own cultural needs. To accomplish this, a regular plan of accessibility to education should be offered to workers in order that they might further and perfect their knowledge and specialties.

Initiatives that would give to all workers the right to study and to all students the right to work in production will cause essential changes in both schools and organizations of work.

Culture and production, science and technology, intellectual and manual work will not be divided by an abyss forever. A general multivalence would allow for a reduction in the number of unskilled jobs, promote improvement and rotation in all jobs, and would accomplish a perspective of social and technological self-government.[9]

In short, these are the new themes: how to work, for what goal does one work, and how many hours should one work. These are the basic questions to be asked in determining a real rationalization of production. Higher education finds itself in the middle of these essential questions. A grave contradiction between a desire for the reform of higher education and the realistic possibilities for such a reform will arise if there are no deep social changes conducted simultaneously in the work process. The true reform of education is hopeless without these changes.

Changes are necessitated by still another factor, one which took hold particularly in the highly developed world and which is the result of the whole contradictory history of civilization. Socialism has to contend with the deepest roots of the problem—with the inheritance of a class history that is at the very heart of its culture—in order to form a courageous new perspective. A widespread and serious work crisis is facing the contemporary world, and we must meet it head on with a new relationship toward work, one which will shake the very foundations of civilization as we know it. People are increasingly critical of alienating work and less willing to accept it. This unwillingness is evidenced by a whole range of phenomena: mass absenteeism, abuse of sick leave privileges, massive slowdowns, deep dissatisfaction, apathy. The crisis has affected the whole working population, but it is most obvious among the young who do not subscribe to the Puritan work ethic and do not accept work as a sacred duty.

All this is the result of the entire development of class civilization, but we have reached the Rubicon. The entire system of society's development over several thousand years is being destroyed. A crisis, which is extremely complex, is the result of different forces; within it there are two entirely different reactions. One is the ultimate result of the effects of a civilization that subscribed to the ideals of consumption. The ideals of an egoistic/prestige-oriented consumption, which diverts the natural desire for a better life into a fight for prestige and conspicuous consumption, produce a narrow layer of parasitic, secure, well-to-do families who do not want to work. On the other side there is a widespread reaction to alienating, stultifying and monotonous work, which continuously drains energy, gulps down the best of life's powers and ties down people to assembly-line production. Work which is far below human ability and education is no longer necessary in the technological society. People are immensely capable of more than partial routine operations. The young, less conducive to the prejudice and indoctrination undergone by the older generations, have healthier reflexes. They express a new and deep dissatisfaction with the nature of such work, and with the ossified hierarchy. The coming generations, not having been affected by the psychoses of poverty and privation as had their parents, anticipate a real utopia, one which is possible and one which is coming to the fore.

But, from this point on, only two directions for further movement are possible, both being completely opposite each other. One is toward a deep transformation of the character and meaning of work, toward work that will be less coercive and authoritarian, that will be freer and offer more room for creative impulse, education, and the development of abilities. The other direction is to the authoritarian tendencies in society; it will be a right-wing wave against the antiwork behavior of the young. Rightists will demand a return to the powerful values of the Puritan work ethic and an authoritarian upbringing: A young generation that is too loose must be bridled, must be governed by an iron fist. The main strength of the rightists' solution lies in their relationship toward the young, who when positive alternatives are not available, use their energies to reject rather than change, who turn to a nihilism that destroys the old without replacing it with the new.

People, when frightened by the explosive growth of instinctive anarchism, will accept authoritarian power. The conservative reaction will first take hold of education. They will reason: all this is happening because too many concessions were made to the young; they have been too indulged. Now we need a strict, disciplinarian school system, from kindergarten to the university, which will finally teach the young how to respect order and work. Naturally, the core of the problem—what is the true nature of the present order and mode of work—will not be questioned. If this prediction is not convincing enough, turn to the prototype of such behavior, turn to the conservative Joseph Strauss and his virulent attacks on the freedoms given to the young at schools and universities.

The whole development of civilization is full of treacherous dangers. An increase in inactivity can cause catastrophic destruction. For, authentic, creative work is the most treasured value and requirement to give meaning to human life—and work as we know it is not such.

4

YUGOSLAV SOCIETY
AND THE UNIVERSITY

Mass expansion of higher education is one of the great cultural achievements of Yugoslav society. A jump from one student per one thousand inhabitants (1940) to one student per fifty inhabitants (1978)—from 16,970 students in 1937 to 242,000 in 1978, together with the fact that from liberation until today 652,000 students have graduated, is proof of the revolution.

On the eve of the Second World War in Yugoslavia there were only 26 institutions of higher education, and in 1979 there were 19 universities and 336 colleges, academies, and schools of higher education (200 colleges among them). While the number of students has increased 23-fold, the number of professors and assistants has increased about 16-fold, from 1,204 in 1938 to 21,000 in 1978. Participation of female students has risen from 3,956 to 157,443—a 40-fold increase, while during this same period, the number of women professors has risen from 39 to 3,744.

On the eve of the war, there were two schools of higher education in two cities; in 1977/78 there were 136.

Graduate studies are advancing too: 8,176 persons have earned a doctoral degree, and 9,796 a masters degree within the time period of 1945 to 1976.

In Serbia in 1845, there was one school of higher education with 62 students and nine teachers. During the 1870s there were three such schools, with 100 students and 28 teachers. At the beginning of the twentieth century, there were 415 students; and in 1939, about 12,000 students and 576 teachers. By 1978, the number of students in the Socialist Republic of Serbia had reached 219,000 (90,000 of which were in the provinces[1]). Yugoslavia exceeds all Europe in the number of boys and girls to whom higher education is available.[2] In comparison with underdeveloped countries, this number is five to ten times higher. Statistics on the number of students per 100,000 inhabitants are convincing witness to this comparison:[3]

U.S.A. (1974)	4,823
Canada (1974)	3,143
Holland (1974)	1,952
U.S.S.R. (1975)	1,908
France (1974)	1,882
Yugoslavia (1975)	1,844
Norway (1976)	1,818
East Germany (1974)	1,813
Italy (1974)	1,679
Finland (1974)	1,552
Belgium (1974)	1,526
Austria (1974)	1,286
Spain (1974)	1,278
Great Britain (1974/75)	1,258
Greece (1974)	1,096
Hungary (1975)	1,023
Czechoslovakia (1974)	982
Switzerland (1974)	972
Portugal (1973)	699

In Yugoslavia the generation within the age bracket of 20 to 24 is about 11 percent of the total population, while in the Asian countries, it ranges from 1 to 6 percent.

But there is one essential trait that is not evident from bare statistical facts. By the concurrence of historical events, the university has a strong plebeian trait. Young people, who hasten to the universities from the poor regions and working classes, carry within themselves strong ideas about more social and national equality. The university becomes the primary locale of our progressive, social, and freedom-loving tradition. Formed in the days of rebellion, during crucial historical storms, it is firmly tied to the battles and, finally, the destiny of its people. There has emerged a center where a generation, in Lola Ribar's words, "follows the ideals of conscious service to the people, as a social duty of the people's intelligentsia."[4]

Strong roots from the significant part of the intelligentsia already within this country's people have contributed to the fact that no other student movement in the world had ever played such an important part in the revolutionary changes of its country. An undogmatic, broad, and open relationship toward the freedom of creation, science, and its intelligentsia is one of the decisive characteristics of Yugoslav socialism. Revolution does not belong to the party or state, but to the class and the people. It is the expression of the total creativity of one society, culture, and civilization. The intelligentsia is not a subordinate fellow traveler who, even at its most loyal, is untrustworthy. It is an authentic, creative force, an equal and organic part of the great historical block of power that aspires to a different state of human existence. We believe that this progressive and deep-seated tradition has its constant driving source of energy, one which is completely contrary to the technocratic structure of the university.

But these bright events, these revolutionary cultural achievements, should not obscure the dark side. It is a fact that the highly educated population is still a narrow stratum—5.3 percent of the total working population. In 1974 the number of employees without any schooling or with only partial elementary schooling was 28.09 percent; the number of employed with only elementary schooling was 20 percent. In addition, we must not forget the bitter fact that in 1971, some 15 percent of the population was illiterate. A fund of superior experts grows from one quite narrow base; many talents are left without higher education, and we are thus not achieving optimal quality in national proportions. For rational, optimal, and speedy development, we need a more effective method of creating experts with a higher education.

Let me introduce still one more extremely important factor that further underlies the essential contradiction. The universities are an asylum for those escaping production. This fact is explicitly expressed in the lack of balance between the students of the nonproductive economic-juridical sciences—35 percent of the total number—and those of the technical, medical, and biological sciences. In 1976/77, only 24 percent were enrolled in all technical sciences combined.

One of the achievements of this development is a true democratization of education, a radical change in its social structure. In the universities of Serbia in 1938, only 3.5 percent of the student body were the children of workers and peasants, but this figure has leaped to 34 to 50 percent.

A breakdown of the social standing of first-year enrollees for the school year 1977/78 at the universities and schools of higher education in Niš and Kragujevac reveals the following:

University and Schools of Higher Education	Enrolled Full-time Students from Families of:		
	Workers	*Salaried Employees*	*Peasants*
Kragujevac	51.0%	29.0%	20.0%
Niš	45.0	40.4	14.6

In 1938/39 the percentage of children of salaried employees and professionals was 64.2%; this decreased to 34.0% in 1970/71. The following table
shows this curve of democratization.[5]

Social Origin of the Parents	1938/39	1951/52	1958/59	1962/63	1970/71	1975/76
Agricultural workers	20.0%	20.0%	18.0%	17.5%	15.0%	13.0%
Workers (in industry and mining)	3.4	8.4	15.3	18.2	18.6	19.2*
Administrative personnel (financial, managing cadres, professionals, and artists)	64.2	54.0	43.0	38.6	34.0	33.5

*Of these the most significant are: workers in commerce, 4.4 percent; workers in services and
work safety, 6.1 percent; workers in traffic, 3.2 percent.

The facts point at the considerable democratization and the lessening of
class inequality. There is not a single level of education that is closed to any
social group. All strata took part in the expansion of education, each
stratum sending a measurably greater number of its younger members to
the institutions of middle and higher education than they had before. This
trend was helped along by the intervention of a society that was able to
create more favorable material-cultural conditions. In Yugoslavia, more
than 88,000, or 36 percent of the full-time student body (and in Serbia alone
25,000 or 30 percent), are recipients of credits or stipends. Tito's fund for
young workers or for the children of workers has granted 13,000 scholarships within five years. Free textbooks are given to about 250,000, or 45
percent, of the total number of students. The social-professional categories
of the parents of students in dormitories are 48 percent from workers'
families, followed by 26.8 percent from individual farm workers (peasants),
and 12 percent retirees.

However, further study of the changes in the social structure of students
shows another side—the persistent maintenance of social inequality as a
long-standing historical phenomenon. The university becomes an important implement in social promotion and therefore a place for competition
among social groups, "a racetrack" where various interests clash. The
university is exposed to contrary pressures and dissatisfactions. For one
group it does not impose a firm enough monopoly and for the others it has
not completely opened itself to the poorer strata, particularly the workers.
In this race the university is not a neutral observer, but a powerful arbiter.

An analysis of facts indicates that the representation of students from certain social groups corresponds to the position of those groups on the ladder of the social structure of society. This correspondence is evidenced by the big differences in how certain social groups are represented in the middle and higher levels of education. There are two obvious occurrences. In all levels of education, the least number of children come from an agricultural background. This fact is a constant in all observations, and special significance should be attributed to it because this background is the largest group within society. This phenomenon is of such importance that one could talk about "the class nature of the social differences between the villages and the cities."[6] Yet another fact is that children from nonmanual workers have the greatest possibility of reaching the higher levels of education and this discrepancy is augmented at each successive level.

The relationship between the groups with the lowest and the highest participation is 1:4.6. This means that the probability that a child of a salaried employee will enter high school is four to five times greater than that of the peasant's child. However, the ranges are significantly greater if the indices are based on a comparison of the percentage of students set up against the percentage of the working population. This range is 1:7.4.[7]

With this information we can make an important conclusion: the degree of decrease of social inequality is inversely proportionate to the level of education. At the lower level of education greater equality is realized, and, conversely, the higher levels are characterized by a lower degree of equality. This iron law cogently demonstrates itself.[8]

Schools for workers as well as technical and vocational schools contain:

> 82 percent of the children of agricultural workers
>
> 76 percent of the children of workers
>
> 58 percent of the children of salaried employees
>
> 24 percent of the children of managerial personnel

Conversely, high schools contain:

> 14 percent of the children of agricultural workers
>
> 17 percent of the children of workers
>
> 50 percent of the children of salaried employees
>
> 53 percent of the children of managerial personnel

The situation at the schools of higher education and the universities is as follows:

	Percentage of Group in Higher Education	Percentage of Group in Universities
Children of workers	33.4	23.5
Children of professionals and managerial personnel	17.4	32.0

There is one more aspect to be taken into consideration—that of the essentially different social structures of different colleges. Although these differences alter from year to year, they are not episodic, but rather they tend to reproduce the existing social strata. There is a rough division into two groups. Participation of working-class children in the colleges of architecture, dentistry, medicine and some language studies is between 3 and 15 percent. Participation of the same group in the colleges of agriculture, technology, metallurgy, forestry, mining, geology, and law is between 40 and 60 percent. Social groups aspire toward those colleges that offer a perceived social status. The dramatic struggles incurred during the entrance examinations at medical schools result not only from the differences between the A and the B students.

The relationship between belonging to a certain social stratum and achieving a higher level of education is not determined simply; it is done by means of the complicated mechanism of selection toward success, by means of the unequal distribution of cultural capital. We have analyzed this subtle social process and for empirical purposes can adduce the following facts. Research done in several teacher's colleges in the Socialist Republic of Serbia points to the significantly different levels of academic success by tabulating above-average marks. At the top were the children of salaried employees, followed by the children of workers from the cities, while the children of the individual agricultural producers were at the bottom. Observing the data on school results in all high schools in 1968/69, Velimir Tomanović[9] concludes that "starting from poorer and moving upward to the wealthier groups of students, there are successively more B and A students, while with the C students the order is reversed." According to the data of the Institute for Education of Socialist Republic Slovenia (Zavoda za školstvo S. R. Slovenije) for the 1966/67 school year (when they were published), on an average 10.5 percent of all students failed and had to reattend the same grade level, but the percentage is higher for children of the agricultural workers (13.5 percent), and for the children of workers (12 percent), while it is significantly lower for the children of salaried employees (4.4 percent).

	Students According to Grades (in Percent)		
	A	B	C
Both parents with higher education	21.0	9.0	11.0
Both parents without school education	1.8	3.8	21.5

Still another nuance should be mentioned, a nuance which unveils an organic connection between basic social processes, and greater access or, conversely, greater restriction, to the university. Changes within society, a greater or lesser push towards social stratification directly influences the social structure of the student body. The percentage of the children of workers within that body is directly linked to the existing social order and until recently did not change. At the same time, the participation of children of administrative, financial, professional, and managerial personnel leaped from 31 to 36 percent within only five years(1961-1965).[10] This trend then changed direction. It was halted at the end of the 1960s. The changes that worked to improve the social structure were continued through strong pressures, conflicts and the intervention of society.

Only by a comparative analysis of one's own needs in relation to all-over world development can we form a historical awareness of the depth of the changes that will occur as the result of future demands; only in such a way can we escape the Scylla and Charybdis of poor solutions. Marx once observed that "the social revolution of the nineteenth century cannot draw its poetry from the past, but only from the future."[11] But if we lack the audacity to face the future as our own, and are unable to make our impression on it, if our image of the future is a lie or is limited then many of the results of our present energies will evaporate, and the educational system will be lost to our youth. The options will be the lifeless alternatives that are so prevalent in contemporary society and that condition a terminus of poor solutions.

Reform cannot be a mere change of facade; it requires fundamental long-term social changes, an integral part of the great cultural revolution of our epoch. Its motto must not be as in *The Leopard*: "To change so nothing gets changed."[12] We cannot forget culpability. But the reform must not be reduced to chameleon-like technocratic alterations, to application-oriented formulae, which under the banner of economic prudence actually halt the development of the university and transform education into a factor that increases social inequality. I repeat, not for a moment do I doubt the necessity of increased economic responsibility, a more cogent rationalization and effectivity of the university. But without fundamental changes, even that request is unfeasible. Finally, neither of the extreme solutions that were expressed in the West and the Far East by the slogans "abolition of the university," "bankruptcy of the university," "down with the schools," brought about the creation of something new. They destroyed the achievements of civilization. The university cannot be abolished any more than could one abolish the system of factories, without the destruction of the foundations of civilization.

But the university simply cannot stay the way it is. We must open up new paths, and undertake an endeavor of deep and long-term changes; we must free ourselves from slavery to the old and create new perspectives, ones which will open up possibilities for more productive solutions. We have to present alternatives in order to find solutions for new directions, and we must begin with those that are the most important to the future of the young—the world of work and society. This necessity is not the result of political demands, or of matters which remain divorced from the university, but it is a result of the combined activity of several social forces. In the first place it is all part and parcel of the new reality which we have already explained—the explosion of science and mass education that causes an ever-increasing gap between traditional patterns and mass higher education. Many irrationalities that appear and create problems at the universities have deep social roots and are an expression of the crisis of the traditions that we have described. Since higher education is becoming so essential to all of society, its impact on this crisis will increase in significance. Among other effects, it shall act as a major determinant in either the obsolescence or the conservation of class structure.

The great social and intellectual endeavor that we call the reform of the university and the trend toward a union of free producers are part of the same process. This process was projected by the Resolution of the Tenth Congress, which announced the need for a socialist and self-governing transformation of schooling and education. (See Appendix.)

The essential novelties of today are therefore the changes that were brought about by the particular development of our society. The university will find itself the center of the new educational system, characterized by the establishment of individual goals at the intermediate levels. There will be a tendency to abolish dualism in education, the differences between high school students and apprentices, disparities that are an expression of great class divisions, for this is the authentic aspiration appropriate to socialist development. It is essential that this basic intention stays preserved, so that class differences are not already fixed among our young. But precisely in order to preserve this aspiration, reform must free itself from certain conceptual contradictions; it must realize that old divisions maintain themselves through new methods. It is essential for the university not only to adapt itself to the concept of intermediate education, but also (and this, at its most developed level of consciousness) to influence the intellectual profile of its future generations in order that they adapt themselves as well.

There is a new relationship: university—society. From a situation in which the state was the only representative of society (the one that decides on funds, number of students, programs) the universities emerge and enter into a network of decentralized and independent relationships with business organizations and social enterprises. Part of the student body will be the result of these direct contacts. The various organizations will provide part of the funds, and will create innovative programs aimed at the idea of a permanent education. This is a path that leads to the destruction of the old patterns formed by class division, the concept of mutually separated activities—material production on one side and education and science on the other. This path leads to a creation of students who are an organic part of both the intelligentsia and the contemporary class of producers. The outline of a new, high-quality education can be seen on the horizon. It announces a great change, the will to develop a self-governing socialist university. All this is not without serious contradictions and risks, for there is always the danger of one-sided solutions. Two trends will be prevalent. One will be expressed by a nostalgia for the university as an institution enclosed within walls, an institution that does not become engaged in direct social activity, in relationships that dirty the hands and dangerously threaten the autonomy of intellectual work, activity that must not be exposed to monopolistic pressure. The other trend, one that we have already described, is the danger of technocratic power over the educational process, the danger of transforming science into a service for those with power and money. The socialist reform of the university, freedom from state tutelage, does not mean that the university becomes a commercial enterprise that buys and sells knowledge and degrees, commercializes science, and transforms knowledge into goods.

The decision to enter into organic relationships with business organizations and social enterprises must be followed with visions and an intellectual framework that will give meaning to the real physiognomy and role of the socialist university. The concept of this great process, of the reform of higher education, can only be accomplished collectively.[13] It can only be the result of the collective creative abilities of the teachers and students of all colleges, for these are the primary instruments of the change. This concept cannot be an administrative act planned in offices that are removed from the everyday school life, for such would be perceived as an enforced outside directive. Only the full participation of all creative powers at the universities and within society can awaken initiative and willpower. Only democratic mobilization of all creative powers can awaken the abundance of initiative and imagination necessary to investigate new and unknown possibilities, and to search for and give concrete answers to the great challenges and grave problems that plague both the university and society. Only by this means can the distinctive characteristics and specific qualities of all scientific fields and different colleges be expressed. A broad circle of varying characteristics cannot be reduced to dull uniformity. Neither centralized control that would restrict individuality and personal responsibility on the one hand, nor a lack of common agreement and unification of powers on the other, could bring forth fruitful results.

The changes are projected for the future, but they must commence immediately. They will start up the processes that will in turn start others, each building on an ever more complex organization. Those concrete measures that will alleviate many irrationalities must be long-term in character lest they do not provide results. It is an illusion to think that a problem might be solved by a slight touch. Without serious attention the problems will accumulate and become intensified. But the proposal that changes must be fundamental and long-term must not be an alibi for their postponement.

The major difficulty arises in the attempt to translate these general concepts and aims into the reality of everyday school life. How do we create a series of concrete measures that can be transformed into actuality? Some elements of more modest efforts, though far from what we know to be our needs, are the subjects of the second part of this study.

Part II

Possible Directions,
Reforms, and Alternatives

5

THE DEVELOPMENT
OF EDUCATION
AND SOCIAL NEEDS

Presently, social development and the growth of education are not progressing at the same pace. This creates a series of dangerous anomalies throughout the entire system, from enrollment to the employment of young individuals.

Already our system of enrollment at the university is a Gordian knot, given the present state of affairs. At the moment of enrollment, all contradictions and discrepancies are focused on and expressed: social differences and regional inequalities, grave discrepancies between productive and nonproductive activities, between future needs and the contemporary situation all cross over each other. Thus, the number and profile of enrolled students are not expressions of real demands, but rather reflect the innate forces and social functions of the university—a place for postponing all the difficulties that the young encounter in seeking employment. Enrollment at the university is a social process that exists outside of any structured directing, and it is small wonder that the entire system has not yet collapsed.

School Year	Expected Number of Enrollees	Number Registered	Number Enrolled	Enrollees above the Expected Number
1974/75	17,030	27,636	21,748	4,716
1975/76	16,033	26,980	21,932	5,899
1978/79	25,779	36,774	27,620	1,841

The application of unrealistic projections would only lead to more difficult complications, until long-term, more productive solutions are implemented. For with that, the gap between the increased number of students and the deterioration of those material conditions which promote quality learning (lack of classrooms, laboratories and equipment) widens. The number of registered students at colleges of social sciences has grown 284 percent beyond the available capacity. At colleges of medicine, the growth is 145 percent; at technical colleges, 142 percent.[1]

The problem of "alloting space" to the young generation, however, cannot be reduced only to the school setting, to the problems of how to sort out classrooms. Such difficulties give warning of the existence of long-term social problems: our developmental policies, the social division and distribution of work, the over- and underestimation of various sectors of work and professions—in short, social differences.

I will now describe several factors that are together one and the same important phenomenon: the large discrepancy between the development of education and the requirements of society. One aspect of this expensive misunderstanding is expressed by the surplus and scarcity of various professions. In some professions we are presently educating surplus cadres, and in others not enough. Data were published in 1977 that indicated that the so-called surplus occupations could be filled by 202,000 individuals, while the expressed need for these profiles was only 35,000. This demonstrates that the educational institutions produce a great number of educated who are not needed in the job market. At the same time the economy was in short supply of a variety of experts for which it searched in vain. It appears that nearly 200,000 people have capabilities in 40 to 50 unnecessary occupations. However, a brief overview reveals only a portion of the picture, while at the same time concealing more important factors. It leads to the easy conclusion that the lack of coordination is only an academic problem, that it is based on a poorly designed system of producing profiles not corresponding to the objectively expressed needs of society. But this is only one facile aspect of the problem. We must subject it to anatomical analysis and discover more appropriate solutions.

THE SURPLUS AND SCARCITY OF PROFESSIONS

Firstly it should be stated that there is no doubt that there is poor coordination between education and forecasting of needs. This is information that colleges themselves cannot provide. We are faced with a need to build a system that will predict the kinds and numbers of professional profiles that will be required in the future. Secondly, today's high schools provide specialties that are too narrow. This conditions additional difficulties because a narrow profile rarely corresponds with the specialty that is at that moment in demand (although it must be acknowledged that students have graduated from colleges where their specialty and the one that is needed is the thrust of their education). But now education and needs appear to be two separate branches, not even belonging to the same tree. This calls our attention to the importance of pedagogical reform, to the problems with narrow specialization, which, if ill-conceived, bring insoluble difficulties to the young professionals. For instance, the registered needs in employment from 1976-1980 consisted of 976 occupations and profiles, while at the same time the whole education system was preparing students for only 250 occupations. However, in this era of rapid technological change, the educational system will never be able to completely educate its students to handle the most specific tasks in the course of their regular studies. For many occupations will become obsolete and new ones will be created in the duration of a professional life.

Thirdly, many profiles at the state level are either in short supply or overabundance. We are dealing, therefore, with the territorial immobility of the intellectual work force. This balance is particularly noticeable between Belgrade where there are many surplus professionals and other centers where experts are in short supply. In forty-eight lesser developed counties of Serbia there are only 2,250 workers with a higher education, and in some economic activities there is not a single employee with one. In ten of the most underdeveloped counties, there are only two to nine (at the most) employed experts who are highly educated.

Fourthly, the employment offices and the commerce bureaus report that many occupations have been in short supply for years, and these include agricultural engineers, electrotechnical engineers, biologists, professors of philosophy, and dentists. The mere adduction of these important professions reveals the problematic manner by which needs are expressed. How could it be possible that agricultural engineers are not needed at a time when we are conducting great projects in the development of agriculture? Are traffic engineers unnecessary when we know that only 2 percent of all who work in the field of traffic are highly educated? Are the professors of philosophy superfluous, when Marxism is taught by geography teachers? Do we not need dentists when patients must wait for several months to be treated by dental clinics? The whole process of determining the actual needs is presently deformed. The image is already distorted in relation to contemporary needs but even more so in relation to the future.

EXODUS—ESCAPE FROM PRODUCTION

At this juncture we can identify the most important discrepancy between the profile that is being created through education and the requirements of society; at the same time we can point to the cause of the discrepancy between surplus and scarcity. It is the mass escape from productive occupations and production, an escape to the nonproductive activities, to administration. An analysis of school enrollment patterns displays this trend in two different ways. Available positions that were left open after the first round of registration into the third grade of intermediate directed education convincingly show the fields suffering scarcities, disinterest for the following professions: agriculture, chemical technology, mechanical engineering, civil engineering, the textile and leather industries, the lumber industry, geology, mechanical-energetics, traffic, the catering and tourist trade, and ecology. In the case of mechanical engineering, mechanical-energetics and electrical engineering, there were at the first term five times fewer students than available places; for ceramics, the refractory sciences, and the production of construction materials, 30 times fewer had applied than were needed.[2]

The economy cries out for the productive occupations, but in vain. At the same time the interest in registration at the colleges of social sciences is convincingly in first place, more than 50 percent of all candidates have applied at the University of Belgrade (a total of 17,709 have registered and 8,485 of these for the social sciences). In Kragujevac 63 percent of all enrolled students attend the school of economics and the college of law. Statistics show that a greater interest in the social sciences is steadily increasing, while the interest in the studies of natural sciences (with the exception of medicine), particularly the technical sciences, is constantly decreasing. In 1975/76 there were 4,500 students in social sciences, 3,000 enrolled in technical sciences and 3,000 in biotechnical, medical and other natural sciences. In 1977/78 the social sciences enrolled over 4,500 students, while the technical sciences only 2,300. This is not to say that an interest in the technical sciences is nonexistent, because 4,073 candidates applied for the 2,860 available places at the technical colleges, and these exceeded the space and teaching capacities of these colleges by 42 percent.[3] In this instance I am describing the imbalance between the social and biotechnical sciences, between the productive and nonproductive occupations.

The universities have tried to alleviate this imbalance by making corrections at the second round of registration. As a result, 44 percent of the students who were enrolled in the biotechnical sciences were above the planned number, as were 16 percent in the medical sciences, 15 percent in the technical sciences, and only 9 percent in the social sciences. But these corrections are of little significance when one takes into account the powerful stream of students entering the universities.

This phenomenon is the result of demands, of the existing structure of the work force. While in industry the number of job openings in one year has grown by 6 percent, financial institutions have increased this demand by 55 percent, and the social-political organizations by 60 percent. While the demand for workers in industry was greater by 6 percent (1978 compared with 1977), at the same time the increase in the nonindustrial enterprises was 40 percent. In the plans for cadres in all work organizations in Serbia (a poll taken of 2,000 organizations), there is a demand for five times more lawyers and economists, a figure far higher than the available capacities of these colleges.

Higher education reflects the image of the existing work structure, the discrepancy between the productive and nonproductive activities as they exist in real life. In Belgrade some 58,000 experts with higher education are employed, and this group is approximately 10.9 percent of the total work force. This imposing power is sharply divided between the two poles: while in the nonproductive activities each third employee has a higher education, in production only one out of eighteen has the same. In banking and foreign commerce, approximately 22 percent of the employees have a higher education, while the total industry of Belgrade employs only 5,340, or 3.9 percent, with higher education (in the chemical industry, 7 percent; in the machine building industry, 4.9 percent; in the food processing industry, 3.3 percent; in the metalworking industry, 2.6 percent; in the textile industry, 2.6 percent).

This picture shows how both parents and children perceive the reality of work opportunities, and how they react to the evaluation of different activities. It particularly shows the odious position given to work in production. Education becomes an escape from production, for positions more removed from the place of production become increasingly more profitable and more secure. One cannot deny people a certain amount of realism.

TERRITORIAL DIFFERENCES AND THE INEFFECTIVITY OF STUDIES

Difficulties rarely come alone. One aspect of educational discrepancy can be expressed by describing the relationship between productive and nonproductive activities; yet another aspect to be considered is the problem of great territorial differences, a lack of balance in territorial development. The ratio between the number of students per 10,000 inhabitants in different locales can exceed 1 to 3.

	Number of Inhabitants	Number of Students	Number of Students per 10,000 Inhabitants
S.R. Serbia	8,848,776	179,054	202
S.R. Serbia (without the autonomous provinces)	5,463,910	111,299	204
Beograd	1,342,946	45,166	336
Zaječar	353,050	4,989	141

	Number of Inhabitants	Number of Students	Number of Students per 10,000 Inhabitants
Leskovac	498,353	7,654	154
Kraljevo	754,959	13,886	184
Niš	636,117	13,462	212
Valjevo	533,357	6,915	130
Smederevo	469,008	4,859	104
Titovo Užice	333,766	5,089	153
Kragujevac	541,804	9,279	171

Out of the total number of full and part time students in the school year 1977/78, 70 percent study in Belgrade, 14 percent in Niš, 6 percent in Kragujevac, and 10 percent in other regions.

On the other side, only 39 percent of the students at the University of Belgrade are from the Belgrade region, approximately 30 percent are from Serbia proper, and 30 percent are from the autonomous provinces and other republics, a situation which exacts enormous expenses.

All these contradictory elements strongly influence a phenomenon that at culmination appears to be a problem of the educational system alone. The discrepancy between the profiles toward which we educate and those required by society, between the surplus and the scarcity of occupations exacerbates the discrepancy between the manner in which education is financed and the mobility of the intellectual work force. This characterizes the present state of affairs.

School becomes a place where one prolongs his stay outside of the working world. Poor work prospects create low motivation in its most basic form and this, combined with the many weaknesses of the educational system, results in a low level of effectiveness. Studies last approximately from six to eight years. Late graduation has become a chronic disease. One can see this ineffectivity when comparing the situation with various other countries. According to data for the year 1968, here are the rates of completion within the expected duration: in the Soviet Union, 60 to 80 percent; in Sweden, 68 percent; in Belgium, 66 percent; in West Germany, 54 percent; in France, 45 percent; in Austria, 44 percent; in Yugoslavia, 30 to 35 percent (40 percent for the schools of higher education, according to the data from 1974.) However, if graduation takes place a year later than expected, 72 percent of the students will have graduated.[4]

But in the last few years various reforms, including closer regulation of studies, the introduction of modular studies, and one-semester courses, show results—there is a certain increase in effectiveness. The number of completions has increased by 8 to 10 percent, the highest number of graduates in the history of the university. The ratio between taking an examination and passing it has improved—at the University of Belgrade the ratio is nearly 60 to 100.

In an analysis of effectiveness, one element of great importance, an element that greatly affects motivation, has to be introduced. The students who receive loans graduate with four times a greater frequency than those who do not, thus showing an entirely different relationship toward studies when there is a motivation.

UNEMPLOYMENT AND WORK PROSPECTS

The factor that kills practically all motivation is unemployment. The work organizations are closed to young experts, even those organizations that do not suffer from financial privation, thus revealing a certain form of social egoism. At the end of 1977, 717,000 individuals were seeking employment, and 450,000 of those for the first time. Nearly 50 percent of them were from 19 to 24 years of age. For over a year 308,900 individuals wait for employment. Nearly 280,000 of these are the educated cadres: qualified and highly qualified workers and individuals with high school and higher education. The number of unemployed looking for work for one open position (in Yugoslavia) has risen from 7.3 to 10.2 percent: in S.R. Slovenia 1.5; in S.R. Croatia 5.1; in the Autonomous Province of Vojvodina 7.2; in S.R. Bosnia and Herzegovina 14.3; in S.R. Serbia 14.3; in S.R. Montenegro 14.7; in S.R. Macedonia 21.7; and in the Autonomous Province of Kosovo 30.3 percent.[5]

The increase in unemployment is the highest among the highly educated cadres. From 1972-1977, a jump of 361 percent was recorded. In 1978 there were 64 percent fewer trainees than in 1977. The lower the level of education, the easier it is to find a job. In S.R. Serbia, 30 percent of all vacancies request unskilled and semiskilled work and these positions fill rapidly. During the time span of 1967-1977, among the total number of unemployed the number of highly educated and individuals with a high school education has increased five times, while the number of unskilled has increased less than twice. The fact that it is easier to employ unqualified labor points to the resistance to hiring an expert work force in many milieus. At the same time, it is an expression of the trend to devalue the expert work force by using cheap labor, as we have mentioned previously.

Among the unemployed, the young prevail—to thirty years of age. Their number grew from 66.7 percent in 1972, to 78.2 percent in 1977. The long and exhausting waits for the results of competitions gradually sap their freshness, and late entry into the work force creates deep social and psychological consequences. At the same time, a substantial devaluation of the educated work force takes place: the educated are employed in positions for which they are much too qualified.

The many-faceted and intertwined causes are difficult to eliminate. These same problems exist also in much richer societies, societies that cannot claim the same excuses, because they provide much greater funding for education. But yet the situation exists, and it is charged with explosive contradictions.

A POSSIBLE TURNING POINT

The assault on education, the discrepancy between the professions that are being educated and the exhibited needs, the escape form productive professions, the ineffectuality of studies, low motivation, and the poor prospects for employment—all are different facets of the same fundamental social process. A better balance and effective solutions cannot be achieved by administrative restrictions on studies, or by halting educational development. The elimination of one danger through such activity would create new and more dangerous ones. Access to education is an expression of democratic aspirations appropriate to socialism, and also a method of increasing the productive powers of society. The rate of highly educated experts in Yugoslavia is below that of Hungary and Romania.[6]

	Portion of Experts with Higher Education among Total Employed, 1971 (in percentages)
U.S.S.R.	7.8
Bulgaria	5.9
Hungary	5.6
Romania	5.4
Poland	5.1
Czechoslovakia	4.4
Yugoslavia (1974)	5.3

The expansion of higher education is a great achievement of Yugoslav society, not its expendable cargo. Although it contains a variety of serious irrationalities, access to higher education must not be administratively restricted or halted. The limitation and restriction of education would deepen many contradictions and create a series of long-term adverse consequences: in terms of the country's developmental possibilities and social relationships, a reduction of highly educated cadres would lead to the decrease of our own scientific creativity and to an increase in technological dependency, to a significant increase in the social (class) differences created by education, to an amplification of the differences between the regions, autonomous provinces and the republics, to an increase in competition for the dwindling number of available positions. It is impossible to restrict the expansion of education through administrative measures. But education cannot be based only on antiquated principles. Simultaneously and gradually new paths should open that will regulate admission to the universities more naturally—ones that will offer quality education and avert many irrationalities.

This is a chain of many links, of which the following are especially significant:

1. fundamental social presuppositions regarding the young professionals' access to work
2. prognostication (planning) and a greater emphasis toward social orientation in the development of education
3. real progress in the organic linkage of studies and work; a greater opportunity for the ones who work also to educate themselves and for those who study to find work
4. a great pedagogic reform—instead of molding individuals into the narrowest specializations (which is risky in an era of rapid technological and professional change), a mobile intellectual work force formed; with a broad educational basis, a series of narrower professional tasks performed with little additional training.

SOCIAL PRESUPPOSITIONS—WORK PERSPECTIVES

More harmony between the development of education and the requirements of society, and more extensive employment of the young—this being the key issue—cannot be achieved if we do not attack the existing organization and division of labor. The first part of this work outlines the argument; the remainder will sum up with conclusions about long-term and fundamental changes and will present a plea for a social compact that will insure the employment of the educated young.[7]

One long-term change requires that we orient ourselves to the near future, to shorten working hours and grant youth more employment. More work by machines and less by people would lead to the greater employment of the young and to the professional improvement of those who are already employed, would lead to a more intensive usage of experts and machines and ultimately to an increase in productivity. Part of the working time would be freed for education in such a way as to gradually broaden the circle of working individuals who would have an opportunity both to work and educate themselves. These are, therefore, the changes that supplement the uniform learning for life with continuing education so that during one's whole professional life a person maintains a knowledge of the course of con-

temporary developments. This is a component of the changes in the character and division of work that, in its present ossified hierarchy, offers little
room to express all potential knowledge, enlightenment, innovation and
talent. In short, more room for the expression of abilities must be offered to
a much greater number of people.

Such a course would enhance departure from the vicious circle in which
we presently find ourselves. New generations cannot find adequate employment because there is an insufficient accumulation of activity to enable the
expansion of production and the creation of new positions. This accumulation is not increasing rapidly enough because, among other reasons, there
is also an insufficient amount of expertise, because of the small number of
expert cadres. The truncation of working hours to make possible professional education for the already employed and to employ the new ones
offers profitable possibilities. In addition to the full utilization of machines,
there would always be one more "shift," that of the educational programs
that have been implemented to fulfill the needs of the total work situation.
This pattern would open a path for parallel solutions to many problems:
essentially increased employment, a network of continuing education
alongside work, an increase in the productive potential of society.

Another side of this new relationship is formation of the consciousness
that a degree does not offer the right to privileged occupations, to favored
positions, but rather to creative work and the development of abilities and
the possibilities for their expression.

Concurrently an increase in remuneration and a respect for work in
material production should develop. Except for the claims for power and
egoistical interests, there is no reason for not allowing the positions of
highly qualified, highly professional work in production to set the standards of the amount for income in all other activities—from administration
and health services to politics and education.

Certain measures can be taken to improve the employment system, and
they are immediately within reach. Overtime hours and second jobs should
be decreased in favor of more comprehensive employment. During the
period from January to November 1978, 10.6 percent of the total number of
employed worked overtime (in S.R. Slovenia 26.8 percent, in S.R. Serbia 6.6
percent). The additional work was paid 1,300 billion old Dinars.[8] In S.R.
Serbia in 1978, an average of 115,730 workers per month worked overtime.
Should overtime work and second jobs be decreased, an additional 100,000
new workers could be employed.[9]

Among other immediate measures, one could eliminate the requirement
of previous work experience, which is a hindrance for beginning employees.
This requirement is often the result of the bureaucratic mind-set. But life
will not stop and wait while we look for better solutions. Thus we must
initiate an organized effort to employ young professionals. This is actually
an appeal to the large work organizations to recognize the law governing

junior employees and the agreement that employment is both a legal obligation and an act of solidarity. Such a law would open new perspectives and allow greater time for more profound and better conceived solutions.

THE LABOR MARKET AND SOCIAL ORIENTATION

Such changes affect various relationships among powers and interests, ones that exist in a system of production and distribution and because of that require a strong social orientation and organization. The method of achieving their concretization is a social compact for the planning and employment of cadres in higher education.

We must insist upon a social compact for employment that would act as the economic/legal base for the new relationship between the increase in revenue (expanded accumulation) and the obligatory employment of young professionals. (Forecasts of required cadres must be mandatory as one of the essential dimensions of all investment projects, and the enactment of a system of planning in the area of higher education—these are its starting points.) Planning for experts—who will increase the production capacities and revenue—is no less important than planning for machines; in the same fashion the investment in education is not an abstraction of resources. Such measures are the starting point for the development of prognostication, for the forecasting of contemporary and future needs for cadres, which is, moreover, one of the founding blocks in overall social planning appropriate to self-managing socialism.

The main problem is how to step from the market-oriented, bureaucratic logic (from the elemental forces of labor markets and the importance of being well-connected as the decisive factors in finding employment) to a significantly great level of social orientation and admittance of the young into work. By no means should this be a return to the administrative allocation of people, in which case the medicine would be worse than the malady. But we should not be sentenced to either the survival of the fittest, or to the supply and demand of human goods, to the elemental forces of the labor market, which often pushes people about like straws. Reality and expectations should be better coordinated. We have a unique social mechanism to which we must give life. Planning for cadres is not a mechanized calculation of needs based only on the existing requirements of work organizations, but a qualitatively different process, an anticipation of future developments and needs. The anticipated innovations are an essential link in the whole metamorphosis of the educational system. Thus universities cannot be passive executors acting only as recipients of the orders for the required number and structure of the cadres, for their profile. For associated labor itself has only begun to come together into an organized system.[10]

The economic enterprises employ 18 percent of the total number of researchers while in advanced countries 50 to 60 percent work in economic enterprises. In 12 institutes and working organizations, there are only 39 researchers with doctoral degrees and one with a masters. Without advanced science, even associated labor will not be able to answer the questions regarding the required profiles of experts of the future. This great operation can only be carried out jointly and in an organized manner by the universities, groups of colleges and developing centers of all of the large economic enterprises. For the foresight of a single enterprise is too narrow—broader resources are necessary. The universities cannot, therefore, merely wait for orders, but they must participate actively in the projection of needs for cadres. In some areas, the task would not be especially difficult as, for instance, in the relationship between medical schools and health services; in other areas the needs are more elusive. Nevertheless, if an attempt is made, at least a part of the needs are being determined.

Let us particularize by advancing one of the possible alternatives. Social forecasting and orientation have two basic levels: (a) professional-scientific forecasting, and (b) self-management decisions [social compacts and agreements] regarding the profiles, numbers, and existing needs. One possible form of professional-scientific forecasting, one that especially should be researched, is the following: universities and those organizations of associated labor that are in a great degree dependent on each other in the formation and employment of experts should become affiliated through some form of basic cooperative. This would be the vehicle to initiate the forecasting of needs.

Prognostication, proposals of plans for the cadres, can be done at the state level. They are carried out by the "Councils for Development and Planning," where three independent forces are represented: (a) universities, or group of colleges; (b) the representatives of the different branches of the economy and social services; and (c) the representatives of the socialist youth and trade unions, who independently research the needs and possibilities for employment of young workers and future producers. It is essential to express all authentic interests and insure that they are represented in a competent manner in order to provide broader knowledge and information. The Councils will greatly rely upon the center for planning (Institute for Planning, Institute for Development of Higher Education).

These working groups will together forecast the required profiles and the numbers of specialists needed in both the middle and long-range future; they will seek ways to raise the standard of the cadres to a higher level.

Then self-management decisions concerning needs, profiles, and numbers of cadres will be carried out at a broad social level within the Republic's cooperative undertaking, where authentic representatives from all branches of activities, the regional social-political organizations, and the representatives of all universities meet. The future of the different branches of science and of certain colleges cannot be tied to the momentary resources of individual enterprises or even to whole economic branches, since individual enterprises constantly experience their own unique oscillations. Under our present practice, it can happen that even if the organizations of associated labor correctly anticipate the requirements for future cadres, they can ignore the obvious and reduce the number to an absolute minimum in order to lessen the risk of short-term over-abundance. In situations like this, even those long-term needs, ones which might be decisive in future development and required for the culture of work and socialist relationship, could be restricted.

Modern life greatly enhances interdependence, a crisscrossing of inter-relationships, close links by thousands of invisible threads. This is the case even for those colleges with strong connections to only one branch of the economy—such as the college of engineering and the engineering industry. But the college educates its mechanical engineers for many other areas, just as the engineering industry has a broad spectrum of other needs: the need for lawyers, technologists, mathematicians, sociologists, and others. These various connections are not one-dimensional. This law of modernity is even more pronounced in other professions. Which branch of the economy corresponds to the school of economics, or to the school of liberal arts?

The prognostication of highly educated experts should not be interpreted as an exact, precise science, both because of the changeability of technology (rendering it unknown and difficult to ascertain) and because of the necessity to preserve personal aspirations and provide a choice of profession. The development of the university has its own relatively independent history that cannot be reduced to vulgarly understood rationalizations—the notion that it can and should provide for the exact number of working positions. The development has also to preserve the opportunity for freedom in choosing a course of study and for a relatively independent development of university and scientific research. One should not be trapped by the illusion that totally precise planning is possible; one should not be enslaved by calculations which can never be exact. Otherwise the demand for "planning" could become restrictive and retard the development of education. It could subordinate the development of education to momentary technocratic interests and could make access to higher education more difficult, could endanger the growth of the cultural/historical sciences and the needs for those sciences that are not so "exact"; further, it could stifle the aspiration for education, a value in itself. All sciences, and particularly the humanistic sciences, are unpredictable; they depend also on the goals and values of a particular society, on the priority of that society's cultural needs and its demands.

Planning is, therefore, very relative; it is conditioned simultaneously by at least three factors: (a) more precision; (b) developmental needs that are difficult to foresee; and (c) the personal aspirations of individuals when put up against the educational possibilities and a choice of profession. Finally, planning is not done in a vacuum, but in concrete economic social situations that impose their own strong influences. At the present, our economic situation is difficult; we are feeling a pinch that restricts the momentary possibilities for choices and narrows the perspectives. In the future, more favorable conditions will be created: shorter working hours, a more democratic division of labor, which will offer better chances to people to work and study according to their affinities and better conditions for intellectual work. Because of this, our present thinking should not be too rigid. An anticipation for the great (though difficult to foresee) changes in the work organization, and a shortening of work hours, is important. An anticipation for that which we foresee but cannot comprehend exactly will create some other prerequisites for the engagement of desires and abilities. Foresight and orientation are built on the principles of flexibility.

Actually two elements are essential. Planning is one element, one form of the conscious intervention of society to secure and increase a definite number of new jobs and to consciously raise the levels of qualifications in the economy, the health services and culture. But, as much as is possible, it is also important to allow people to study what they want. For when people can freely choose a profession, they will accomplish more, they will be better motivated than if they were to be forced. The power of motivation often makes up for any other deterrents.

For the future, as much as we can foresee, it is both possible and indispensable that we develop an essentially greater level of social orientation, instead of developing merely the elemental forces of the labor market and its dependence on connections. The starting points on the way to realizing this request are a social compact governing orientation (planning) and employment of young professionals, and the creation of a flexible system for the prognostication of needs. Its two supports are: (1) expert prognostication, a creation of a joint body of colleges and branches of the economy—councils—where all this would be made possible, and (b) a level of decision making, the creation of an assembly, a parliament of education, where all authentic protagonists would be represented—individuals from all branches of activities, socio-political communities, and all colleges.[11] Prognostication is by its nature flexible, not rigid and precise. This is merely a germ, a rough prototype of a more mature, finer form that might be developed later on in the course of existence.

EDUCATION AND WORK

A greater degree of congruity between social needs, individual development and higher education is possible only through innovation—that of developing an organic connection between study and work.[12] Even at this early date, we must begin to create elements of a future in which science will actually be a direct productive force, and the differences between manual and intellectual activity will be substantially decreased when work—as an innate human need—and learning will be part of an undivided whole. In the future, an increasingly greater portion of the younger generation, after initial training, will shift to work and will alternate work and learning in many different forms. This great notion of humanistic education has become closely related to the general trend of civilization, to the development of technology and knowledge. From youth, each individual will be accustomed to a rhythm of life that incorporates regularized education and provides him or her with successively further knowledge. Periods of learning will alternate with periods of active professional work. We will do away with the antiquated pattern of a working life whose stages follow each other like seasons: (1) childhood, (2) obligatory schooling, (3) vocational or higher education, (4) full time employment, (5) retirement—vegetation.

But we must take concrete and decisive steps toward the linkage of study and work, and our efforts must come from two different directions. One should be a gradual alteration of the socio-economic position of students, from one of student to student trainee (students/working people). Another should be a steady expansion of the circle of producers-students. This development has been completely neglected; it has been relegated only marginal importance within education, although it is entitled to a decisive role. When these two efforts are applied simultaneously, they will develop into more massive proportions, and in front of us will appear the pattern of a new university, the university of the future.

Gradually, from year to year, a work perspective will be introduced to an ever-greater portion of successive generations. At the beginning the students of the final years will be particularly affected when the results of the first half of their studies are seen and when they are introduced to the basic problems of their professions. Working prospects are realized through self-management agreements between the universities and the branches of the economy, or social organizations.[13] A commitment to provide study/work has been resolved by the resolutions of the Party Congress, but it hovers somewhere in the future and moves steadily further away as we approach it. Can we now proclaim mandatory leave for productive work for recent high school graduates as a requisite for entrance to the university? I think we cannot. For among other reasons, work would be perceived as a punishment, a difficult coercion forced on the individual, as if it were purgatory on the way to paradise.

By the self-management agreement between the university and the branches of the economy and social organizations, systematic working prospects become available.

By contract and based on competition, students receive a loan, which is in fact a payment in advance ("advance money"), because the loan will be reduced commensurately with the student's educational success.[14] The amount of advance money, or loan, would depend on two factors: on the result of one's work—success in studies or a successful participation in scientific research, and on the family's financial situation. Through such an agreement, a kind of pre-employment relationship, a practicum is created. Through this method, the need for work experience in order to achieve employment is satisfied and at the same time the great hurdle of finding it is eliminated.

The other side of the contract is the commitment by the student/trainees to work for several years for those enterprises that granted them loans. Through this procedure, the great lack of territorial coordination could be alleviated. Presently, 82 percent of all unemployed graduates are concentrated in the Belgrade area. An arrangement could be made by which priority for employment in the Belgrade area be given to those experts who have served professionally for several years in the provinces, thus creating a strong motivation which would better equalize geographical expertise. According to one recent poll, a vast majority of people are more prepared for a temporary change of place of living than a permanent one. In addition, were geographic distribution a factor in offering scholarships and loans, as well as a consideration for registration at the universities (under equal conditions), the same purpose would be served.[15]

The establishment of a socio-economic relationship between students and a society such as I am describing is realistic. For, there are already some 3,000 loans going to cadres every year, while the number of graduates for one year is 6,500. This proposal would mean that part of the student body in its final years of study would have an opportunity to receive payment in advance (a loan). But in this arrangement, particularly during competition, more objective criteria and evaluatory systems should be introduced, and the democratic participation of both the universities and especially the students themselves should be insured. The loans for the cadres should be followed by many so-called social loans to be alloted, as is now the case, to the students from poorer families, as an act of solidarity to alleviate social differences and to equalize conditions for study. Loans are given now to more than 25,000 students each year. This proposal is not unrealistic; it draws from the germs of existing practice, and these need only be developed and refined. The educational taxes levied on the enterprises, hospitals and communes that in this manner directly educate experts for their future needs should be lessened in correspondence to their participation.[16] So long as study/work maintains the present student status, it remains an empty shell, a mere declaration. Freedom from complete material dependence becomes an exit route from one's minority, an assumption of personal responsibility for one's own future. Students will no longer be divided into golden youth who can allow themselves the luxury of eternal education and those poor who suffer and early on lose élan and strength. Herein is also presented the foundation for a liberating, less authoritarian structure in the pedagogical process.

Study and work are the only healthy bases for solving the problem of part-time studies, a problem presently incorporating a chaotic tangle of vastly different motives. Part-time students are, decreasingly, individuals who are involved in work; their umbilical cord with employment is practically severed. This status is transformed into "lower-class students," a kind of punishment for being less successful. The portion of part-time students in the total student body for the school year 1974/75 in Serbia was 27.1 percent at the universities, and 67 percent at the institutions of higher education. The number of part-time students who are unemployed has increased 42-fold, and at the schools of higher education 90-fold (during the time period 1964/65—1974/76). The composition of this group has changed significantly; in the school year 1964/65, unemployed part-time students were less than 1 percent of the total part-time student body, but in the school year 1974/75, the rate of unemployed increased to 45 percent.

THE PRODUCERS AND STUDENTS

Another direction, that of presenting systematic possibilities for education side by side with work as a general condition, rather than as an exceptional one, will have to gain in importance. In the future the centers of higher education will receive people from employment as well as those who have achieved intermediate education and wish to continue, and those who have graduated and are returning to refresh their knowledge, narrow their specialization, or enter post-graduate studies. But decisive steps must be taken now in order to initiate the innovations that will be the imperative of the future.

There are presently three very important reasons for the young to flood the universities: (1) difficulties in finding employment; (2) society's neglect in promoting study and work together; and (3) the low value given to work in production. Many students would not rush to the university but would rather find employment and continue their education later. For this to be possible, decisive changes must be made in the following areas: higher incomes for work in production; great possibilities for the employment of the young; and a socially regulated generous system of work/study—these are absolute necessities that cannot be avoided. If these conditions are not fulfilled, we will never be able to break from the vicious circle: the number of students will grow higher and higher, and the material basis of education smaller and smaller. There will be a downward slide in educational quality, and the institutions will be brought to the point of bursting.

A more sophisticated analysis of matters as they stand now reveals that the differences between early entrance to work in the factory and the continuation of education are actually profound differences between two lifestyles, a great gap of social circumstance. The transition from the worker's qualifications to the university is a transition from one class to another. It is made even more severe both by the attitudes of workers themselves, who look upon their upwardly mobile colleagues as defectors, and at the university by the nature of the pedagogic system. Only the rare exception who pays the price of great sacrifice makes this social *salto mortale*, this leap upward to a higher position in society. This is why we have a great exodus "from production and out of production." This is not, however, only a transitory difficulty; it becomes a problem that reaches the very basis of the social structure. An array of occupations that are in short supply forewarn of a crisis in every branch of manual work, occupations that are increasingly left without a new generation of workers. This problem cannot be solved by sending educational rejects into productive occupations, the ones who are stigmatized with failure, the ones who are paying for marginal success in academia by the punishment of their entrance into the factory, and the ones whom we expect, as if by some miracle, to later become the bearers of the production development of society.

If we stay indifferent and impassive, a new and insidious clash must be expected. The world of the employed, who, due to many circumstances, could not attain education, will be less in favor of allocating large funds for such education. The relationship between the allocation and use of funds, scrutinized by social statistics, shows the following picture:[17]

Group	Total Employment (%)	Allocation	Use	Minus-Plus (%)
Workers	78.0%	384,933	261,027	−32.2
Salaried employees	22.0	201,910	351,399	+14.0
Agricultural workers		133,476	170,142	+21.0

The connection of social success to education will be felt as an ever-increasing burden on one's own difficult situation; by their own hands, labor is supporting the education of others who will tomorrow demote them on the ladder of social promotion. A question will be asked: where and when will workers as a social class be educated? We must not forget that nearly every second worker has only a primary education. (The number of workers without schooling or with only primary schooling was 41.5 percent in 1974.)

We must approach these vital problems from yet another perspective. The poorer material conditions of less qualified workers, their justified opposition toward inequalities, the inherited characteristics of the wage laborer, and the resultant psychology that emerges from all these elements together create a desire to destroy differences, regardless of the beneficial results of creative work. This psychology creates a resistance toward experts, toward science and technological changes, particularly if in this development the laborers do not perceive of any benefits for themselves. In addition to this, nearly 30 percent of all employees hold positions above their qualifications; they were promoted to positions that were at least one level higher than their schooling justified. A huge proportion of these employees are office workers who were advanced by virtue of internal regulations that substitute tenure for professional qualifications. The same attitude is applicable to that part of management that instinctively resists the wide acceptance of professionally educated people. Within the organization, which is by law self-managed, there is a tendency to create a techno-bureaucratic top, a government obscured from general view that aspires to grasp a monopoly on decision making and the management of resources, in spite of a watchful public. Such behind-the-scenes manipulations create social connections that support each other in the conquest of privileged positions, and the acceptance of new members to their ranks is based on the principles of obedience and mediocrity. This pattern can develop into a serious closing of ranks; it can produce a front of conservative resistance to a broader engagement of highly qualified working power and knowledge.

We have, therefore, every reason to promote and encourage through normal means the constant improvement of the top level of professional knowledge of all who are interested and show abilities and results. Gradually, from generation to generation, there will be an ever wider circle of individuals who from their youth until retirement will become, one after another, the producers, the students, and the transmitters of experience. No one should be sentenced to spend his life filled only with the monotony of unskilled labor. The motivation resulting from greater possibilities for education is not less important than the incentive of a higher income.

The question, then, is which steps we should, and could, take to make the beginnings of such a future possible.

I suggest the following concrete measures as a pattern for the stimulation of occupations in production, for the solution of the problem of scarce occupations, and for the future of aggregate learning side by side with work.

1. Many privileges to study should be offered now to those who enter into material production. In the near future, all working people should be given 150 paid hours a year free for education. Shortened working hours are granted according to the results achieved, to good work and success; enough free time to complete a certain cycle of education is given as a reward. In this way people will be widely mobilized, their aspirations toward better expertise and knowledge will be realized, and the rewards will not be the privilege of only a small number of chosen ones.[18]

2. For the difficult and critical sectors in material production, the number of free hours for studies will increase to 300 per year per person.

3. The same will be the case for all employees who work in underdeveloped regions.

4. Work becomes a springboard that naturally facilitates entrance to the

university. Employment in excess of two years exempts an applicant from the entrance exam, thus enabling him to enroll directly into the university.[19] This bonus will encourage early entrance into production without closing off possibilities for further education. This offers a chance to the able workers and salaried employees to continue their education, the interruption of which is very often more the result of circumstances than personal inability.

5. The universities should audaciously meet the real need within the working world for great pedagogical reform—they should develop a freer and more intensive form of teaching (organization of summer sessions for instance) and a pedagogical method more suited to the producers/students. The creation of the "open university" becomes an order of the day. The producers/students are not left to their own resources.

A limiting factor to such advances is the fear of cost increases. But fear hampers foresight. For by reducing the pressure now placed on the universities, by earlier employment and entrance into productive work, the duration of studies would be substantially shortened due to the stronger motivation, and the burden of financing the younger generations (now placed on associated labor) would in the future be diminished. The resultant increase in productivity from a better qualified labor force would act in the same direction.

We have to turn toward the future to exploit effectively the possibilities and prospects that would serve as the educational standards for both young and adult.

A new path, although announcing possibilities for better solutions, is far from idyllic. We have to be aware that it is replete with the dangers of vulgarization, partiality, and the unknown. Determination should go hand in hand with prudence and maturity.

6

THE UNIVERSITY, SCIENCE, AND THE DEVELOPMENT OF SOCIETY

The development of research has been stormy and contradictory. While before the war there were only fifteen research centers, within two decades a great expansion occurred, and as a result, 493 research centers (260 of them independent, 37 within the academies of sciences, and 196 within economic organizations) were formed. In addition to this expansion, the various colleges contain a great number of instructional units—institutes, seminars, and laboratories. Within one decade, funding for scientific research has doubled.

The number of employees in research institutions has risen to 36,600, of whom 10,000 are researchers. One reason for the great industrial leap accomplished by Yugoslav society within these three decades is that thousands of scientists and researchers were engaged as active participants in this endeavor.

In S.R. Serbia in 1977, there were 237 research centers with 13,585 employees, of whom 5,000 were researchers.

The number of researchers per 10,000 inhabitants—one indicator of the degree of progress—has risen from 5.8 in 1965 to 8.1 in 1974. From 1968 to 1970, those European countries in the middle of the economic ladder had about 10 researchers per 10,000 inhabitants, while the most developed countries of Europe had 15 (Switzerland, 20.1; Holland, 15.3).

However, more recently a decline has set in and the suggestion of a very dangerous trend has started to appear: a decline of independent scientific creativity.

Education and research are the two functions of the university, which not only transmits but also creates knowledge. However, research has increasingly fallen away from the universities; it has become an auxiliary activity.[1] Except for the occasional part-time activities of a few individuals, the vast research potential remains unused.[2]

This development is part of a broader trend. For example, mechanical engineers transfer into commercial departments, and thus research departments become units of commercial services. From factories, we hear that we do not need many engineers, technologists, or mechanical engineers, but that we do need more technicians for the routine operations. Out of the total number of researchers, only one-fourth does research; a disproportionate number of working hours are devoted to other purposes. From year to year, there are increasingly fewer researchers/teachers in the technical-technological, biotechnical, and medical sciences within the ranks of university personnel.

There is a pronounced trend toward aging (nonrenewal) within the research cadres. In the field of the basic natural sciences, nearly half of the research cadres is over 40 years of age (1976). The participation of researchers who are over 50 is rapidly increasing. This situation is particularly worrisome when we know that in this area the period of greatest productivity is usually between 35 and 40 years of age. In the research/developmental units of working organizations, there are only some 15 percent of researchers under 30 years of age. In the decade of 1965 to 1975, the participation of researchers under 30 in research institutes has decreased by nearly half. In some of these areas of research there is not even a new generation of scientists—in geology, in textile research—while in the humanities, only one out of twenty researchers is younger than 30. The same is the case with biomedicine, where only 5 percent of the researchers are younger than 30.

In S.R. Serbia (without the provinces) within the Independent Scientific Research Organizations [*Naučno istraživačke organizacije* (NIO)], the participation of scientific workers/researchers under 30 years of age has decreased from 20.6 percent in 1964 to 12.6 percent in 1976. Within the same period, the participation of researchers over 40 has increased from 33.5 to 52 percent.

Behind these symptoms lies a chronic malaise of rank-closing, a lack of rejuvenation. This situation is exacerbated by the fact that the master and doctoral degrees of sciences are obtained in ever later years of life. From 1967 to 1976, the average age for achieving a doctoral degree has increased from 36-38 to 40-43.[3]

What is behind all of this? What are the underlying causes that limit the engagement of knowledge and science?

All these indications are part of the broader and deleterious trend of the technological development of society. We must face it openly and fight "a decrease of our own scientific creativity and an excessive orientation toward merely receiving foreign solutions and licenses; we should not be hypnotized by the foreign patterns in technology, urban development, and consumption."[4] This is that type of knowledge that, as a rule, keeps us one step behind the latest discoveries, which maintains us in a subordinate role. It is known from experience that only those industries that in their own laboratories search for innovations have at their reach the most advanced knowledge. "To buy a foreign license means to buy a ready product, and this is not the acquisition of the invisible, untouchable part of research that is embodied in the license—the research ability and the theoretical knowledge."[5] An excessive reliance on borrowing deadens the creative potential of one's own science and technology and maintains economic backwardness.

One false perception of the world economy has influenced such attitudes. The assumption is that as a younger partner of world corporations, one would automatically expand outward to the world market, that one would become an exporter. But such has not been the case. Close links, if they develop into a form of technological dependency, do not increase, but to the contrary, decrease the possibility of expanded technological-economical exchange, particularly with the Third World, where our chances for exchange are great. Restrictive contracts, dictated by the companies, limit the usage of licenses, and forbid the expansion of the acquired technology.[6]

Technological dependency is an enemy that has to be conquered over and over again in order to escape from the vicious circle of underdevelopment. For one should not forget that the transfer of technology, like the ancient god Janus, is two-faced. On the one side, it is a means by which knowledge is transmitted, and it serves as a breakthrough into contemporaneity. At the same time, though, technology in the hands of transnational companies is the strongest instrument of exploitation and technological colonialism. I have already described the trend toward dividing the world into a few regions where the centers of knowledge and innovations develop, while the remaining centers stay at the bottom of the pyramid and are expected only to imitate and become merely executors of routine work.

This development is one of the main reasons for the unemployment of the younger generation. This is the reason for the frightening brain drain that is occurring without a trace of remorse. This is a reason for the emigration of the scientific, expert cadres who have become a surplus in their own countries. The Third World grows into an auxiliary reservoir to the world laboratories. In this fashion, technological dependency and the lack of one's own research activities combine in deadly fashion with the hyperproduction of scientists and experts precisely in those societies where they are most needed.

Gradually this development creates its own material and social basis. An array of powerful narrow interests is formed, interests that find their way to an easier profit by copying licenses, even though this practice is contrary to their own long-term good. The excessive importation of licenses is an ever-growing factor in the heavy encumbrance of the balance of payments; annually the owners of foreign licenses are paid some 300 billion Dinars [or approximately ten billion U.S. dollars]. The number of licenses that are acquired to duplicate the same production and technology is very often between three and ten and coincides not only with the number of republics and provinces but also with the number of larger enterprises. Thus, the country as a whole usually pays two to three times more than is necessary.

Technological dependency acts as a depressant not only on economic results but also on the social psyche and culture. An ideology of dependency forms a satellitic mentality, which, after a certain amount of time, deadens needs and never sees the possibility for emancipation, for alternative modes of development that are better suited to the needs, potentials, and advantages of one's own society. An apathy occurs, even an aversion toward national sources of innovation. This attitude influences the abilities that are in demand—it appears that highly educated people are superfluous.

When one's own research and innovation are lacking, when only routine work exists, when repetitiveness at all levels of the working process is all there is; then it would seem that the experts are indeed unnecessary. Engineers transfer to commerce, a master-builder senses atrophy, and research abilities and talents within commercial enterprises wither away. Passionate researchers, innovators, turn into loners, into quixotic characters. In many countries the number of innovators and rationalization experts has reached 25 percent of the total number of employed, while in Yugoslavia it is 0.2 percent.

This creates serious consequences with the social relations between the engineering-technical cadres and the skilled workers. The development of one's own innovative abilities requires collective engagement. Experience, intuition, and physical dexterity combined together play a direct and valuable role in the construction of the new. An innovative working process lends a new quality to work; it develops people, releases previously stifled abilities and talents, mitigates class differences, creates human contacts, a spirit of an association among producers. All this also influences the character of education, develops need for knowledge, which becomes as natural as breathing, and which demands the development of education alongside of work. And conversely, when the atmosphere of creativity is completely absent, engineers and experts become merely a part of the hierarchy of power, a privileged commercial apparatus and ultimately superfluous.

A PATH TO ONE'S OWN CREATIVITY

It is well recognized that a significantly greater reliance on one's own power is difficult to accomplish; the developed countries hold 96 percent of all information and scientific innovation. But the emancipation from a critically dependent status in the international division of labor is the only healthy strategy for survival and development. For dependency is not a fate; it is not necessarily unavoidable. We have great research potential (about 10,000 researchers, nearly half of whom are at the universities) but they do not yet exist as an organized force. Yugoslavia has more researchers than the whole of the African continent; it is an army that is nearly as large as the number of active researchers on the Latin American continent. But this great potential does not act as a unified body; it is dispersed among fragmented institutions. More than one third of the independent institutes have fewer than ten researchers while another third has 10 to 24. Only one third have more than 25 researchers.

The scattered nature of our program is even more evident when we add the fact that a great number of institutes hire part-time collaborators, university professors whose number is several times greater than that of the permanent researchers. Such fragmentation of human potential and funds cannot produce as fruitful results as would a concentration of all potentials on the vital areas of research. The average funding per one employee in the institutes in Yugoslavia is $5,600, while in the more developed countries it is 3 to 4 times greater.[7]

There is a need for deliberate change, a more mature conceptualization and strategy in the development of science. A more fruitful combination of the inevitable transfer of technology (knowledge) and the greater participation of our own creativity is indispensable. Creativity that corresponds to the needs of the socialist alternatives in the organization of production, in energy, in the production of raw materials and food, in urban planning, in rural/urban relationships, in the advancement of health and culture is better than the mere transfer of knowledge. This aim cannot be realized all at once, with merely a hasty push at the stern, but gradually by way of selective and creative transfer. Instead of across-the-board purchasing, a selective accrual of licenses that presuppose the application of our own knowledge should be initiated. Knowledge should be imported only to the extent that it stimulates the development of one's own research, not so it stifles it. Parallel to this development should be a great concentration of research resources around those sectors where we have comparative advantages in the world economic scene, where the production centers can be encouraged to use more national technology. This plan is not contingent so much on financing (at least in a substantial number of fields) as it is on expertise and on a conscious strategy of development. The countries that have taken these steps have achieved great results.

The universities play an indispensable role in this conscious activation of research potential. They are still the centers of the greatest possibility for research development. Of all researchers, they employ half.[9] (Forty-eight percent are at the universities, 34 percent in the independent institutes, and 18 percent in the research-development centers in economy.) The configuration of research cadres is even more obvious when observing the concentration of doctoral degrees. Out of a total of 2,654 people with doctorates, 72 percent are employed by universities, 26 percent by research organizations, and only 1.7 percent by research-development units in economy.

Stressing the unavoidable role of the university in research is neither a demand for the return of science to the university, nor a request for its monopoly. It is in the interest of the university that each large work organization become also a research center and a partner. For were the possibilities better exploited, the experts educated by the universities would be in demand by the hundreds of research centers that exist throughout society. If in the whole of society research stagnates, then there is no place for higher expertise. This is not a demand for a parasitic subsidy, for a second income for professors, but rather, it is an aspiration for the participation of science in social development, for the possibilities for creative work. All this can neither be accomplished by private initiative nor public solicitation, but must be the work of a well-thought-out orientation, which differs from our present course, of a conscious and total change.

It is already possible at this stage to adopt a few concrete measures in a direction that would open up different perspectives for research:

1. transform the university into one of the centers of systematic research activity
2. establish increasingly closer ties among the universities, the groups of colleges, and the corresponding institutes
3. create institutional connections among the universities, the institutes, and the research-development centers in the economy and social services

These are the first steps toward a powerful triangle: education—science—development.

THE COLLEGE: A COLLECTIVE RESEARCH SCIENTIST

The starting point for this concept is to initiate inherent changes in the colleges. Colleges should be enabled to perform systematic scientific work; they should be transformed into a *collective research scientist*, into one of the centers for scientific research. They must perform research not only in the service of pre-existing knowledge or momentary necessity but they must also be pioneers in the search for new developments, new knowledge, future technologies, sources of energy, urban development, health and culture. The aspiration toward the discovery of new possibilities binds into a whole the fundamental research that extends into both developmental and practical solutions—a subject of interest to working organizations. In practice, the college would become a rich system of scientific information from whence the decision-making centers are empowered.

All this, therefore, is not a division of fundamental and applied research, but a search for new developmental possibilities that contain the characteristics of both. A sphere where the joint participation of colleges and institutes is unavoidable (as much because of the relative independence of research) is a necessity for the discovery of new developmental possibilities. Society consciously creates its strategic intellectual reserves; in addition to responding to manifest demands, it concentrates its research forces on those points that are not in strict economic dependency on the current and exclusively prevailing needs. These intellectual reserves are aimed at new possibilities, at those fields of research where the great scientific revolutions, the great breakthroughs, can be expected.

This level of pioneering research is primarily financed by social funds, contrary to projects connected to the individual work organizations. The relationship between the Self-Management Community for Education and the Community for Scientific Research—one now typified by complete separation—is seen in a new light. In the future, these communities would be part of a whole. The decisive influence on the formation of research projects and their financing (from the point of view of the universities) would not be in the hands of those removed from the colleges, a situation that at times reveals privatism and the small-enterprise mentality that would limit funding to higher education, but it would rather be in the hands of the colleges as collective bodies. For research is a legitimate part of college activity and must also be financed by the Community for Scientific Research.

The entire activity of the colleges must be permeated with a research orientation in order to bring about the participation of a particular science in the improvement of a particular area of social life. Each college, or a group of colleges collectively, would have its "white book," which outlines the manner in which work and technology could be enhanced in industrial development; in civil engineering; in mechanical engineering; in electronics and cybernetics; in the production of energy, raw materials, and food; in the improvement of housing and urban development; in health and particularly in the preventive health services; in work organizations and public services; in the enrichment of culture; in contemporary pedagogical methods; in innovative techniques for learning foreign languages; and in other areas as well. By marking out the forms of knowledge and kinds of experts that are needed, the colleges become the champions of a higher level of work; they influence both public opinion and the decision-making centers.

All this activity cannot be achieved without a change of spirit. Work in research must become a fundamental component of evaluation, professional advancement, and the determination of income. The process must involve the engagement of students, particularly the students in their final years of studies and graduate students, the organization of "Young Researchers" and creation of joint research teams. The Community for Scientific Research should allocate 10 to 15 percent of its funds to student research within each such project that it finances. Graduate work and doctoral theses must be oriented to the vital problems of science and development, rather than remaining closeted within a bookish and sterile citation mania.

I am suggesting a climate of creativity where the spirit of the contemporary man of science is formed, not a commercial buying and selling operation. A research mentality and a material basis for that research are indispensable. If we do not resolutely take this path, our intellectual level will inevitably decline, the criteria for the evaluation of scientific results will become debased, narrow egoistic interests will erupt, and the whole will degenerate into bitter fights for money, prestige, and position, and science will become forgotten.

Presently, both the state/bureaucratic and the commercial university stifle scientific zeal in their own different ways. They reduce motivation to a force that, rather than being innate research, is one that is only the result of orders or remuneration. The intellectual profile is exchanged for one of management of businessmen. In our present course, professors and their assistants will become dependent on scientific contractors who apportion the social funds for research, and this must not be allowed. Scientific work demands its own, inner motivation, its own ardor and autonomy, all of which are subjective qualities and therefore gravely imperiled by the climate of managerial power and profiteering. If such continues, the intellectual creators have no choice but to either pay tribute to it or retreat.

Another step that is a natural continuation of this effort is the alignment of colleges or the groups of related colleges with their corresponding institutes, thus establishing joint research projects. The unification of associations and education is a creative maneuver. The colleges and institutes have the immediate task of examining their organizations to determine the form that joint cooperation will take—from the self-management agreements to the more complicated forms of the organizations of associated labor. Some very modest beginnings of this cooperative venture already exist, but they are the exception rather than the rule. Cooperation between colleges and institutes is now very rare; it exists in only 8.6 percent of all research projects. A systematic alignment of the colleges and institutes would vastly enhance the research base, would make possible the linkage of education and research. The institutes would gain the immediate ability to contribute research results to the educational process and consequently add to its enrichment.[9] The combination would result in a more economic and more rational form of education and research; it would create an organized force of participation in social development. With this participation, the educational base from which the cadres draw their resources would be widened; such activities as education within study groups and work with advisers could be initiated with ease. And, conversely, the professors and collaborators could devote more time to research and scientific work.

These connections gradually expand to include also the economic groups and social services. This powerful research potential concentrates around key projects. In establishing such an organization, we are faced with two tasks, both of which are interrelated. Firstly, we must form systematic institutional connections among the colleges, institutes and economic organizations, and the social services. One possible direction to take in this regard is to develop basic units within the self-managing research organizations, each unit acting as a center for collective long-term research. One unit might draw from various areas of expertise. For instance, the college of mechanical engineering would combine with its corresponding institute, with the machine-building industry, the colleges of civil engineering and architecture, and their corresponding institutes, and the civil engineering and construction industry.[10] Another possible direction is to establish coordinating bodies among the colleges, the institutes and the branch associations formed in the Economic Chamber.[11] From these initial forms of cooperation, initiatives would be born that would lead to permanent programs of education and research. The second task at hand is to examine the role and future of the educational process. Higher education, were it connected to the organizations of associated labor, would be better prepared to solve our various other problems, and thus the possibilities for growth through a more rational framework are created. Higher education could produce those cadres that can, without any difficulty, be employed by the corresponding organizations of associated labor. Altogether this would create a foundation for the insurance of the education of cadres, promote contemporary teaching methods, and better utilize the laboratories and resources of the organizations of associated labor.[12]

When the extent of cooperation between colleges and other organizations of associated labor is reviewed, it could be stated: all colleges have made significant efforts in concretizing their cooperation with the organizations of associated labor; the forms of cooperation between the colleges and the organizations of associated labor are different, and they depend on the specificity of the college and its organization for such cooperation in question. But still there are only a few examples of such cooperation throughout longer terms—the majority of them are of a temporary character.[13]

At the University of Belgrade, joint efforts between the colleges and the economic sector took place in only 19 percent of the projects.

But, when we judge the extent of cooperation with the centers for development in the economy, we must keep in mind that it is not a one-way street dependent only on the will of the colleges. Contemporaneity is not merely a fictionalized utopia. The economy is just entering the age of the formation of large centers for research and development. Therefore, this is a moment of embryonic development for both sides, a moment that must be stimulated by actively advocating centers for development in the economy.

Within one decade (1965-1976), the number of research units in the economy has increased by 70 percent, and the number of research cadres has grown threefold.

	Scientific Research Organizations in Economy
Before 1918	3
1945–1949	11
1950–1959	40
1960–1969	115
1970–1974	36

This growth is already a significant force, but still incomparably smaller than that within the economy of developed countries. Approximately 18 percent of all researchers come from the research centers in the economy. This concentration, however, reaches a density of 60 percent in some other countries.[14] The dearth becomes even more evident if one adds the fact that in Serbia there are 2,000 people with a doctor of science degree, of whom only 19 work in the research-developmental centers in the economy. These shortages are confirmed by the results of one study that shows that the polled organizations of associated labor announce their preparations for large increases in production. According to their plans, the number of researchers should be increased from 30 to 80 percent.

But social development is never one of only technological growth. The development of the cultural, historical, and social sciences, those disciplines that cannot be so directly connected to certain groups of colleges, is of exceptional significance. Because of this development, it is as important to search for specific solutions that express the peculiarities of these branches. The path described is therefore one that must be taken but not the only one. For there are activities and occupations that are not practiced on a large scale, but that have exceptional scientific and cultural value and therefore must be nurtured.

This discussion has related primarily to institutional networks and organizational issues. The decisive matter, however, one that gives real content to all that has been said, is that there be a statewide organized concentration of research potential around the key projects of development within middle- and long-range plans. These forces are now diffused, and we face the task of transforming them into powerful scientific teams and research collectives. Concurrently, with the adoption of middle-range plans for development, we must establish a social compact that directs us in determining the manner and the form by which our research potential participates in the key programs of development. A social compact would provide a substantive basis as well as initiative to form this powerful triangle: colleges—institutes—developmental centers in economy (social services) in the developmental programs for the Republic. It would provide a path to the greater utilization of our own scientific activity as required by the needs of society, a path toward independence and away from dependent development. At the same time, there is a great responsibility which must be borne by scientists to arrive at scientific results.

This is neither an easy nor a comfortable undertaking. The many vexing difficulties that will of necessity arise will not be solved in a day, and new ones will continue to appear. For there is a force of conservative inertia that weighs heavily on our mentality and provokes distrust on both sides. On the one side, the work organizations tend to close ranks.[15] On the other, there is pressure among those within the university to maintain the long-lasting tradition of the "nonengagement" of academic science in social development, the tradition that science is a privilege of the elite. Both reactions are powerful hindrances to the introduction of organic and equal connections between the world of the economy and the world of science. And there are yet further dangers—from the enclosing of science into the academic halls on the one side, to commercialization, the technocratic control over science, or the transformation of it into a service for the rich on the other.

Science that is deeply engaged in solving social rather than esoteric problems, that attends to vital needs, is an end for which we must strive. But we must at the same time insure the indispensability of relatively independent research. In order to perform its social function, scientific thought must have freedom. Closer ties with practicality do not connote subordination to narrow-minded pragmatism, to a bureaucratic/technocratic tutelage, which requires of science that its expertise define a technical rationale for already preconceived decisions regardless of their wisdom. When research demonstrates rational choices, then it is easier to overthrow monopolistic interests. Such interests cannot be easily sustained when they are unmasked as parasitic and irrational. From this revolt stems the important role of independent scientific research, which is able to decisively effect developmental possibilities and searches for innovations.

In conclusion, I wish to say that one of the fundamental questions of the future of society is an understanding of the concept of an expanded reproduction that is not reduced to material ends alone.[16] The expanded reproduction of knowledge and human abilities becomes a working principle. Marx's concept of our spiritual horizons contains one great idea: the notion that with the development of industry, production itself is transformed into scientific and experimental work. A basic flaw of any economic system would be to reduce expanded reproduction to materialistic ends at the expense of expanding the reproduction of knowledge.

7

THE ECONOMIC BASIS
OF EDUCATION

The economic and material basis of higher education is an intricacy of relationships. Yugoslavia has set aside enormous funds that have been the material basis for the great growth of education in the last three decades. According to data from OECD (Organization of Economic Cooperation and Development), Yugoslavia holds a prominent position among those countries that set aside a sizeable part of their national income for education. The percentage set aside for education in Yugoslavia has increased from 2.1 to 5.86 within twenty-five years. A more accurate picture of the measure of this achievement can be seen when this figure is compared with the percentages from other developed countries. At the beginning of the 1970s, funds set aside for education were as follows:

	Percentage of National Income
Holland	7.6
Sweden	7.4
Finland	5.9
Belgium	5.6
Bulgaria	5.1

	Percentage of National Income
France	4.8
Hungary	4.6
Austria	4.4
Italy	4.0

In all levels of education, however, there is one general law: the law of an inevitable increase in costs. This increase is not only the result of an inefficient educational system. Research conducted throughout the countries of Western Europe shows that in the last thirty years, the ratio of increase in the number of students, the number of teachers, and the amount of expenditures in educational production stood at 2:3:4 respectively.

The law does not exclude higher education. Fundamental changes in the relationship between the growth of education and the expenditures for it could be effected if the greater part of studies were conducted alongside work.

In addition to the general trend, there are a few adverse circumstances that are detrimental to the economic aspects of education, and more specifically to higher education.

The growth of funds for education in the time period from 1965 to 1975 was the lowest in the S.R. Serbia (without the provinces).

	Percentage Increase in Funds for Education
Socialist Federative Republic of Yugoslavia	589
Bosnia and Herzegovina	683
Montenegro	587
Croatia	572
Macedonia	500
Slovenia	583
Serbia (without the provinces)	552
Socialist Autonomous Province of Kosovo	786
Socialist Autonomous Province of Vojvodina	591
Socialist Republic of Serbia	586

This trend became even more serious recently, with rampant inflation, and material development (particularly within the larger universities) has been halted or dangerously reduced. Our investment in new equipment is not more than 3 percent of total educational expenditures while it reaches 18 percent in other countries. The investment in total funds for education in the Socialist Republic of Serbia has dropped from 23 percent in 1962 to 7 percent in 1974. Physical space for one student is about 4.50 square meters, while the world average is 14 to 18 square meters. At certain popular colleges, for instance, the College of Law, it is only 2 square meters per student.

DISTRIBUTION OF FUNDS AND THE "POWER PLAY"

Higher education ranks unfavorably when compared with other social activities—its position in the power structure leaves much to be desired.

The percentage of total income in social activities in 1977/78 was as follows:

Education	25%	
Institutions of advanced education		41%
Higher education		23
Social security	36	
Health care	39	
Culture, art, information	39	
Athletics	88	

In precise contradistinction to this concentration of funding, the concentration of highly qualified individuals is the greatest in education. The ratio of the structure of qualifications is:

in economic activities	1:73
in social activities	2:02
in educational activities	2:19

Under existing conditions, when income in material production does not set the standard throughout the entire system for the level of income in other fields (I refer particularly to excesses within administration), the dissatisfaction of teachers is justified—for the level of expertise and income are in inverse proportion.

Income is determined now on the basis of two principles. One of them is remuneration for work performed—both in terms of results and the complexity of the work performed. Another is according to one's position in the hierarchy of management. There are enough indicators that point to the fact that this second principle is weightier, that it encompasses whole activities, and that it creates a ladder, on the bottom of which is material production. Within such a system, it is inevitable that comparisons are made with activities that are unjustifiably privileged, thus harming motivation. Inadequate remuneration for personnel in education has one more rather invisible consequence: assistant professors are increasingly recruited from the well-to-do families. Only they, by virtue of family support, can compensate for the poor salary. Thus, the supply of the talented scientific young generation becomes increasingly limited.

Colleges are not in a position where, by their own activity or by their contribution to science and education, they are able to influence the earning and division of income in any fundamental regard. They are subjected to a bureaucratically deformed budgetary system of financing characterized by a lack of objective measurement, by subjectivistic decisions, and by power plays in the allocation of funds for salaries and capital growth. Under this system there are large and unjustified differences: while the college of law is allocated 400,000-500,000 Dinars per one student, the school of economics is allocated 900,000. Gaps are created between the individual colleges and professors, and they are not justified by any real differences in the quantity and quality of the professors' work.

The internal distribution of funds in colleges often displays an image of subjectivity, lack of objective measurement, and poor working norms. Salary policies, without a more realistic basis for judging real content and without respect for some substantial peculiarities of scientific and pedagogic work, can lead to vulgarized solutions. This is how the great disparities are created—from the enthusiastic, intensive scientific and pedagogic work of many professors, which does not find equivalent remuneration, to the cases where income is earned for an inadequate job done hastily in several hours per week. The work performance at the university is very often exclusively a matter of individual initiative, of a personal rather than social norm.

EXCHANGE OF WORK AND SOLIDARITY

We are faced with a twofold task: to correct the irrationalities of the existing system and to build an economic base that is adequate to the changed status of higher education. The task, however, requires a thorough examination of this maze of complicated relationships in order not to eliminate one set of irrationalities and then create new ones. We are advancing into new and unknown territory; we have only a general notion of our direction, and our audacious plans must be tempered by calm and mature deliberation.

There is one important perspective, one signpost that marks the new route: the direct free exchange of work, free from bureaucratic, budgeted financing and free from the budgetary dictates of the state, which acts as the only arbiter directing the economics of education. People from within the educational system become the protagonists, the subjects who through their own activity create the economic basis of their life, create a more just evaluation of their work, and enrich the quality of student life. At the same time, such activity destroys the walls that for centuries kept the universities from direct contact with economic and social life. This economic relationship becomes a new and strong tie to connect the intelligentsia to the class of producers and education to work.

A change of socio-economic relations, a reform based on the free exchange of work as a foundation for a different social position of working people in higher education is in question. . . . The change will lead to a new system whereby the colleges, through their own activity, create and build on new sources of revenue, for the present form of income does not depend on real results of work, but on the decisions of different commissions and self-managing interest communities.[1]

The economic aspect of the free exchange of work must be part and parcel of its working content—there must be programmed and planned connections between the educational associations and work, where the needs and the forms of their relations are responsibly established. The whole structure of needs rests on two major aspects discussed in previous chapters. They are:

—the participation of science in developmental programs and the innovation of knowledge so that it constantly prepares vital individuals, the bearers of future developmental projects; and

—self-management agreements between the colleges and work organizations by which the new status of students is institutionalized—their pre-work relationships and pre-income arrangements as well as the future structure of work/study.

The content of these connections is not reduced to the commercialization of degrees, or the marketing of knowledge and working power, but directly aims at historically overpowering bureaucratic capital relationships. Money will not save us from the clutches of the statist university; freedom from the state is not gained through the creation of a commercial university, but by the unification of the socialist associations. This involves constant cooperation among the different organizational bodies. Contracts insuring the participation of enterprises in monetary allocations are based both on the contribution of the university and aspirations of the enterprise. The university's contribution will improve the level of expertise in the enterprise and discover innovations that will free us from the yoke of foreign licenses. But all this is one large phase during which economic relationships will be historically changed. Only people working consciously can assure that the free exchange of work is an authentic socialist endeavor rather than a system of profiteering.

A basic understanding of the necessary changes is increasingly important because, although this new path is accessible to everyone, it is not accessible in the same degree to all colleges; colleges will always have differing levels of direct contact with the economy and social services. For some, connections outside the colleges are easily available but for others more difficult to make. There are data that indicate that colleges have already started the free exchange of work and that they realize about 15 percent of their income from this activity. But while these funds reach 24 percent in the colleges of engineering, they are only 2 percent of the income of the colleges in the social sciences.

Among the three economic sources—direct exchange of work, financing through the self-managing interest community (SIZ [Samoupravna interesna zajednica]) and citizen compensation for study, the basic source will be the Republic SIZs. The educational needs in their totality could be determined and planned for—and consequently the basic part of it financed through broader social insight. In this, it is possible to create a policy of solidarity in satisfying needs and to develop a standard whereby collective needs are decided upon by society as a whole. We must constantly keep in mind one of the central roles that education can play in acting upon the decrease or increase of inequality. In order to avoid the creation of a new upper class through redistribution, we should keep in mind the basic principle of solidarity's formula: from each, according to his ability—to each, according to his work. For both, different abilities and different possibilities for a greater contribution are not only the result of natural differences, but also arise from essentially unequal possibilities to develop those innate abilities alloted to the members of different social classes. The policy of solidarity is a socially coordinated attack on fundamental inequality, where unequal opportunities for education are inherent in the system. Gradually, but steadily and concurrently with the increased wealth of society, solidarity creates more equal conditions for the development of abilities and consequently of production. This attitude differs from statism, which regards the individual as a permanent child, and from capitalism, which has left him to cutthroat competition.

We must closely scrutinize the manner in which the funds for education are accumulated. There is in contemporary society a fundamental contradiction between the region and sources of educational funding. The individual's locale becomes more restrictive as a direct consequence of greater access to information, expanding educational opportunity, and the increasing mobility of the intellectual work force. From an early age, youth live in a new world of information; each day aided by television cameras and the press, they are introduced to a new corner of the world. Naturally they crave independence and broader experiences. The economic system of education molds individuals into predetermined patterns.

Generally speaking, if an individual is born in a certain place, he will go to high school there, enter a local college, work either in a factory or in administration, and retire. The pattern looks simple, but, in fact, it is a truly complicated entanglement. For, from the point of view of the economically underdeveloped regions, there is a loss of the best human power, the ones who would be the bearers of future development, and they are beginning to experience their lot as a great inequality. To solve this problem with much more equity, the regional development of industrial and cultural centers is necessary. A better concept of student apportionment and quality education within entire networks and a much freer transfer among colleges is indispensable. Rather than remaining as isolated centers of activity, the educational system must incorporate the whole of modern life.

We must investigate the possibilities to accrue considerably broader funds on the state and national level, and, without too much hair-splitting, balance the disparate financial costs of education in separate regions. The contributions should be proportioned to the number of students in each area, but it is natural to expect that the more developed and richer regions would participate with more funds.

A dictate announced by the Republic Community for Directed Education will introduce a change which should correct an array of irrationalities and introduce a new economic base for higher education; simply speaking, it will acknowledge "the cost of education."[2] It should create an equitable socio-economical basis for education, which compares to the status of working people in other areas of life and work. It should stimulate more productive and more rational work, work of higher quality, alongside a more effective use of the means of production. Reimbursement for work is not a spontaneous dictate of the market, but rather a cost arrived at by self-management agreements.

It would be premature at this point to discuss the cost of education in detail. Its concept is as yet unformed, its fundamental effects and as yet unknown elements are being studied; they will eventually be the subject of an all-encompassing public discussion. We shall limit ourselves, therefore, only to two elements.

A thorough study of the relationships between the financing of institutions (branches of scientific activities) and their programs is truly in order. For if programs are financed without an understanding of broader needs, an array of more difficult problems could develop—such as the fight for an ever-increasing number of courses, or conversely, the elimination of scientific branches and areas of education which are not popular but are yet essential to the technological and cultural growth of society. Another key problem is how to determine the different values of the very routine activities that can be easily measured and that of scientific and pedagogical work, the work of the visionaries and creators, which is basically unmeasurable.

Income, which is automatically connected to routine operations, has become nearly the only regulator of participation in teaching and research. The number of points earned is self-explanatory; each act has its justification, which legitimizes the differences in income. Routine activity becomes the alibi for imposing excessive examinations on young scientists. Success in examinations becomes the student's primary task, thus removing him even further from the creative process of research. Such activity determines a greater or lesser share in the distribution of income, and all seems to be in its proper place. "Cost effective" schemes, however, cannot replace a collective program which in a well-prepared and academically stimulating manner engages all of the most valuable qualities of the colleges. Income cannot remain removed from a collective program of working norms and plans for scientific-pedagogical activity; it must concern itself with the most rational engagement of each member of the collective. Income is reward for quality and quantity of such programmed work and not only the regulator of mundane participation in the pedagogic process. Such measurements are essential, for totally objective measurements do not exist. It is important to do away with the ever increasing routine of quantitative activities, which so easily replaces the more creative ones, which are more difficult to measure. We must avoid being smothered by record-keeping. Only in this manner can the introduction of economic planning press for the most rational use of material resources; only then can these resources give greater results, and the true product of work be evaluated.

The third source of income is the fees that citizens pay for study, primarily the tuition of part-time students. One part of the fees from part-time students is a legitimate charge for the expenses and energies of the colleges, which also contribute to society by accepting an excess number over their capacities in order to keep part of the young generation off the streets.[3] But at times, these fees are an expression of the commercial appetites that work against the interests of the students, that increase social differences, and that orient students toward a civil-servant mentality. The School of Economics in Belgrade has ten times more part-time students than all colleges of technical and natural sciences put together.

The race to raise tuition rates and the constant introduction of new forms of tuition are not permissible. The fees must be regulated by social norms; they must stay within the framework approved by the self-managing interests communities. Tuitions have to reflect the actual results of work, teaching, programs, and number of hours offered to part-time students.

It is unjustified in principle to allow a situation in which the poorer students, the ones who are already disadvantaged, would be yet again penalized by high tuition. A social criterion should be introduced for those students whose families pay all expenses of studying, a social compensation based on a scale tied to success in education and the level of income. Depending on the material circumstance of a student, the expenses for education should be borne either by the families or by funds set aside for assistance.

We need a more rational and a better understanding of student living standards in order to offer some solutions for its improvement. In illustration, I will suggest a different approach to student nutrition. Instead of maintaining one unwieldy bureaucratic institution, the same huge funds by which nutrition is subsidized (65 percent of the resources are given by the community, and 35 by the students themselves) could be given in the form of coupons. These coupons would subsidize the meals of students in restaurants throughout the city. Many working organizations already have such a program. The problem here is not only the more economic usage of funds, but an important fundamental principle. The students should live together with the rest of the working society; they should not always be separated in secluded refuges. The student center could maintain smaller and more modern cafeterias where the students could go if they wished.

8

SELF-MANAGEMENT
AND THE NEW MONOPOLIES

An exceptionally important element of reform is the development of self-management within the colleges and the universities. The totality of this element is many faceted. Particularly important at this point are: (a) the direct participation of the faculty in the process in order to assure the expansion rather than the restriction of self-management; and (b) the true participation of students in an effort to actualize that which is now only a possibility. These two elements lay the foundation for an organic whole.

A new chapter in the history of self-management at the university is made possible through self-management initiatives based on the Associated Labor Act[1] and especially by the development of student participation in the self-management process.[2] By adopting this act, we would face only the tasks of the perfection and correction needed to insure an effective and vigorous mode of life and work.

But, of course, reality is rarely so straightforward. In actual practice, there is a tendency to restrict the direct participation of faculty in the decision-making processes. The order of the day is to curtail the democratic forms of decision-making and suffocate the faculty with reams of paper-work that channels energy toward ends that are only rarely vital or even rational. The tendency of bureaucratization takes different forms: a concentration of power around the counseling bodies; limited participation in the election of deans; a restriction on the influence of the public in faculty selection; the dependency of the colleges on the *SIZs*.

Almost invisibly over the years, a significant shift of the decision-making center of powers has taken place, and today it rests almost exclusively in the council, presently the only body with the right to make central decisions. Until recently, representatives from the social community and a selection of students comprised half of the council. This situation underwent significant change when the students were given equal participation both in terms of numbers and authority, while the representatives of the social community were reduced to one-third. But the council is still a body with a strong behind-the-scenes concentration of power. Scientific/teaching councils—in which students also take part—are reduced to consultative units without decision-making power, even though they are dealing with vital issues that require socially and professionally responsible decisions.

Today, a very narrow circle of faculty who are council members are the primary participants in the decision-making process, while the broader circle, which formerly took part on an equal basis, is shunted aside. The fundamental flaw of the earlier period was the exclusion of students from authentic participation in self-management. A serious flaw of our contemporary system is in limiting the direct participation of the faculty to a very exclusive circle. This trend was reinforced by the manner in which deans are elected; from the authority of the broad college collective, this power was transferred to the council. In similar fashion, an increasingly smaller circle of the council selects new faculty at the expense of the broader influences of the scientific and student populations. The scientific/teaching councils nominate the candidate for faculty position and this nomination is very often decisive. But the final selection is carried out by the council, which at the present comprises only a small number of professors. At certain colleges that are divided into several small organizations of associated labor, the authority in the selection of faculty is transmitted to the organizations of associated labor. Thus, recruitment into the teaching profession, one of the most important functions that any counseling body might perform, and which was heretofore under the direction of a broad university and scientific public, is now decided by an increasingly narrow, almost nepotistic circle of a few. The process is being transferred from the mainstream of scientific and pedagogical life to a limited sideshow.

In short, this circumstance means that direct participation in self-management decision-making processes is being curtailed. This phenomenon could lead to the monopolistic control by small groups and to the expression of the broader circles of creative powers within the colleges. Likewise, some dimensions of self-management that have been developed by the university (for instance, the direct participation of the faculty) could wither away. This will encourage the emergence of informal groups that will attempt to influence key decisions and advance the psychology that promotes the notion that the only duty befitting a serious professor is his specific expertise. The rest of the community would assume all other responsibilities.

It is essential, therefore, that further self-management changes do not limit direct participation in self-management, but rather develop forms that will express the uniqueness of the university and will include the direct participation of the faculty and all working people. The selection of professors must be a task of the colleges and not of small, narrow units.

An alternative (which should be a subject of public debate) is the possibility of forming the council on more realistic principles. The representatives of the social community should be official delegates from those large economic associations and social services on which the colleges naturally depend by virtue of their activities. This would be a new bridge in a more direct linkage of school and life; it would facilitate the forecasting of needs, assist in promoting continuing education, and aid in assuring the participation of colleges in the developmental projects of the large working organizations.

The authentic participation of students in self-management (this including also the educational process) is a great achievement—a new chapter in the history of pedagogy and in its transformation from an authoritarian to a democratic system. The active participation of students in teaching as well as all of the other aspects of college life has a crucial influence on what type of personality, what type of future producer, and what type of social being the university means to form. Work at school is not only the preparation for a future life, but is life itself. Participation in self-management requires the devoted energy of students and, lest this energy be channeled into superficiality, an active life within the organization and a great sense of responsibility. Now it is of fundamental importance that we be less preoccupied with the formal side of the issue and more with the real content of the authentic participation of students in self-management and the pedagogical process. Thus a working institutional network is formed—from informal gatherings to the conferences of delegates at the colleges, and the participation of student delegations in the educational scientific councils—and it becomes a fact of life. One important social reform has been created whose real content will depend on people who are giving it life.

There are difficulties in the actualization of student rights. On one side there is some distrust in the readiness of students to be socially responsible when it comes to questions of educational planning and programming. On the other side, there is no efficient system of delegate selection that will assure a strong self-management organization capable of accurately expressing student needs. An active student life at many colleges is hindered by the organization of teaching, by the low demands placed on everyday work because of poor working conditions, and by the lack of real motivation due to the limited possibilities for employment. All of these factors undercut vitality of student organizations. Under such conditions, it is difficult to secure a thorough understanding of the basic interests of students and their maturing process, and it is especially difficult to insure their presence in all phases of decision-making and finally establish their strong influence in self-management.

Until now the emphasis has been on the form of participation rather than on its content. It is an indisputable fact that students are able to participate competently in discussions about educational plans and programs, about the regime of studies, the organization of teaching and practical work and about the evaluation of the pedagogical work of the professors and collaborators. If everyone, particularly the professors and collaborators, supports the work of the councils of each year of study (groups, sections, divisions) where the students and faculty jointly and directly take part in discussions, if all this is understood as a natural process, there would be much less distrust and a much more real and qualitative participation.

MORE RATIONAL FORMS OF ORGANIZATION

A self-managing interest organization should be based on the fundamental functions of the colleges and their substantial interests and needs; any reorganization should avoid merely shifting functions about, which takes an enormous amount of energy and does not lead to any essentially new content. Innovations must act as a stimulus toward more effective modes of education and toward developing the centers of economic organizations and social services. The fundamental principle in the proposed partnership is that the colleges are the autonomous foundation for higher education, the purveyor of educational and research activities. All other, more involved forms of organization are only a derived and voluntary expression of those common functions, interests, and needs upon which the colleges base their agreements. A complete absence of coordination would lead to a discrepancy within education programs, and a lack of coordination in the development of areas of common interest for several colleges (the development of basic sciences, acquisitions of expensive equipment, effective graduate studies). The introduction of more thorough coordination is urgently needed in order to enable the colleges to play an active role in influencing new social conditions. When gradually the connections between the colleges and the large and complicated groups in the economy and social services take place, their mutual cooperation will be indispensable. A common participation in research projects and future projections for the development of higher education is pressing. Some suggestions for possible alternatives include the following.

1. The colleges become autonomous and act as the fundamental bearers of all educational activities; at the same time, they will increasingly become an open system of connections to the other areas of life.[3]

To establish closer ties of the colleges to the corresponding schools of higher education and the centers of secondary directed education is one of the immediate tasks. With this accomplishment, all levels of education would be tied into one organic and more harmonious whole. The forms these ties will take will be determined by practice itself; presently it is important to start activity in this direction.

Another important task is to enable colleges and their institutes to perform more effectively systematic research work of importance. It is essential to create a program with functional ties to the corresponding independent institutes (by self-management agreements or by the formation of associations).

These ties will gradually broaden to include the economic enterprises and the social services. The colleges will participate in their developmental programs and all organizations will work together on the projection of profiles of needed expert cadres, innovation of knowledge, and continuing educational programs. The actual form of these connections will develop gradually through practice. The basic communities of our self-managing interest organizations are possible prototypes for many colleges.[4]

2. Another complex alternative is the formation of scientific/teaching councils that link related colleges and departments (such as colleges of engineering and natural and mathematical sciences, colleges of medicine and bioengineering, colleges of social sciences). Scientific/teaching councils, formed out of groups of related sciences, would make possible the coordination of all that is common, while at the same time make allowances for specific applications to particular professions. The councils would be an important bridge in forming common criteria in research, in the promotion of interdisciplinary research and studies, in graduate education, and in publishing activities. An assembly of all scientific/teaching councils would function as a forum for the consideration of the general and common problems of science and education. The councils would also be open to the institutes, which link themselves to the colleges and also to the bodies of the chamber for the development of scientific work and research.

Another alternative which can be anticipated through the Associated Labor Act is the formation of work organizations out of the groups of related colleges. This structure presents a possible direction for the development of future forms of linkages with further refinements based on the needs and the demands of the colleges themselves.

3. A broader form of organization of directed education is at the regional and the republic level. Presently colleges are not represented in the Republic Community for Education; consequently, the Republic Community for Education is structurally incapable of satisfying the authentic needs of the economy and the society. It is incapable of establishing the true programs and common planning to satisfy needs. Alternative structures are possible and existence itself will determine their forms, but regardless of the configurations, there are some requisite features. Basically, they concern two aspects: the level of professional/scientific forecasting, and self-management decision-making. The most important requirement is that the organi-

zation deal with real content and strive for spontaneous and relatively simple interrelationships in order to avoid being smothered by a flood of bureaucratic debris. And above all, it is important that the structure is not a mere facade which shields the real centers of decision making from public view.

A feasible alternative is to integrate into basic units the colleges and those organizations of associated labor on which they depend. Together they could project the needed profiles, the educational programs, the research projects, and the plans for the employment of future experts. The basic organization of associated labor[5] could be allied with more specific self-managing interest communities.[6]

At the other level stands the regional and Republic Community, where (particularly at the level of the Republic) basic and fundamental decisions regarding overall needs are made.

A fundamental change in the character of the SIZs and the manner in which they make decisions (now characterized by subjectivism and power plays) is called for. In certain essential aspects, the manner in which decisions are made at the republic level does not reflect any greater quality than decision making at the state level, and when one considers the broader responsibility of the task, the charge of inferiority is not without justification.

The problem is not with the people within the system, but with its structure. Colleges do not have any influence over the SIZs. Out of 160 members of the Council of the Republican Community for Directed Education, colleges of the University of Belgrade are represented by only two, even though they comprise 65 percent of the students of all Serbia. There is not a single representative from the College of Art; students are not represented at all. In key educational decisions, the SIZs are a mere facade, behind which lie the real centers of power where the decisions are made, and where the responsibility for those decisions remains unchallenged.

A thorough change of the character and structure of the Republic Community is indispensable. It should consist of authorized delegates from:

—the branch associations from the economic and social services,

—the social-political communities and the Assembly of the S.R. of Serbia, and

—all colleges and universities including student delegates.

Only thus can SIZs become an assemblage of real planning and decision making.

9

A GREAT
PEDAGOGICAL REFORM

The inner being of the university, the content and manner by which knowledge is transferred, finds itself torn between the same two radically different cultural-historical orientations that the university faces in legitimizing its purpose to society. On the one side, there is the urge to broaden cultural horizons and widen the theoretical basis of the profession to create a pedagogy that instigates intellectual growth and a critical and creative spirit. Formation of a personality that can carry on independent research, make decisions, and perform management is the goal. The other side is oriented toward technical preparation for the job and rapid absorption of the crumbs of knowledge. The production of an obedient work force trained to execute semi-intellectual components of a routine work operation is the goal.

Life asks difficult questions: What is the university? What are its goals? What is the character and meaning of a higher education appropriate to authentic socialism? Which abilities and what type of personality does it mean to form? What direction in social development does it mean to promote? These are not merely pedagogical questions. The answers are not sought in pursuit of a higher quality of knowledge, but rather in pursuit of a better way of life. Education has become a decisive factor in the fate of people and society, for it develops independent growth, assists the entrance into contemporaneity, and creates individual identity. If it fails in this task and succeeds only in the formation of obedient drudges, then the result will be the sterilization of creativity at an early age to the detriment of both personality and society and a halt to the development of society's productive powers. To hinder the young in their individual searches and to prevent them from coming to their own conclusions may well result in a later inabilty to produce innovative work.

The kind of personality and society that this invisible pedagogy promotes is manifest in the content of knowledge and how it is transmitted—through the social relationships within pedagogy. How and what is studied holds the individual and society at stake. Of course, the content of knowledge is many-faceted; I shall explain only the relationship between general/theoretical and the narrow/specialized knowledge and how together they effect the intensification of the socialist content of culture and knowledge.

In its best form, the most important purpose of higher education is to create and transfer a type of knowledge (education) that contains:

—a broad perspective of culture, an introduction to the fund of the most precious achievements of civilization;

—a theoretical basis for a future profession (that profession being interpreted in a broad sense) and the presentation of a practical knowledge that is based on a comprehensive theoretical background; and

—the development of the ability "to learn how to learn," to think and search critically, to comprehend intellectually the meaning of the actual.

This is an effort to understand the world through a contemplative analysis of the scientific foundations of the processes of production, and the economic, social, cultural, and moral relationships that permeate these processes.

Without this effort education becomes degraded, and those cultural values that ennoble the profession of education are lost. The emotive aspect of human life becomes degraded, along with the intellectual and moral character of education, which strives to form emotionless human machines. In a truly graphic fashion, this process is described by Charles Darwin in his autobiography:

Up to the age of thirty, or beyond it, poetry of many kinds . . . gave me great pleasure. . . . I have also said that formerly pictures gave me considerable, and music, very great, delight. But now for many years I cannot endure to read a line of poetry. . . . I have also almost lost any taste for pictures or music. . . . My mind seems to have become a kind of machine for grinding general laws out of large collections of facts, but why this should have caused the atrophy of that part of the brain alone, on which the higher tastes depend, I cannot conceive. . . . The loss of these tastes is a loss of happiness, and may possibly be injurious to the intellect, and more probably to the moral character, by enfeebling the emotional part of our nature.[1]

THE MEANING OF HIGHER EDUCATION

The desire for a general education usually remains unfulfilled because an all-pervasive force—the trend toward super-specialization—enjoys both technical and social justification and works against generalization. But the aspiration for a broad cultural-theoretical basis of professionalism is an essential characteristic of the best version of higher education. From antiquity through the Renaissance and up to today, this aspiration has been a part of our great cultural tradition. It is an expression of the need for broader knowledge that acts as a counterbalance to the narrow specialization that is so often integral to individual professions.

Greater general knowledge is a means by which the ability to perceive the whole is developed and retained. No effective ruling class has divided knowledge and talents into small fragments without also developing the ability for synthesis. Higher education must be transmitted to the masses of youth and to the class of producers who are the bearers of a new society; it must hand down the most precious cognitions and the best intellectual values, which will become enriched and radically altered by the new. And this synthesis must be one of the cornerstones of the culture of professionalism. Earlier society developed by virtue of the spiritual forces of a relatively small number of people, but nowadays, in the midst of the scientific and technological revolution, the intellectual powers of a small number of people are inadequate. There is a practical need to gradually engage the intellectual powers of an ever increasing proportion of the population.

Marx's idea of a polytechnical education—of the formation of free and versatile personalities—is based on this philosophy. At the very core of his humanism is an aspiration to create a society in which everyone is able to develop those abilities that lie dormant within each of us. This aspiration is not an inherited myth of utopian impossibility. It coincides with the strongest trends of civilization of our era and with the imperatives of the scientific-technological revolution. This notion is considerably more topical today than it was in a time when it was expressed as a faraway anticipation. A new era has always had its originators—people who had foreseen and desired it. The concept of polytechnical knowledge was an indication that exclusively narrow specialization was recognized as a trap. This idea was a signpost toward the industrial-collective culture of the future, toward a humanistic imperative that dictates that new generations organize as free producers collectively in control rather than under the control of production and social relationships.

The only culture that can survive a series of rapid technological changes is a vital, inventive, and critical one. It responds to changes by shifting human work toward the creative activity that is inherent in the scientific-technological revolution and thereby creating work that becomes more intellectual.

The Structure of Labor in the Factories in 1926

	Duration of Training				
	Not More than a Day	*1-8 Days*	*1-15 Days*	*From 30 Days to a Year*	*Up to 6 Years*
Percentage of workers	43	36	6	14	1

When the early and later periods are compared (that of the early industrial civilization with the era of automation), the following model of the qualifications structure is obtained:[2]

	Classical Mechanization (% of Workers)	Total Automation (% of Workers)
Unskilled	15	—
Semiskilled	20	—
Skilled	60	—
Complete high school education	4	60
Higher education	1	34
Postgraduate education	—	6

A professional education with a broadly based knowledge of the principles fundamental to the profession enables the individual to perform different tasks. It should not happen that people be victimized by unforeseen changes in production methods. A contemporary expert is not a technological serf tied by invisible chains to the destiny of a technology that might change overnight; rather, he is qualified for an array of professional functions which branch out from a broad professional base. Modern production by its very nature demands a variety of abilities and roles and a broadly mobile work force, in contrast to the old division of labor, which pigeonholes the individual into partial tasks. Contemporary practices continually make the narrowly specialized workers dispensable. The professional scene is ravaged by a scourge that replaces old occupations with new, which are no more secure than the previous ones.

The possibility for variations in working roles and the formation of experts who are alternately able to accept responsibilities for several narrow specialties must become a fact of social production, and education must assist in its realization. Instead of prematurely educating workers into narrow specializations and then placing them into the reserve work force when their expertise becomes obsolete, we should create experts whose general-professional education qualifies them to work in several technologies and provides them with knowledge of broader technological processes. The very nature of modern technology has made polytechnical education a crucial issue for contemporary experts. It is essential that we cease the practice of premature specialization and the resultant unadaptability; all abilities must be encouraged in all possible directions. There exists a broad panorama of occupations, but their nature is such that the majority require a skill that can be acquired in a short time by one with general professional expertise.

I do not deny the inevitability of narrow specialization, nor am I supporting the production of amateurish know-it-alls—an expert who knows everything about nothing. Rather, I am suggesting the avoidance of premature specialization in regular schooling and the acquisition of it later on, concurrently with work or toward the end of one's studies. The character of knowledge is such that, even when it goes into the depth of one specialty, it always offers an awareness of general presuppositions about the meaning of science, and the place science commands within the realm of human thought. No matter how specialized one scientific area can become, it still rests on the core of fundamental principles that are basic to the entire field. A truly educated man is someone who knows a little about everything; he is not someone who early in his education learns the myriad of details and facts attached to a narrow occupation, facts that will of course change several times during his professional life. A truly educated man, along with gaining expertise in a narrow occupation, learns about its foundations and understands its basis—the source of his specialty.

The scientific-technological revolution demands highly developed abilities, yet at the same time it contains the potential for offering liberation from alienating, super-specialized, degrading, and monotonous work.[3]

The intricate relationships among the character and content of knowledge, the manner of its transmission (the content and method of pedagogy), and the direction of social development is demonstrated by yet another phenomenon. We have stated that the role of the university is not merely education; it is also one of bringing about the maturation of a science that conquers the peaks of world knowledge and audaciously detects our own needs and solutions in a manner that is not merely derivative of foreign patterns. For if we only borrow, there is no need for any highly qualified and educated individuals, but only a need for drudges and technicians. There can be science of quality. But it must be inspired by the new human needs of our time and society. It must be engaged in an ever-deepening socialist impulse and in audacious innovations in all professions—innovations inspired by new human needs for more humane cities, for better housing, for more humane use of technology, and for more humane health services. It is of decisive importance that the university form personalities who are not only the masters of knowledge (which we have stressed), but also masters with a deep social feeling, who search concurrently for the best technological and humane solutions. The education process links knowledge with fundamental humane values and with the real life of people; it seeks to improve living conditions—in production and consumption, in culture and education.

These reflections on the character of higher education and, specifically, on the relationship between general/theoretical and narrow/specialized knowledge are not merely academic. To the contrary they are extremely topical and important. They are painfully felt at a time of far-reaching changes, especially in the realm of secondary education. The university will soon be caught up in a maelstrom of new forces; it will find itself in the middle of a new educational system; and it will be faced with the inevitability of connecting all levels of education into one harmonious whole. But higher education cannot simply accommodate itself to the purpose of secondary directed education which is directed at ready-made and definite results. The university is the most developed ideal of educational worth, and it must actively influence the intellectual profile of the future generations.

DISCREPANCIES BETWEEN SECONDARY EDUCATION AND THE UNIVERSITY

The changes underway throughout all of secondary education are so great, so contradictory, and so alive with social impact that a thorough analysis of them is mandatory. It is necessary to understand the different aspects embodied by the reform—namely, the two contradictory trends that are the substance of both its concept and its practice, and more directly, its contradictory view of the social and professional division of labor. The reform is of great relevance to both education and society. Its dimensions must be understood in order also to understand higher education and the necessary corrections that must be made in order to prevent higher education from becoming merely a mechanical continuation of previous training.

The central idea of the reform is an aspiration for the true democratization of education by abolishing social discrepancies within the younger generation. It is of utmost importance to understand and encourage that aspiration. For the differences between the high school student and an apprentice and between the high schools and the vocational and workers' schools signify not only the differences between future occupations, but more significantly, between two different ways of life, between two classes.

Of all students who completed high school in the school year 1968-69, one-third continued their education at the university and the schools of higher education. But a breakdown of this third reveals the following:

92 percent were high school students

34 percent were students from the technical and other vocational schools

0.7 percent were students from the schools for skilled workers

After a decade of changes a certain amount of democratization has resulted: by 1977 the number of high school students had decreased to 78 percent, and the participation of graduates from the school for the skilled workers had increased to 6 percent.

The differences between the high schools and other schools permeate the very substance of educational quality: courses in general education in the high schools comprise 75 percent of the curriculum, while in the vocational schools and the schools for skilled workers such offerings are sharply reduced to around 20 percent. Only because of social intervention in the 1970s did it increase to 40 percent.

The new commonality raises the level of education of the younger generation as a whole and introduces into it the powerful elements of poly-technical, social and production-technical education. The differences among the different types of schools are abolished—all schools of secondary education prepare the individual for higher education. The traditional school structure is fundamentally changed, and the new structure provides a considerably broader access to secondary and higher education. Innovative secondary education states that its goal is to qualify young people for occupations and to make employment possible, thus greatly reducing the legion of wanderers who are not prepared for any trade. Overall planning within education signifies a change of course; it foresees a considerable increase in training for occupations in production and a decrease from 64 to 36 percent in training for occupations not directly related to production.

The introduction of commonality results in yet another factor: the territorial distribution of high schools has created great differences in the possibilities for acquiring an education. In 1976, twenty-two counties in Serbia were without a single school of secondary-level education, and nearly every second student attended school outside of his locale; in Vojvodina the same was the case for three out of four students.

In many underdeveloped counties, where there were previously no high schools (truly an educational wasteland on the map of schooling), there are now facilities for the first phase of secondary education. The number of students in high schools in less developed counties has increased by 40 to 60 percent. We should not forget the importance of these increases to the development of these regions.

But there is another side to these progressive initiatives that could deform and endanger their fundamental purpose. It is the extensive fragmentation of educational profiles—an overzealous specialization that perceives education to be connected to a precise task. Such fragmented training is too archaic for the contemporary work force. Education cannot be based on the transience of technical tasks, which often change faster than the time needed to educate workers to perform them. It must transcend a technology that cancels out a whole array of old professions and creates new ones overnight. Nowadays even the technocratic reformers look for a versatile worker who can perform interchangeable (partial) tasks.

Young people who stay fixed to a precise task are exposed to the mercy of each technological change, and their expertise becomes a dispensable "surplus occupation." In the words of Prvoslav Ralić:

Do we want education to become a means of adaptation to the inherited mode of production; do we want to assign education the function, I stress *function*, of maintaining current class divisions and the existing technical division of labor and, consequently, the revival of class society? . . . Directed education should not be reduced to technical specialization. It would be a doubly expensive structure: first, it would be very expensive in practice because on-the-job training (already a practice in much of the world) is possible within a much shorter time period. It would also be expensive in a human sense, because instead of polytechnically-educated individuals, we would get workers who are "well prepared" to be "an extension" of existing machines. These individuals could well become a good human basis for a future restoration of the technocratic orientation in society. The goals of the reform of education should not be to take expertise and "parcel out, fragment into specialities, and divide up into small pieces" a form of education which will effectively transcend the division of labor rather than be controlled by it, an education which will resist "fach idiotism."[4]

Secondary education is a battlefield of the two conflicting orientations — one attempts to abolish class divisions, and the other fixates on the extremes of the narrow division of labor and through it the maintenance of class differences. Milan Kučan has succinctly identified this pivotal point in his criticism of secondary education and offers a suggestion for its correction:

We all agree that schools should educate for work and that this principle is acceptable to all. But this concept must be defined with more flexibility and clarity. During the course of education, a student not only must acquire knowledge necessary for the execution of a narrowly defined task or the work operation but also must understand the whole of the production process. He must understand the entirety of the production and socio-economic relationship within which he acts so that he will be prepared for further changes and developments in these processes and relationships.[5]

A task of education is to offer students a basic knowledge of the scientific foundations of the technological and various other processes in 30 to 40 basic occupations or professional areas. A reduction in the excessive fragmentation of profiles is mandatory. This must be an axiom of the movement for higher education.

Another matter crucial to secondary education is the character and fate of practicums in production. In workers' schools, work in production had comprised a fund of 1200 hours of vocational training in workshops or factories. This has now diminished by nearly tenfold to about 120 hours per year and has been transformed into excursionary trips to factories that merely clutter the curriculum without accomplishing any training. A mastery of the practical skills of a vocation cannot be acquired at school but must be achieved through practice commensurate with that education that is the springboard to the profession. Once more this demonstrates the necessity for a gradual and organic linkage of work and education and for expanded possibilities for education alongside of work throughout an entire professional career.

A third crucial matter is the enormous overload of a myriad of indiscriminate, unwieldy, and dull material forced on students. Thousands of unnecessary details from one class to another must be deposited in the memory banks and learned by heart—as if the students were a bottomless reservoir ready to store up the totality of knowledge. They are smothered with information that very often is not justified on either scientific or educational grounds. A fundamental reform is yet to come, and it will reduce the quantity but increase the quality of the units of knowledge. It will occasion innovations in study and curricula. Perhaps the most subtle aspect of the reform is the necessity for a great cleansing that will ennoble the content and method of teaching. It is necessary that great changes in pedagogic activity occur lest the reform remain superficial. Enormous amounts of strictly formalized knowledge and extremely abstract and academic concepts (particularly in the social sciences) are transmitted to legions of workers and peasants' children, children who belong to a different subculture and are the bearers of different values and experiences.

This really is a collision of worlds, a social conundrum, which often, without intervention, leaves thousands of teachers helpless; the teachers are inspired by the most ennobling mission, but they are, by virtue of their experience, deeply rooted in a different subculture. The reform can be carried out only by a great movement of enthusiastic teachers who will audaciously develop a new pedagogy that incorporates new approaches to studies—approaches that are sensitive to the masses with different cultural backgrounds who are entering schools and, more generally, to the new needs of young people.

There must also be a reaction to a certain decrease in the educational level among some students who enroll at the university, for the diversity of backgrounds now being accepted into colleges is such that the general educational experience of some students is inadequate to the continuity of a university education. But the importance of the fundamental achievement must be kept in sight—the heightening of the educational, cultural, and professional level of the majority of the new generation, which was earlier denied that privilege. These achievements are like the roots of a plant that does not immediately bear fruit. And what should be done in the meanwhile? To solve these problems the colleges should develop an array of well-thought-out pedagogical programs that will compensate for the voids in education and prevent the deepening disparity between the vocational aims of secondary education and the higher education that follows.

So far we have discussed both the obvious and the obscure problems facing us in our educational system. But we must be aware that the contradictions that are now reflected in secondary education are most deeply rooted in the social system, and it is here that the main entanglement lies.

Let us start, however, with simple facts:

There is a need for metal and foundry workers, but the parents' and students' perception of desirable occupations places administrators further up on the social scale. For years economists and lawyers have been at the top of the scale—the absolute stars. Typically, the populace of industrial cities aspire for administrative training. In that city, which is the center of the metal and mechanical engineering industries, two-thirds of the students are studying economics and law; colleges of mechanical engineering contain the fewest number of students. According to available developmental plans there will be a lack of one thousand mechanical engineers within five to six years. It is also known that lawyers and economists are already on the waiting lists of employment offices. In the Belgrade School of Civil Engineering only one student from Belgrade has enrolled.[6]

Overnight the openings for education in the administrative, bureaucratic-technical, economic, commercial, trade, translating, and archival and museum professions were filled by the best students. The projections for enrollment in production occupations fell very short of expectations.

	Percentage of Enrolled in Relation to the Planned Number
Mechanical engineering	66
Mechanical engineering and energetics	65
Civil engineering	51
Mining	46
Metallurgy	22

The politics of enrollment in high schools have strongly skewed aspirations in the wrong direction.

	Production- and Service-Oriented Professions	Nonproduction Professions
Planned number of openings	69%	31%
Enrolled	53	47

The exodus from the villages has been exchanged for an exodus from the production professions.

We have arrived at the crux of the problem. The aforementioned differences between schools have been replaced with differences between the elite and production professions.

"The simplest explanation is—everyone migrates to where income is higher and where there is less work and a better life. It is obvious that this is a deep social problem which cannot be solved by the educational system alone."[7]

On one side there is an effort to eliminate these differences. Yet on the other, differences are still preserved in the form of fragmented profiles, in the old division of labor and in the contrast between the nonproduction and production occupations. This great clash between revolutionary and conservative principles is a source of much tension.

Still further analysis of the social structure would show the nature of events. What has actually happened? What are the dangers and how can we avoid them? It is quite obvious that the very foundation of the class ranking of occupations which was accomplished through fundamentally different types of schooling—through the high schools and the vocational and worker schools—has been shaken. This mechanism almost automatically secured either working or intellectual occupations. Vocational and workers schools were sending the majority of new students to workers' occupations. Both the parents and the children accepted the situation as predetermined fate. Children from the families of intellectuals, managers, and highly placed administrators rarely joined labor. But the new uniformity within secondary schools has drawn all youth into a broader education. The masses of the young—from the workers and peasants to salaried employees—are suddenly, through the introduction of a general education, offered a broader perspective and a new world of culture. Aspirations have been stirred, and possibilities exist for the continuation of an education that will now depend only on personal ability, and, of course, on the new system. It is a gigantic aspiration that has been awakened.

The aspirations of students from all secondary schools have become quite clear. The new school in the Province of Vojvodina also prepares students for work in production; yet following the reform, 90 percent of the whole generation from the region continued their education while only 10 percent went to work. But the problem now is how to recruit cadres for positions in production, particularly those labor intensive occupations that, thus far, have been the purview of a particular class. This problem foreshadows a future crisis in whole sectors of material production, and it will be manifested in several ways: directly, by workers migrating out of these occupations and indirectly, by reluctance to accept what apepars to be a severe punishment for academic failure. Finally, these occupations cannot be learned at school nor during the 120 hours per year that are allocated for excursions to factories.

Criticism of the educational system is coming from all sides. Some are dissatisfied because they have lost the monopoly over entrance into higher education that was provided by a secondary education. Admittance to the university is more complex, the risks are higher, and competition greater. This segment wishes to conserve the old divisions of labor and old organization of schools. Another type of criticism does not originate from the past. These critics disapprove of narrow, fragmented, and archaic superspecializations and the fragmentation of profiles. They foresee a serious conflict between education and the needs of our era. People no longer believe in the justification and certitude of the class division of the young. But intuitively they feel a future crisis developing regarding occupations in production—a crisis in the functioning of a society that cannot survive without an industrial base. The class system that automatically formed workers and occupations in production and provided manpower for these occupations with apparent ease has been fundamentally shaken. A new system providing these occupations and workers to fill them has yet to be developed. How we shall progress is unclear. It is expected that the education system will solve the problem—a most profound one—of the manner by which we carry out production in society.

A dangerous imbalance exists but there are two possible solutions, both of which require audacity. One solution requires placing a higher value on labor in material production and offering strong incentives to enter work in production. A part of this initiative should provide for the opportunity to study in conjunction with work, for the possibility of shortening working hours, and for a leave of absence of one to several months each year for education.

The other solution is to implement certain corrections in secondary directed education: (a) to abolish the extensive fragmentation of educational profiles by reducing them to thirty to thirty-five broad and basic professions that will allow for later adaptation to an array of narrow specialities; (b) to do away with the ficticious practicums and replace them with genuine work, during which one can learn the skills of the occupation for which he or she is being prepared; and (c) to revise the bulky subject matter of the curriculum so that it provides better preparation for higher education.

Presently one of the most important tasks of the reform of higher education is to create appropriate teaching programs (teaching content) based on the new principles and the participation of all forces of the colleges. The programs should make up for the gaps in general education that are characteristic of students from certain secondary schools. The purpose is to avoid discontinuity from one type of education to the next. This is an important step that cannot be postponed.

Higher education must create and transmit knowledge which contains: (a) a broad cultural orientation, familiarity with the most valuable cultural achievements of civilization; (b) a theoretical basis for a widely defined profession; and (c) the development of learning abilities—learning how to learn, how to think, and how to research critically. Narrow specialization enters the program gradually and naturally toward the end of the studies or later on concurrently with work.

All of these changes together form the essential characteristic of higher education; it must not be broken into reciprocally unrelated fragments and must not be reduced to mere job training.

This concept directs and guides a system of teaching that encompasses two organically connected cycles. The first cycle presents the foundations of professional knowledge, and it contains: (a) broad cultural knowledge, and (b) the theoretical and scientific basis of the profession and the practical work to be performed. Depending on the specific occupation, it may last for several years. The broader cultural and scientific construct of the first cycle of education fulfills yet another need. Beyond its ostensible purpose, it is able to correct the shortcomings of certain educational units in directed secondary education. It should be very effective in providing correction since it is dealing with more mature individuals. The students become acquainted with the great world of science and culture, and their intellectual fund begins to contain more than narrow technical facts.

To connect its particular body of professional knowledge with the broader cultural and theoretical-scientific ideas, each college will have to apply its collective creativity in its own peculiar and inventive fashion. The first cycle is not a separate unit of fixed duration. It is an intermediate step. The purpose of a general cultural education is not exclusively the presentation of knowledge, but is also the development of intellectual and creative abilities, the critical mind and the ability to associate and investigate—in short, the development of those intellectual abilities that help a person think and search better. The great riches of human civilization and the wonders of nature and its laws should be explained to the young in order to strengthen their intellectual abilities and stir their imaginations. All innovators were individuals with broad general and professional backgrounds. These abilities provide an all-encompassing productive energy closely integrated with a general cultural and theoretical perspective. One of the gravest pedagogical delusions is that the colleges should offer technical knowledge with specific factual content but without forming intellectual horizons as well.

The second cycle is characterized by diversification and a degree of specialization (alongside the continuance of certain general theoretical subjects); it provides a broader scope of elective subjects, both from the student's major college and other colleges.

Periods of work and the final period of studies (the second cycle) will merge into a single whole for an ever-increasing number of students prior to entering into a contractual relationship. This practice must incorporate two elements. First it must take students through the research/developmental centers, through the laboratories, through the construction bureaus and analytical departments, and through the areas in which practical research and development are executed and where the profession advances. Secondly, this practice should take students into the factories and operative departments. If it is to be expected that the future experts have a spirit of innovation, then during their studies they must get acquainted with these activities (as well as with the other parts of the working process) in order to be able to fruitfully integrate research and production. Every economist has to go through the analytical centers, every practicing sociologist must be exposed to research practice regardless of the nature of his future position. He must be well prepared to understand the fabric of sociology—the research.

The university and the associated labor bodies strive to form such an intellectual profile. Only in this way will research be demystified to those who work in the plants, and, in the same manner, the plants will not be an unknown quantity to the researchers. In this way, the university turns toward the future—a future where there is a qualitative change within society where personalities as social beings are formed, and where the integration of a profession with human social values is realized.

With regard to proposition for the levels VI and VII (the social compact of a unified basis for the classification of occupations and professional qualifications)—propositons for the introduction of education by levels, it should be said that, if adopted, it should never lead to the dismemberment of the wholeness of a general professional education at the university level. A merger of the first two years of study into one can be introduced only where there is justification for it, where a general professional education and some practical knowledge of the profession actually enhance the learning process. These matters can be solved individually—from college to college, from profession to profession. In any case, such decisions should not be an obligatory norm for all professions. In many cases such mergers do not have any real meaning and only serve to break the wholeness of education.

These matters are of true importance when studies are tied to work and when work is an intermediate step in a program that educates for the same profession. This is not to be considered the final step in education but rather a step in between that seeks to encourage further perfection—particularly in the work situation.

It has been suggested that the schools of advanced education act as a first level of university education. However, the two should not simply merge *per se* into some combination of their present structures. Any upgrading of advanced education will not be accomplished by merely conferring on it a higher status while retaining the original physiognomy. A deep inner transformation of the whole character and content of teaching is necessary, for schools of advanced education and the university do not only represent two different levels of education but also two fundamentally different types of educational quality. The difference is between the production of broad experts and narrow practitioners, between a scientific-theoretical education and a narrow technical one, and the difference between a narrowly directed education that becomes obsolete after a certain amount of time and a broader, all-encompassing education.

From all this we should come to a fundamental conclusion. The entire process of schooling, from the grade and secondary to higher education, should be a continuous flow along a path of development to the peak of the profession. Each lower level, whenever possible, should prepare for the higher ones; each should be a bridge leading ultimately to education alongside work. We should not discriminate between the different types of schools; we should not divide them up so that some prepare for only a lower category of labor that traps individuals into a life without any possibility for further education. Until recently, our school structure mirrored a stratified social structure. There is a need for a great change that will gradually present broadened opportunities for all youth and workers. In principle, secondary directed education has opened such vistas, and the initiative should be further perfected. The individual of the future should enjoy a life of work and education as a norm of development.

THE COMPARTMENTALIZATION OF KNOWLEDGE

The major limitation of the existing pedagogical process is its increasingly greater fragmentation of the scientific disciplines—its tendency to disconnect and isolate subjects. Contemporary science developed through the continuous branching out of separate sciences in their attempt to incorporate the ever more specific, but this trend dangerously narrows each area of research. This development has brought about a rich harvest; it has accumulated many significant and also very practical cognitions. But when the pendulum swings too far to either extreme, the pluses change to minuses. Ever narrowing subjects of research and compartmentalized units of knowledge appear. Knowledge is divided into more confined fragments and is dissipated into bits of information that cannot offer whole perceptions about man, society, or nature. The subjects of study often consist of information acquired through chance rather than through conscious planning because world knowledge grows with such incomprehensible speed. The structure of knowledge in all subjects is constantly razed by the acquisition of new knowledge. There are always new subjects, and facts become instantly outdated. The attempt to achieve an interdisciplinary approach is, at the same time, an admission of the inability to comprehend the whole of a cognition and a mechanized attempt to overcome it.

This entire development, however, is not only the inevitable consequence of the evolution of science, but also the consequence of class-divided labor and the social function that it maintains. Just as there is a fragmentation of labor in material production, there is a fragmentation of thought in intellectual activities. It would appear that the whole world has become parceled out into the subjects of the university curricula. But compartmentalized subjects and the intensive fragmentation of knowledge are not always conditioned by objectively different areas of reality as much as by the number of professors who need an intellectual specialty to justify their professional status. This is the most significant source of scientific imperialism; everyone aspires to a command post in his or her specialty, and everyone denigrates the significance of other subjects, which are viewed as vassal disciplines. Therefore, the reform remains indecisive. All too often we stop at compromise because we become weary; we know that agreement must be reached, and we know that our time and our means are limited. Tactics become all important, and one who is inept at them is silenced.

Fragmentation is perpetuated because it also has a useful social function. It maintains an expert in his extremely narrow framework of thought. He need only occupy himself with small improvements of one limited part of the social machine, and he remains protected from the view of society as a whole. An understanding of the totality of human existence is lost, along with an understanding of societal progress and the necessary measures that can influence the direction of evolution. The ability to explain the significance of each narrow phenomenon as it relates to a broader view is left behind and the narrow specialist very often shirks the most important questions. They do not belong to him, and thus he is not responsible for answering them. In this way, decisive solutions to straightforward social problems are consistently shunted—with a disclaimer of responsibility—from one scientific discipline to another.

An industrial psychologist, for instance, will occupy himself with his own narrow research on how to achieve the psychological motivation for greater work efficiency. But such social factors as exploitation, oppression, and the character of work that maintains foreign economic colonization—factors that are the chief enemies of all motivation, of any desire to increase intellectual or physical effort—stay completely out of the range and competence of the psychologist.

What is to be done? It is clear that we cannot take the nihilistic attitude of underestimating certain sciences, because they are altogether one vast body of knowledge. It is not suggested that certain sciences negate themselves. To the contrary, each specialty should develop its own methods of research to the maximum. But this should not mean that any field of research should be sentenced to describe only isolated segments that—uprooted from a broader social context—are left without any real sense and meaning. Only when fitted into a whole do the separate elements obtain their full definition; only then is their function discovered and their social and human meaning made apparent. By the same token, research of partial phenomena brightly enlightens the wholeness of the social condition and the nature of our principal social relationships. But how do we achieve a correlation between an array of separate phenomena (sciences) and the broader social and natural whole?

We are faced with several mutually connected orientations in a long-term and all-encompassing pedagogical reform:

1. the organic blending of separate sciences and general theory resulting in a broader cultural-professional horizon
2. a change from the mutual isolation of various sciences to interdisciplinary connections and permeations
3. connecting the functions of the same and similar scientific branches of different colleges
4. greater flexibility and freer selection of subjects—the possibility for a freer choice among narrower professional roles so that they branch out from one broad professional basis

THE MEANING OF MARXISM

One of the most important means by which the individual social sciences can be connected to a more complete understanding of society is to adopt a theoretical orientation with a vision that comprises a more complete outlook on nature and society—its structure and its developmental trends. In this respect, Marxist theory stands out in importance because it applies a broader humanistic attitude that bridges the differences between partial and whole cognitions. It is not a body of thought that exists in a vacuum, for it both informs the sciences and is equally informed by them. In one direction Marxist theory enriches the separate social sciences that bring their categories to the Marxist analysis of the basic patterns of our epoch and their contradictions.

The fundamental categories of one science—its theoretical structure—are put in juxtaposition with these basic problems. The juridical and political life and their institutions, for instance, are observed in the light of the fundamental categories. They are observed to determine how much they act in the service of the reproduction of the class structure, or in the retention of bureaucratic monopolies, or—conversely—in the service of overcoming them. A true image of juridical and political life is not achieved by the mere descriptions of these institutions, by the descriptions of their norms, which exist apart from real life and the world. The fundamental categories all relate to the totality of Marxist thought—from the philosophical conception of alienation through the theory of classes to the economic theory of exploitation. It is theoretical thought that is not fragmented, or enclosed within compartments of separate and hermetically sealed off subjects. For instance, Marxist thought regarding production in society can be relevant to other disciplines.

The distinctive trait of bourgeois theory is expressed precisely in the fact that it has separated all social sciences from their material basis: the economy and production in society. The same can be said for the basic philosophical questions of man, for the meaning of existence, the meaning of history; these problems cannot be left to one isolated area of philosophical study, for they also imbue other areas of knowledge. An ever deeper Marxist orientation is a great intellectual process that can be achieved only through collective creative effort. Its goal is the advancement of each discipline, and it never acts forcefully to prescribe or censor. This is a true opportunity to intensify, enrich, and modernize general theory by the mutual participation of Marxists and economists, sociologists, lawyers, political scientists, psychologists, and philosophers. Through this we can greatly enrich Marxist theory, which is empty without the support of the individual sciences.

This is only part of the problem. For in order to accomplish enrichment of the Marxist vision of the world and achieve a broader humanistic application of the sciences, we must devote great energy in defining the relationship between Marxism and natural science. It is a subtle relationship that usually suffers from simplified solutions and vulgarizations and is frequently at the mercy of bad extremes. One extreme is to reduce Marxist education to a body of thought totally removed from professional education and treat it as a separate subject with its own teachers. Another is to view it as a certain kind of ideological, Zhdanovian control over the individual sciences which all too often develop their own Lysenko in the simplified attempt to establish that a few general canons give answers to all the secrets of the world, from the movement of the stars to the action of the atom. The relationship of the general to the specific is, however, fundamentally different. A general theory is an important regulator for true research in each subject, and through theory the field of study enriches, develops, tests, and corrects itself.

It is even more important that we not reduce Marxist education to dealing with the relationships between specific subjects but rather that we work toward a humanistic orientation within professions and toward the transformation of those areas of life to which the young generation will devote its knowledge and talents. A key question arises: what kind of knowledge is needed for a great cultural transformation? Marxism then acts as a synthesizer between a broadly based humanistic culture, whose primary ideal is the improvement of the living conditions of producers, and professions as a whole: medicine, engineering, biology, and economics. This relationship cannot be reduced to an artificial network of several general canons, which are presented in the introductory lectures on biology, geology, or chemistry as the keys to all the world secrets. This is a continuing problem and only the real experts in the profession can find the solutions to it. There are no clear-cut rules for successfully applying a certain programmatic, ideological attitude to scientific cognition in a calm, intellectual fashion. The real integration of ideology and subject matter does not occur unless touched by a creativity and originality unswayed by outside thinking.

Therefore the enrichment of the Marxist approach requires the diligent study of new relationships between Marxism and the fields of medicine, biology, and nuclear physics; study is required into the relationship between engineering and society (the scientific-technological revolution and contemporary society); studies are needed of the urban crisis and a more humane organization of living space and activity that includes a new perspective in urban-rural relations, the ecological crisis and the search for a new harmony with nature. One possible form such an approach might take is to provide common graduate studies in Marxism that would unite economics, law, philosophy, and political science and then start building bridges toward the natural sciences.

Our new research methods should also be applied to the manner in which Marxism is taught. It should be more audacious in both content and structure. It should not be reduced to the rote memorization of bare definitions and their regurgitation in examinations. Active study groups should concentrate like a magnet around the great theoretical and humanistic themes.

After a period of neglect there were great advances made in Marxist education. Many new courses in Marxism were introduced in all colleges, and there was a genuine effort by many faculty members to make Marxism more relevant to the young. But there is the further necessity for a great collective effort to improve the intellectual level and quality of teaching. There is a need for a collective effort to overcome one form of the impoverishment of Marxism—the loss of a possibility of communicating with the younger generation, an inability to sustain them emotionally and intellectually, and a feeling of repulsion toward Marxism on the part of the young.

Marxism is looked upon as a body of thought for which there is no actual need, and which is imposed by outside forces. It is perceived as some form of civil-servant-ecclesiastical opus that offers an idealized picture of the world and is suspected to be some kind of social cosmetic that is at variance with everyday experience. Real answers to the complex and difficult contradictions of the world, life, and the creation of a new society based on socialistic principles are not given. A Marxism that is separated from life, from the great social, economic, and political struggles of our era becomes lifeless; it becomes information that is needed only for passing examinations and is perceived as useless to real life. Another extreme to which Marxism is subjected is its interpretation as a form of abstract thought that ends in total negation and dispiritment, one which seeks neither answers nor solutions and leads finally to total resignation.

In the broader perspective, the world has been experiencing an onslaught of nihilism and despair—feelings that deny the very possibility of a new society and the meaning of revolution or socialism. They are notions that proclaim the ineffectuality of Marxism and forewarn of its ultimate collapse. The social and cultural foundations from whence these thoughts arise is the bourgeois world; they are a great offensive launched by the bourgeois intellectual right-wing.

But serious conflicts within the extremely difficult beginning stages in the formation of socialism have contributed to this sentiment; the crisis within bureaucratic socialism has even caused wars among the socialist countries. Early socialist theory was characterized by a strong trait of optimism. There was the conviction that the development of socialism would be nearly automatic, and would come about as a natural result of the growth of productive forces within bourgeois society. The anticipation was that these forces would simply be taken over by the working class with the overthrow of state power. The depth and profundity of the break with the old society and its class civilization could not be foreseen.

Many of the principles of organization and patterns of consumption of class civilization—such as the division between intellectual and physical work, and the division between managing and the mere execution of duties that perpetuate power over people—remain deeply rooted within the new society.[8] Of decisive importance is the attitude that we form toward this entire phenomenon. Marxism is neither a factory of illusion nor a factory of despair. It is a critical understanding of reality, of the world and of one's own society; it searches for new solutions and the forces behind change. We want to promote an awareness of the inevitability of even deeper changes that involve a total break with the old bourgeois world and with its ideological descendants—the bureaucracy and technocracy still within socialism.

This criticism of empty intellectuality is not a lament for things lost but is rather a criticism of obsolescence within our own methods. We are presented with a renaissance within Marxism, which is becoming richer, fuller, and more brave. It is providing us with a way of life that can open up new vistas, and our maturity of experience can enhance the possibilities for a freer life for all people and all communities. Marxism is not mere quotations but the most advanced theory of our time. It is a theory that expresses what we have yet to achieve and what we may become through conscious efforts and continuous struggles. "Marxist thought and science is not a dogma for us. But it is a means of management and orientation in all situations no matter how complex they might be."[9]

One of the greatest dramas of our era is taking place—the clash with all past forces. It is taking place daily and in each area of social life; its themes are seen at each step. Any research that ignores this drama is lifeless and devoid of all vitality. The great mission of Marxism is a struggle for a real understanding of reality. It aims to make the young truly experience our era and its great events and to make them understand that they are not merely raw material being processed by history. Dissatisfaction alone will not suffice to effect a transformation of the existing system, nor will it be accomplished through malaise toward this world. It is not enough to discard. One must create, must search for the meaning of life, must be engaged in a struggle over each small detail of the new because innovations are not presented to us on a silver platter. This is not merely a utopian impulse. The sparks of a new mode of life flicker all over the world. They are found in the great social movement of the workers, intelligentsia, peasantry, youth, and women, and in the historic fight for self-management.

From our point of view, the future of Marxism and its relationship to other subjects rests not in the introduction of one or more new courses of study but rather in the attitude of the young toward their entire profession and in the development of a desire to further advance their fields of work through the acquisition of greater knowledge.

BRIDGES BETWEEN SUBJECTS AT THE DIFFERENT COLLEGES

My emphasis on the importance of the connection between the separate sciences and a general theoretical framework is not an appeal to abolish separate subjects. Rather, it is an expression of a need for more cooperative interdisciplinary work—work that will not endanger personal, intellectual creativity but will broaden the field in which it can be expressed. A variety of disciplines, departments, and collectives of teachers and students should function together in an effort to solve truly significant problems, thus breaking down the barriers between subjects. If the problems themselves provide the impetus for cooperation, the barriers among the subjects will diminish. This approach will offer analyses closer to reality and will satisfy the natural need of the young for a more complete world view—one of the most important requirements of our time.

For instance, instead of treating only the narrow concept of *housing law*, it should be possible to assemble cooperative efforts around a real life problem. For experts in disciplines ranging from the economy, sociology, and urban development, to psychology and the law are all concerned with and are able to affect housing conditions. It is possible to collect into one whole a diverse body of fragmented knowledge that joins economic reality with such components of a critical analysis of housing policy as criteria for distribution, urban problems, esthetic concerns, legal statutes, and the social principles that underlie them. Such preparatory studies would create not only experts conversant with legal codes but also experts with a highly developed understanding of society. For only a broad sensitivity towards human needs and only the energies of thousands of workers—together with material growth—can insure that this important dimension of human life will be solved by principles that are neither profiteering nor bureaucratic, but rather are based on the needs of the producers.

The intermingling of subjects would eliminate redundance, would save time—this most precious commodity of our era—and would permit more concentrated training within a shorter period.

An important aspect of pedagogical reform is a functional connection of basic sciences at the different colleges. Valuable results cannot be achieved by the total isolation of similar scientific disciplines. The lack of connectedness among the basic sciences (mathematics, physics, chemistry, biology, linguistics, Marxism, sociology) cannot be in agreement with the many serious demands of these fundamental disciplines. In the near future, such divisiveness will be even more of an obstacle to development. The forms these connections take can differ. One form could be an agreement concerning certain subjects common to the basic disciplines—particularly Marxism, national defense, the same basic natural sciences, and so forth—in order to make their content richer and of better quality. But at the same time the content must preserve those specific characteristics that link them organically with the totality of teaching within their specific college. Communications can be channeled through the councils for teaching and research (or common chairs), which may constitute the backbone of one profession (as for instance law or economics).

This is a subject of concern among the colleges. Deeper changes in the essence of the university require more thorough deliberations and this in itself will create a common basis for a number of professions. One form of cooperation that is already in existence in this level is the universities' scientific/teaching councils of related colleges: colleges of engineering, medicine, bioengineering and the natural, mathematical, and social sciences.

Still the decisive influence on the structure of these subjects and their relation to the whole of teaching, as well as to the choice of faculty, is the final right of the major college. The intercollegiate councils of faculty influence the content and the professional level of teaching as well as exercising a degree of coordination between teaching programs and research. But these connections stay within the realm of one profession. These are not administrative matters; they do not lead toward uniformity and the impoverishment of subject matter. The teaching programs are an autonomous decision of the various colleges, but during the proposal stage there is professional coordination and mutual influence. Yet this will not lead to a rigid uniformity that removes a subject from its organic dependence on the total purpose of a specific college.

FLEXIBLE TEACHING AND FREER CHOICES

Reform offers students a significantly freer choice of subject matter and disciplines not only within the major college but also within adjunct colleges in accordance with needs presented by a life that is no longer divided into the same compartments that our curriculum reflects. We must take into account the new rhythm of professional life. Many narrow specializations will disappear overnight and then reappear in new combinations that our rigidity in teaching cannot follow. We cannot create a new university for each new profession. These needs should be met by combining the separate branches of science at the different colleges. This changing situation creates a need for constant deliberations to improve the relationship between the general theoretical basis of the profession and the manner in which narrow specialization is acquired.

In this light we have to observe the relationship between core (required) content and free choice; as part of the teaching method we must observe the results of the various combinations of study elected by students and observe their growth. The young are not only the students of one isolated college, but they are part of a whole university. From the first days of study, instead of molding the young into a narrow specialization (a practice full of risk), we must leave many professional paths open to them. Education will become more flexible, more differentiated, and more adaptable to change. The experts of tomorrow are not prisoners of one narrow specialty with an unknown destiny. The philologist need not be only a teacher. He can work in publishing, in book dealing, as an editor and translator, or as a social worker.

Single-handedly, the university can act to prevent over-investment in an unknown future. The university can prevent the onerous burden of inadequately educated people and the disparity between the required and the available experts. Rapid changes in technology and the transformation of existing patterns of life require the formation of a mobile work force which is intellectually and psychologically prepared for the return to education. These past changes need constant improvement and new combinations among disciplines, the ability to perform team work, and adaptability to the job. However, the endeavors in this direction are paralyzed by the overly rigid forms of teaching that are becoming increasingly more expensive.

An educational system that is more flexible and more differentiated and that contains a greater variety of educational programs has become an imperative of our time. Studies and the structure of education should be formed on the basis of subjects and in flexible modules, incorporating offerings from different colleges. But this does not mean that the pendulum should shift to an extreme that leads to abolishment of the system that is its mainstay and the foundation of a profession (its infrastructure). The educational program is not a bazaar of modules (units) unconnected by a common perspective. Education is not a wide swath through a jungle of programs chosen by the student according to his particular wants. Education for a profession has its systematic foundation, its nucleus of general professional knowledge (its infrastructure), and its narrower subjects (modules), which are connected to its base but which are more freely chosen from within the major or adjunct colleges (a freely combined superstructure).

Of course lip service given to these aims is not enough; the sciences must begin to develop bridges between each other that connect their common aims. Mathematics for the sociologist has certain specific traits that differ from those of electrical engineers. Some of the programs at the college of mechanical engineering are creating ties to certain specialties in agriculture. The students left to themselves will be unable to identify these connections unless the subjects are joined through bridges that link together complete professional programs.

When the core courses in a given professional program are linked together harmoniously, and a free choice of subjects among an array of colleges is offered, then the students' professional development is greatly enhanced and the petty technical division of labor is ovecome. Such a program provides possibilities for specialization that are unavailable in a narrow and fragmented program that only offers training in smaller segments. A broad view greatly enriches the entire professional outlook.

Presently only training in specialties exists. For instance, law is divided into the detailed branches of criminal and civil law, and these are broken down even further until, for instance, we find an expert on water resource law. A specialist, however, must also be able to work backward to the general. He should be molded through a liberal combination of the parts of other professions so that he becomes a new professional whole. Economists and lawyers should be introduced to computer techniques; a philologist should be able to perform social work.

Specialization should not be achieved exclusively through the fragmentation and impoverishment of subjects, but rather it should act to enrich understanding and should provide training in the ever-new combinations of different areas of knowledge. Specialization should expand rather than narrow the professional outlook. It should open rather than restrict new possibilities for employment. Specialization of this nature would act as a force to overcome the division of labor (the division of knowledge) instead of maintaining the ongoing fragmentation of both knowledge and professionalism.

In addition to this advantage, a freer choice enables the young to develop their own tastes and abilities. It motivates them, and through this motivation they influence the choice of subject; they contribute to their own development, and they develop a certain autonomy—which is not the case when they submit themselves to a stiff and rigid educational program. Through free choice the students participate in the formation of their own education; they create their own educational program, both according to their inclinations and to the available prospects for work. They are formed to be freer, more autonomous, and more independent personalities. At the same time their personal inclinations have not restricted them because they have acquired a broad professional base—the foundation on which a specialized superstructure is built.

In addition, a more flexible system of education opens up other alternatives that should be carefully researched. One is the possibility of abolishing the rigid semester system and introducing a number of smaller time blocks (units). In these shorter time periods, the training should concentrate on several closely connected subjects in logical sequence for optimal effect. The courses could be repeated within one school year. Either an introduction or continuation of the training could be offered at the beginning of each such time period. The advantages of such a system are manifold. Firstly, a more thorough review and mastery of subjects is possible because of the concentration on smaller units of information. Secondly, the individual could progress at his own speed because he could choose the number of courses he wished to attend during any given time. In an educational system divided into semesters, the school facilities and laboratories remain unused for three whole months because of vacation. In a system of more flexible time units, teaching at full capacity takes place throughout the year. As a result the teaching capacity of the university increases by nearly one third. Such fuller usage could greatly save funds. Nevertheless, we should be careful when we examine such alternatives because they may contain hidden weaknesses.

The broadened accessibility to institutions of advanced and higher education is one important element in the development of a more uniform territorial distribution of the centers of cultural and intellectual life. It has opened up the possibilities of education for the young, particularly for the young from poorer families. A wider span of members of the same generation entering the assembly halls of the university has greatly increased. But this cultural expansion has contained certain weaknesses: all too often development has been completely rudimentary in nature and, in fact, numerous institutions have simply duplicated each other. These circumstances have had two negative effects. First, educational centers have fallen into competition, and, second, local funds are not being used economically.

Any future direction cannot halt this development because there is a fundamental need for intellectual, cultural, and scientific growth and for a more equitable distribution of the centers of intellectual development throughout the Republic. The basic problem, though, is the development of the underdeveloped regions. Today the formation of individual centers of education is as important as yesterday's development of factories. Today's development is a path of human development. But it is of utmost importance to develop in a well-thought-out manner, to secure full quality in the advancement and enrichment of these institutions, and to prevent a rudimentary growth that can only produce adverse results.

This means that the centers for higher education must not be mere copies of already existing colleges but rather colleges that express particular needs, possibilities, and specificities. They must be an expression of originality and must offer professional training that in itself is capable of attracting students. The University of Belgrade, which has an extremely well-developed network of colleges, should not strive (except in very rare instances) to open up new colleges. It should strive instead for new combinations and functional connections between the existing colleges in response to new professional needs. Nowadays, creation of new professions is a very real event. But this does not mean that a new college should open for each new profession, but rather that there be a recombination of activity among the colleges, institutes, and the new scientific disciplines.

PERMANENT EDUCATION AND THE OPEN UNIVERSITY

We have arrived at a point that marks a radical change in our whole approach toward education. Education is no longer just for the young. It is not the final, lifetime sufficient, the total of knowledge acquired during one's youth. The foundation of traditional education has been upset, and the structure has started to crumble. Education must be envisaged and organized as a continuum that spans the larger part of life—a continuum that will progress alongside other normal activities. The greater part of our lives shall be a process wherein study and work alternate. The previous system that created educational automations for a brief period in preparation for the rest of a working career will be supplanted by a continuous process of education and a renewal of knowledge as society develops.

This development is a radical innovation. It is a totally new idea of this century that has spread throughout the world and has become a *spiritus movens* in the development of civilization. The society of the future will be increasingly a society of education. Education therefore has become as much a problem of society as it is of the school system. Innovation in education is not merely a new approach to learning but a new approach to society. Its development should not be left to chance, but rather it should be handled with the same resoluteness with which we traditionally handled the education of the young.

There are two significant forces which underlie this development.

Since the time of Newton, the fund of scientific knowledge has been rapidly expanding. Initially this fund doubled every fifteen years, but today the cycle has shortened to every few years. Within the working life of an expert in any given technical field, the fund of specialized knowledge will change several times. During each decade, individuals are faced with so many all-encompassing physical and intellectual alterations that no earlier explanations suffice.

The techniques for transmitting knowledge from the old to the young, from fathers to sons, that were used by so many successive generations are no longer effective. As a result we are increasingly forced to find new methods for this transmission. An example of the exponential growth of knowledge vividly illustrates the history of the continuing obsolescence of knowledge with each generation: the half life of an engineer has shortened from ten years for the generation that graduated in 1945, to only five years for those who are presently graduating.

The obsolescence of knowledge grows proportionately more rapid with each successive year of graduation. For instance, ten years following graduation, the class of 1935 would achieve a 40 percent obsolescence of knowledge, and for the class that graduated in 1970, this figure would be close to 70 percent. Dr. Robert L. Hillard, a top expert on educational broadcasting for the United States Federal Communications Commission, goes even further: "Knowledge expands so fast that the sum of all human achievements for the child born today will be quadrupled when he graduates from college. When the same child turns fifty, this sum will be thirty-two times greater, and ninety-seven percent of all knowledge will have been discovered since his birth."[10]

Continuous education is a strategy of the cultural life of an individual and modern society. For the first time in history, great cultural transitions are taking place within a shorter time period than the working life of one man. It is no longer possible for teachers to transmit on a one-time basis the whole of cultural life. They have to offer an education that will progress alongside a rapidly changing civilization. Education must be organized so that it offers the possibility to return to school at any time to improve an understanding of one's profession, to acquire a higher educational degree, or to change profession totally. An endless renewal of the reservoirs of knowledge and a constant return to the source must be a continuous process or must occur from time to time during an active professional life.

Education throughout life silently acquires the force of a revolution and therefore prepares individuals for participation in society and clears the way for democracy and the society of self-management. Cultural enrichment is no longer a luxury or privilege; it becomes a working assumption that people are taking the responsibility for their lives into their own hands. The widened groupings of society will no longer accept the notion that cut-throat competition at a certain phase in early youth must determine the fate of a person for his or her entire life. Education throughout life provides an opportunity for a higher education for those who were previously unable to acquire it and for those who were prevented from succeeding merely because of differences so minimal that they were often expressed at the third decimal of a grade-point average.

When education becomes continuous, the concepts of success and failure change. A person who did not achieve at a certain stage in early youth will be given another chance concurrently with his intellectual and social progress. He will not be given a life sentence in the ghetto of failure. His future is not sealed at youth. Continuous education is a practical system for organizing a growing program of study combined with work.

In many countries such a program is a new aspiration. It is taking root and is expanding the possibilities for higher education to the populace regardless of age and social status. It is presenting opportunities to different age groups, thus providing effective incentives to combine work and education—to open the doors of the university to those who already have work experience.

In Sweden and Norway, the universities are open to anyone who is 25 years old and has worked in a profession for at least four years regardless of whether or not he has any secondary education.[11] Time that is spent in returning to education at the institutions of higher education should be considered active years of work experience. Under this system men and women should receive a personal income during the study period and they should be recipients of health and social security. Pedagogical reform should be one of liberation; it should gradually reorganize colleges into centers for permanent education and should seek new forms for transmitting scientific knowledge. The time has come for the university to open its hallowed doors.

The content of teaching programs, the length of courses, condensed teaching, the criteria for enrollment, correspondence courses, summer schools, evening classes, a stronger emphasis on self education, a new pedagogy that credits work experience and nonacademic (but nevertheless real) competency in a given field—these are the central themes in the discussion about a permanent educational program.

Under such a system, time, space capacity, and intellectual potential would be utilized more rationally. In the future the institutions of higher education will have more diverse study programs, and their organization will have to become more flexible.

Recurrent training will enable us to shorten the educational cycles. More condensed study should be understood as an integral part of a process of learning that extends throughout the whole of a man's working life and will enable a prudent reduction in the duration of basic studies in higher education. It will condense the same number of subjects into shorter periods of time and will tie the periods of active work to study.

Permanent education is too wide a field to expect that the university will be the only bearer of all forms of higher education. It will play the leading role, but it will also act in concert with the educational centers of the organizations of associated labor and particularly with the "open university."

Ten years ago Great Britain started a far-reaching educational experiment—the birth of a dream. Today the dream is alive in many countries. The dream is a university that consists of only part-time students. Its students—adults, employed people from all professions, from all social classes—follow lectures over the radio and television, and receive printed educational material and other literature. Only from time to time do they actually go to the university itself, but nearly all attend during the summer session, pass their examinations, and receive degrees that are on an equal footing with those from other universities.

The Open University, which was looked upon at the time of its founding as a risky venture and viewed with skepticism by the more conventional universities, was widely seen as a weak issue in education. Ten years later many countries contend for the honor of being its initiator. Its students are older than twenty-one, they are full-time employees, and their studies are most frequently conducted at home. The Open University offers them a variety of courses: literature, the natural sciences and mathematics, and a variety of social and technical programs. Each main course is divided into thirty-four weekly "units," and each "unit" is comprised of correspondence courses, one radio program, and one television program. The Open University mails specially written courses that contain teaching units and the problems that the students must solve. The students also receive written outlines developed by university professors. The radio and television programs are aired via the BBC twice a week: the television programs are transmitted between 5:30 and 7:30 p.m. every weekday, and are repeated over the weekends. Experience so far has shown that the dropout rate is 9 percent, and the percentage of failure 10 percent. A degree from the Open University is obtained following four years of study.

THE CONTEMPORARY EDUCATIONAL TECHNOLOGY

Students are the key to the success of the Open University. But at the beginning, the initiators of this project doubted that students would have the energy to spend 400 hours a year in study for a six to eight year period—the time needed to complete the program. Fortunately, these fears were not realized because the most striking characteristic of the Open University students is their determination to study and their aspiration to excel even in the most difficult educational material in order to be successful at the examinations.

The reform of education must take into account the concept of the Open University, a program which will, through standard correspondence courses and the use of modern media, enable many people to achieve a quality education alongside work. It should be especially directed at individuals older than twenty-one and with several years of work experience. An immediate task at hand is the formation of a commission to develop the concept of the Open University.

There is a need to introduce the innovations of technology into teaching; radio, television, other audiovisual media, and computers should all be employed as sources of information. A strong incentive to adopt these means is the very number of students, the mass programs of study. The explosion of knowledge imposes a similar incentive. There are literally thousands of new facts being discovered constantly, and knowledge can no longer be merely memorized or transmitted through lectures. New technology, an ally of the cultural revolution in education, is essential to educational reform. Close to 80 percent of all information necessary to the educational process could be transmitted through new educational technology. A rational application of technology could significantly reduce the cost of higher education.

If the university wants to become an organizer of continuing education, it must seek different vehicles of communication. With the aid of new technology, self-education will play a greater and greater role in the education of both young and adult. Innovative educational techniques must use the power of technology, because technology is fundamental to all systems that acknowledge the importance of self-education. A computer is an instrument that transforms teaching into a highly individualized process. Computers can rapidly transfer and verify information; they are extremely useful in simulation and experimentation. In short, the computer is particularly adapted to the transfer of knowledge, the very activity that presently engages 80 percent of the time of all teachers in all educational systems.

The young live in a society that is becoming increasingly more technological but their time at the university is given over to machines from the nineteenth century. Higher education, a process that claims to be the transmission of all knowledge, is, with few exceptions, still living in the era of the handicraft trades. The abyss that separates the young from the contemporary technological achievement with which they live is already too deep. Is it actually possible in these times to imagine a developed industry, an efficient administration, and a contemporary educational process that is not utilizing the instruments that are offered to us by technology? Yet institutions of higher education are applying this technology only in exceptional cases.

Colleges must develop a program of modernization through cooperative funding ventures with other colleges.

BRIDGES BETWEEN THE ACADEMIC CADRE AND PRACTICE

Mass higher education imposes the need to engage a broader circle of gifted artists and experienced experts in teaching. In this way the funds for teaching will be more rationally used because expertise within the university will not be based only on full-time faculty, but also on the expert abilities of professionals, who could serve on a part-time or temporary basis. The need is clear; in only five years (1967-1973) the teaching load increased from twenty-three to twenty-seven students per teacher, and the number of students per collaborator increased by almost one-third (from twenty to twenty-nine).

The increasing number of graduate students working on research projects in practice, and the establishment of organic connections between the university and the developing centers in the economy and social services, present good opportunities to attract part-time instructors from outside into certain aspects of teaching and research. But it is important to both these instructors and their students that they retain close ties to their profession, for it is essential that they keep in touch with the realities of the working world. Every society should include among its educators the most talented artists, scientists, physicians, engineers, and innovators. But we must carefully develop the procedures and measurements that will maintain a high intellectual level and that will prevent the occurrence of private arrangements and political maneuvers. Such practices could lead to monopolies within the universities and eventually compromise and prevent this reform. It is necessary, therefore, to reach a self-managing agreement at the university level (or at the level of the related colleges) that could serve as a framework for this practice.

The proposal that the profession of education be occupied by other than full-time teachers is not meant to lessen the importance of professional pedagogical work. But we must begin to examine the student-teacher relationship in a new light because the faculty cannot continue to exist in its traditional form. A great deal of instructive work will be carried out by the students themselves, who will be aided by programmed tests and machines. The role of the full-time teacher is to provide cultural inspiration and research leadership. No student can by himself achieve such training, and no technology or technique can replace the great role of the educator.

Another aspect of reform is related to the career of a university assistant. Is the odyssey from one phase of schooling to another, from one level of study to the next (each totally separated from life and practice) the only way to create future professors? And how does this phenomenon influence educational politics? Subjectivism is inherent in a system that permits individuals the overwhelming power to select their intellectual successors. Under current practice the pool of talented assistants evaporates and what remains is individuals from well-to-do families, who have parents willing to assist them through the difficult years at the assistantship level. The less fortunate, in spite of their talent and gifts, will have to forego the dream of an occupation in research and teaching. Reform should require that all assistants practice their profession for a year or two directly or soon after graduation.

Two radically different pedagogical orientations have existed in the university from its inception to the present time. One is aimed at the formation of the creative and independent personality with broad intellectual and professional views. It thrives especially during social and cultural upheavals such as, for instance, the Renaissance, the French Revolution, and the beginning enthusiasm of the socialist revolutions. In a time of social calm, it does not disappear totally but goes into remission. In a limited form, it stays within the elite universities such as we have already described. The remain-

ing universities are led by an authoritarian pedagogy (repressive socialization in a sociological sense), and their substance is student passivity and
mechanical learning; in short, they form a routine, dependent, and obedient
labor force.

THE NEW PEDAGOGY

The pedagogical system rests on three pillars: the teaching program
defines what is considered knowledge; pedagogical methods define a legitimate way of transmitting it; and evaluation measures acquired knowledge.[12]
But these three factors do not occur in a social vacuum. Broader forces
penetrate each part of the system, and pedagogical relationships correspond
to social ones.

Pedagogy is both a technique for the transmission and acquisition of
knowledge and a force by which personalities are formed, socialized, and
groomed for future roles.

The relationships in the pedagogical process are at the same time social
ones. Students are prepared for the relationships that they will face later in
life as citizens, workers, managers, and parents.

The whole history of pedagogical relations reveals its double life. It is a
creative form of the transmission and acquisition of knowledge. But it also
educates for either freedom or oppression; it forms either a liberated and
more creative personality or an obedient executor of orders. Viewed as a
social force, pedagogy is either a means for liberation or a means of
oppression.

There is no need to waste words showing the connections between this
social relationship and the direction of development in a given society—its
orientation toward the association of free and independent producers or
toward bureaucratic collectivism.

This criticism of the pedagogical system is not primarily directed at
teachers; their abilities and aspirations differ, as is the case in all professions.
Rather, the criticism is concerned with the system, with the prevailing social
relationships in pedagogy and with the never-ending reliance on obsolete
traditions. Many teachers do their jobs well and with honor. They transmit
broad areas of knowledge; they do not shirk the responsibility of keeping
up in their subject area and they do their best at equitable grading. Many
teachers invest a lot of effort in teaching; they try to make their lessons
interesting to students in order to be able to transmit knowledge effectively.
The best of them add yet another quality to their work: they are full of
enthusiasm for their subject, and they wish to transmit that enthusiasm to
the young with the hope that the lives of their students will be enriched in the
same way that their own lives have been enriched. Lectures by such teachers
can be rewarding experiences, even within a basically authoritarian system.
All of us can recall such a teacher. But we all also recognize situations where

a relatively unimportant subject is transformed into an artificially insur-mountable barrier and where an examination serves to promote arrogant and petty powers. One should never forget that the young can tolerate an overload of subject matter more easily than they can injustice.[13]

So also when dealing with humanity, pedagogy reveals its two-sided nature. It is an avocation that contains the finest, the most noble—nearly artistic—ability to form other personalities. It is an avocation that has already received enough censure. Conversely, education can also be a trans-mitter of the authoritarian socialization that is inherent in its nature.

But to return to the analysis of the pedagogical system, it is apparent that the patterns of authoritarianism are still predominant. The student is under-stood as an object. This status is strongly reaffirmed by the phenomenon of mass studies. There is an interesting opinion—one that supports the thesis that high and low tides of human pedagogy are linked to major social developments—which states that the students of the years directly following the war were the closest to the ideal of the school of under-standing. According to this ideal, school initiates a love for knowledge and prepares the young to find their way with greater ease into the future. As described by members of the older generation, the postwar school was more mature and more intimate; there was less hierarchical dependency, and the teachers attempted to establish contact with the young.[14]

Reform must inspire a creative pedagogy that will be less permeated with hierarchical relations, an authoritarian mentality, and the passive status of students. Unfortunately the large number of students in and of itself makes it more difficult to realize these changes.

We can already discern the outlines of a pedagogical alternative that will include not only a rejection of the old methods but also a gradual structuring of a new and more democratic school. Or, in the words of the students themselves:

Our stand is determined by the awareness that we must continue our struggle for more rights; that the ability to achieve more complete creative expression is above all a matter of changing the old "objective conditions" offered—or forced on us—by the traditional university. . . . The obstacles that deny truly equal chances to mature and that prevent the full creative affirmation of the gifted will disappear.[15]

Only through the vital pedagogical creativity of all participants—the teachers and the students alike—will the renaissance of the school become possible; this is particularly true under the difficult conditions of mass education that present seemingly insurmountable obstacles to many changes. Education on a massive scale strongly favors a pattern of teaching in which the student is not an active participant. Time is needed to understand and nurture the new democracy; of all possible systems a dictatorship is the one that requires the least time. But our main orientation is without a doubt: "The formation of individuals [as reiterated in the student's resolution] does not require that we fill their heads with facts, but rather that we awaken their intellectual curiosity, develop their sense of responsibility and their ability to think critically, and stimulate a spirit of initiative, imagination, and creativity."[16]

Our task becomes even more necessary with changes in the character of knowledge.

It is not only a matter of selectivity and a decrease in the volume of knowledge imposed on us; we are not talking about the impoverishment of education. People have a need for even more knowledge in order to satisfy the demands of the future. But all knowledge should not be "inventoried" in the minds of students. Today one need only "press the button," and an enormous amount of information can be obtained. Because of this a general education and its content should stress usage of knowledge over the retention and memorization of a mass of facts. Today, learning should contain more than rote acquisition. It must encompass the understanding, comprehension, and identification of information, and it must transform that information into generalizations, phenomena, principles, and laws. Students must know how to use and apply what they have learned and how to communicate it to others.

Contemporary education insists less on the acquisition of specific amounts of knowledge and more on the development of universally applicable abilities which impose discriminatory judgment and which serve as the instruments for the further acquisition of knowledge. Our understanding of knowledge changes constantly and the need to wisely organize new information is pressing. Science and technology develop at such a rapid pace that within a lifetime of one generation professional knowledge becomes outdated. Because of this, less emphasis should be placed on the extensive acquisition of knowledge and on the detailed particularities of data and events. Printed materials, computers, and other contemporary technical aids will render the memorization of detail unnecessary.[17]

A culture of silence exists within today's educational system, but an alternative to it is taking shape. The culture of silence excludes rather than attracts students; it deadens rather than arouses their interests. According to the new alternative, classes are not merely lectures (subjects) presented to passive students (objects), nor are they the simple deposit of material into data banks. The lecture is not authoritarian *per se*. It may become so if the lecturing technique is so used to impose sacred knowledge *ex cathedra*, rather than impart knowledge to students. Lectures can be better adapted if they are used along with other techniques of learning such as seminars or group studies.

In addition, students are well able to accomplish preliminary work in many subjects themselves. An interest in a new theme around which there is collective preparation is aroused in advance. The teacher points out the key issues or problems to be discussed and puts particular stress on the more important controversial issues. The student discussants, aided by the teacher, prepare condensed reports on different aspects of the theme.

In such a fashion, the academic structure is fruitfully combined with spontaneous initiative. The natural need of the young to search for knowledge independently, to explore the world and society, and to develop their own ability and their own critical awareness is met. Especially for students in their last years of study, it should be possible to develop this approach in certain subject areas. With such a practice the authoritarian form of teaching will disappear.

The difference between the classical lecture form and student participation—heretofore two totally separate activities—is mitigated. On occasion, study groups can link lectures and exercises into one whole. The study group is also present and active in lectures during which separate themes are presented by the collective of teachers and student-discussants. The lectures grow into a dialogue, into a discussion about the theme, which expands with participation. The teacher is an organizer and a leader of the young, who learn to search for knowledge by themselves. Dogmatic pedagogy, which is perceived as the imposition of absolute and burdensome knowledge, is replaced by participation, independent research, and free discussion. This cannot be the practice in every teaching unit, but it is difficult to find a single branch of science void of key themes that penetrate the very core of its expertise. These themes can act as true stimuli for posing problems, arousing interest, and initiating the active participation of students in the dialogue.

The essence of the university is the purveyance of a form of education that will qualify people for creation and research rather than for routine execution. With this purpose in mind, science and teaching must not be divided into two separate sectors but must be an organically connected whole.

One's own research activity is education in a microcosm, where the researcher reproduces, processes, and acquires knowledge not through mere transmission but through individual practice. In finding solutions to certain types of problems, the routine part of work receives less attention and the emphasis is on understanding relationships and connections within a given field. There is a fundamental need to allow students the opportunity to conduct scientific research work while they are being educated and to channel the most gifted students into the more sophisticated scientific projects. This need is connected to the indispensability of work practice, which all together promotes understanding of the real basis of life, averts onesidedness, and offers skills in the basic instruments in production. It bridges the abyss between the long period of learning and the later period where work is the only activity.

Our attitude toward examinations will also change. Examinations often become a mere tightrope act. One consequence of the system is that the students cram facts shortly before the examination "trying not to move their heads too much lest knowledge leaks out too early." One student from the college of electrical engineering candidly describes the process:

Studying is actually arranged so that it is primarily reduced to preparation of exams; an exam is a fetish to which everything else is subordinated. Students will never say we are studying mathematics, or we are learning biology, but always, we are preparing for an exam in mathematics, or biology. The most successful students are those who study the professor's preparatory units exclusively and then spew out the answers. The most important lectures of the course are the first and last ones because this is when the professor tells all about his exams and what should be done to pass them. The most popular assistants are the ones who work with the students on the examination exercises and give them (behind professor's back) a few tips on the oral part of the examination. But there are also departments where the exams are kept like guild secrets which are transmitted from one generation of students to another. . . . Isn't it logical that knowledge acquired so mechanically is reproduced in the same manner later. . . . The examination procedure is perfectly adapted to mechanical reproduction. . . . The ones who study differently often give an odd impression and with more effort achieve less. Students are required to learn countless patterns of constants and schemes by rote when they can easily be found in any handbook.[18]

Of course, everyone needs to evaluate his work, to see where he stands and how far he has gone. We are talking about the nature of this evaluation—about the character of the examination process. It could be both a verification that knowledge has been acquired and also a useful and instructive termination of study. But our examining process stifles nearly all efforts to apply methods which would be more appropriate than are today's endless testing of lecture matrial. A book learned by heart is not a guarantee that the subject was learned too. The examination should be a test of knowledge and the ability to apply it. Instead of our formalized methods of today, several other forms will develop. Active participation in a study group will serve as a collective testing of knowledge and understanding and, particularly in the case of seminar students, there will be a collective discussion of individual research papers. In this way more evaluation would take place throughout the entire study unit. Experience in literature searching and gathering together material for a report is more useful to the majority of the students than is the accumulation of details.[19]

Such participation requires trust, a great effort, an active intellectual contribution, and motivation on the part of the students—in short, responsibility. Only such measures will prevent examinations from becoming superficial, and students from becoming indifferent if not indolent. We are faced with truly the most difficult problem in academia: the problem of authority—how to progress from enforced discipline where all decisions are imposed, to a self-discipline borne out of a more democratic relationship between student and teacher. There are major problems with enforced authority, and the students are aware of them. They are able to recognize authentic authority and do not oppose, but to the contrary, respect it because it has developed naturally through mutual endeavor.

The gaps lessen among all those who must of necessity participate in different roles. The students are not excluded from active participation. The barriers that sharply segregate students from teachers diminish—as they must, for nothing can be achieved when those who work together remain apart.

MASS PARTICIPATION AND THE QUALITY OF STUDIES

Teaching, particularly teaching of the social sciences, should not be merely the input of information into data banks, but a spark that will light the torch of knowledge. Quite simply, these sparks are a teacher's work. However, the formation of the new pedagogy will require more than prescription. It is a manifold research enterprise still in the stage of inception, but already promising a broad array of solutions. It will require different social relationships in the educational process, and in order to achieve these relationships, we must have social forces that are so motivated that they awaken new interests and ideals.

These demands are essential. But immediately we face a dilemma which is exceptionally difficult. Is it possible to achieve a high level of quality when the present growth in the number of students is not matched by a growth in space, capacity, equipment, and number of faculty, and when pedagogy has yet to develop a response to this massive growth?

It is possible to state, because it is already a fact, that mass enrollment *per se* does not effect a decline in quality. There are many universities in the world that are large and still maintain a high quality of education. Tomorrow, millions more will enter the university. Will the democratization of culture continue without a dangerous decline in quality? In the near future a university education will be more generalized. If the level of quality were to drop significantly, then it would seem desirable to compensate for the loss in quality by forming elite universities. Yet that would again lead to stratification and the formation of a technocratic elite and would not solve the primary problem. This is not the direction we wish to take. If a university education becomes standard fare, it is essential that the level of quality still be maintained. In other words, we must guard against the mediocrity which this universality might invite.

The whole string of changes stretches out in front of us: the development of work possibilities for the educated, the merger of study and work, the introduction of educational technology, the transformation of colleges into scientific-research centers—all this will enhance motivation, the true force behind achievement, and will strengthen the active role of students in the professor-student relationship. Without waiting for these changes to occur, we need to search audaciously for a variety of new solutions, for the answer to a problem in one field of study will not necessarily transfer to the next.

No later than the senior year, we must introduce the study group as the basic unit for the whole of teaching from lectures, practicing, and group research to examinations. Such a measure now seems impossible, not only because of the character of pedagogy, but because of the nearly insurmountable problems of the shortage of space and faculty. The pedagogical reform must demand funding for more teaching faculty (such as we have described) and for more space in order to be able to take the first steps in the formation of study/teaching groups, if only initially for students in their senior years.

Such a collective work group will prove to be one of the most significant aspects of the democratic school. The techniques of group work stimulate participation and free creative energy. This point is of a far-reaching significance that surpasses all other techniques in learning, for it is decisive in the formation of personality. The pedagogical culture is deeply imbued with cruel competition, with unrelenting tensions and with an egoistical individualism that does not discriminate in its methods of achieving success, degrees, and awards.[20] Cutthroat competition is far more important than cooperation, collective awards, admiration for the success of others, and mutual assistance. How can we expect those who survive twenty years of such battle to be miraculously transformed into well-developed personalities with an understanding of society and a desire for the solidarity that is a trademark of self-management and collectivism? There is so little of such understanding in contemporary civilization, and the lack of it so impoverishes and alienates people.

A form of pedagogy that is not authoritarian, which has more collective spirit and aims at the active participation of students, is a far-reaching investment in the future development of society—in the type of experts and personalities of the future producer and social being. For only through the active and collective participation of the student will independent personalities and creative professionals engaged in self-management develop. This is of crucial importance for all aspects of social development. A high quality of belief in the future and the assumption that education and life is led by the golden thread of a searching spirit is crucial to our youth and will greatly influence our ability to develop our own creativity and our own identity as one of self-managing socialism.

10

THE UNIVERSITY
AND THE FUTURE

It is possible to argue that it is not a function or a duty of the university to participate in the orientation and employment of the cadres, or in the planning for scientific development and implementation of the work-study principle. It could be argued that these are matters solely for society to solve. The university's job is to receive orders regarding the numbers of students to admit, and the profiles of the cadres desired, and to deliver these goods to the market. We do not believe that such an attitude corresponds to the contemporary scene, let alone a future that is developing rapidly—practically before our very eyes.

We will be faced with two tendencies. One will be expressed in nostalgia for an exclusive institution that does not enter into direct social contact and engagements. Contacts are said to "dirty the hands" and endanger the autonomy of intellectual work, and, in fact, such is actually the case when monopolies enter into intellectual activity. On the other side, there will be pressures from a civil-servant mentality that would see the university transformed into a service for those who have money and power. This is the trend of commercialization that aims exclusively at the sale of services for the best price. The free exchange of labor—an essential principle of social development—may become vulgarized and twisted. The expansion of the university, with a decisive orientation toward connections with groups in the economy and social services, must be followed by a clear understanding of the possible contradictions of such a process and must be conducted through joint efforts lest negative results occur.

The university must create an active concept of its role and function in society. This is not a request for a privileged position for science and the intelligentsia, but neither can there be acquiescence to the notion that the university only acts to receive orders from the patrons, the state, and the technostructure. Education and science are neither a service nor a civil service institution. They are not only a superstructure in themselves, but also one of the fundamental levels of social practice.

An active position in society should be built. Colleges are society's centers of knowledge regardless of any shortcomings that they might exhibit. They must initiate an active role for themselves; they must influence the formation of consciousness, public opinion, the self-managing, decision-making centers in the economy, social services, and politics. They must act in cooperation with associated labor to whom they send the young cadres, who are the best educated segment of the contemporary class of producers. The colleges must more profoundly influence social development so that we might gain the opportunity to reach the height of world knowledge and provide for our own needs. They should create an awareness for the types of cadres that will be needed in the future; they should foresee the direction of the development of science and attempt to raise the level of the existing professional structure. The colleges should be the champions of a higher level of education, and they should fight for the central role of real knowledge. This means that they should at the same time enact their own profound reform, a revitalization of the role of science and intelligentsia in society, for only through reform can they become an organic part of the contemporary class of producers and associated labor. Such an active attitude is not adopted for narrow class interests but for the needs of society and for the future of the young. An activist attitude in all areas is a presupposition of our system; it insures its life and development. We have built a whole network of institutions, but human activity is the force that will give it real content and life.

All points that we have touched upon have shown that the reform of the university—a self-managed, socialist university—and the technological and cultural advancement toward a community of associated producers are both part of one and the same path. The path is open; great potentials lie within the colleges, but they will not develop by themselves. Only people actively and energetically engaged can do this.

We are talking, therefore, about a long-term series of breakthroughs. It is necessary to understand the seriousness, the true intent, the difficulties, and the length of time necessary to enact these changes. Fundamental changes at the university cannot be brought about through decree. Concrete measures can efficiently solve immediate difficulties only if they follow the direction of long-term policies.

We must be able to act simultaneously on two wavelengths. One is the long-term and audacious plan of gradual but fundamental change. A reform of higher education is in essence a change of revolution, history and civilization. But concurrent with this general understanding, we must enact immediate concrete measures, the first step in this long and complicated chain of events that will open the way to changes and that will solve the amassed difficulties of everyday life. These concrete measures, the preliminary work, are prerequisites for accomplishing the deeper changes that are waiting for us and that will be felt acutely by the next generation. The first steps are to ascend toward the higher education of the future. A realistic radicalism that is neither foolishly utopian nor hopelessly practical is indispensable. The fundamental and revolutionary transformation of higher education cannot be accomplished overnight, nor even in a week; it is a long-term process.

The supposed fact that funding for such reforms is unavailable deserves further thought. We should extensively analyze the economics of education in order to determine the expense of supporting the legions of unemployed people and unemployed experts, who endured years of schooling followed by years on the waiting lists of employment offices finally only to find jobs for which they were not educated. It is realistic to assume that the type of university that we propose, with mass education alongside work, with the increased work productivity, with shortened years of studies due to significantly increased motivation, can in the near future lead to a healthier educational economy. Of course, we must also form a new consciousness, we must develop mature projects and healthy solutions, we must organize our forces and establish social perspectives. All this should not be taken as an argument in favor of postponement. These activities must start now. They must be intensive and must be tested in practice.

We must guard against an attitude of realism (actually pragmatism), which is so closely linked to existing relationships and interests that it appears nothing can undergo a profound change, and everything is totally imprisoned by the existing order. In difficult times there is natural nervousness that tends to look upon all radical solutions as an unnecessary luxury. We must bear in mind that a narrow vision and the administrative measures that would limit education may solve one problem and at the same time provoke two new ones.

The true era for education is the future, and it is a possible future. Investment in the future should not be sectarian and overzealous; it should not serve a conservative front that opposes everything. Collectively we should build our concepts, and we should win over people without selectivity. There is not one group or person today who can alone offer definite, secure and totally mature answers to the needed changes in all areas. A collective effort is important. We must start to think about it, and we must start with changes; we must initiate a new mode of thinking and practice, and we must create a new consciousness. Of incalculable importance is that a change of such magnitude be at the volition of the people; it should be accomplished through their own deeds; they should accept it as their own and not as an act imposed on them from above.

The awakening of all forces is possible only if the principle motivation is the enrichment of the lives of both students and faculty and it works for a fuller and more meaningful existence—one that expands the future of the university and so also of the young and society. As was stated at the outset, it is important to unite all our abilities and energies in order to accomplish the great tasks of the moment and to understand the creative needs and aspirations of our era.

APPENDIX

Excerpts from the Resolution of the Tenth Congress of the League of Communists of Yugoslavia (LCY) on the Socialist, Self-Managing Transformation in Schooling and Education.

The entire socialist schooling and education should be such that it profoundly contributes to the formation of the free, universally developed, socialist personality. It is an indispensable factor in the development of the socialist self-managing social relationships and of the forces of production in society.

A self-managing constitution of schooling and education, an organic and functional connection of all parts of associated labor and education in the framework of the united system of associated labor, and an active role of schooling and education in social reproduction in the speedier development of the forces of production and socialist self-managing relationships in production are today the basic thrust of social action that aims at fundamental changes of educational activity. Schooling and education must both overcome its separation from the other spheres of associated labor as well as its status as "communal consumer." Schooling and educational work must be evaluated in a free exchange of labor according to its contribution to increasing the social productivity of work and advancing the general society and culture. Long-term consideration of the needs of the cadres and educational needs must be based increasingly on the needs of the development of the economy and other social activities, on the scientific research of labor, on the study of educational processes and on the problems of employment.

The League of Communists pleads for the consistent application of the principle of solidarity in education in order to alleviate the influence of the differences brought about by the environment, the position in distribution, unequal educational standards, and the family situation as it applies to the possibilities and conditions for education. It pleads particularly for the workers and their children. . . .

The changes in the system and the policies for the development of education must, by their basic orientation, contribute to the fuller realization of democratic rights to education. We must hasten the realization of the principle from the Program of the *LCY* that an equal opportunity be offered to everyone, and particularly to workers and women during the whole working life to decide on and prepare themselves for an avocation suitable to their abilities and in pursuance of the interests of associated labor. . . .

The League of Communists propagates the idea that education becomes a right and obligation of workers in associated labor. Organizations of associated labor are required to ensure various material and organizational conditions and concessions for the education of workers. . . . The development of our society requires that the entire educational program be basically oriented toward education for work and through work. . . . Because of this it is necessary that the entire younger generation join work and social life earlier and continue their education alongside of work, or return to school from work in order to overcome the separation of education and work. . . . It is necessary to enter education from work, or to participate in education along with work. According to this need, the periods of learning will be alternated with periods of work.

In realization of this task, special attention should be given to the affirmation of the socialist, self-managing, and humanistic content of education.

Socialist self-management in schooling and education must be a right and the obligation of all participants in this activity, and this, above all, assumes the active participation of pupils and students in the educational and self-managing process; this will overcome the hierarchical and authoritarian relationships in schooling and educational organizations.

In higher education there is an urgent need to speed up work in research as a basic condition and an integral component of a contemporary and unique scientific-educational process. This requires an integration of the irrationally scattered educational and scientific units and stronger and better equipped institutions which will be able to keep pace with the world development of science.

In developing directed education it is necessary to search for and nurture the various forms of connecting the current intermediate, high, and higher education and establish common educational centers. At the same time, it is indispensable to combine the traditional forms of education with extracurricular ones (evening schools, correspondence courses, workers and peoples universities, usage of radio, television and other contemporary media) and strive for an equal evaluation system of acquired knowledge and expertise.

Translator's Note: In the original Serbo-Croatian edition of this text, a second appendix was included, which consisted of an excerpt from Steven Rose and Hilary Rose, "The Politics of Neurobiology: Biologism in the Service of the State," in *Ideology of/in the Natural Sciences*, edited by Hilary Rose and Steven Rose (Boston: G. K. Hall, 1976), pp. 71-86. In Pečujlić's words, the text was to "illustrate how the malevolent side of science influences the directions of research and ideology even in the natural sciences."

NOTES

1. THE UNIVERSITY AND THE NEW REALITY

1. Radovan Richta, *Civilization at the Crossroads*, p. 332.—Trans.

2. Richta, *Civilization.*—Trans.

3. Edward F. Denison, *Accounting for United States Economic Growth, 1929-1969.*—Trans.

4. Richta, *Civilization*, p. 304-5.—Trans.

5. Cited in Richta, *Civilization.*—Trans.

6. Cited in Richta, *Civilization.*—Trans.

7. The Jugovinil factory in Split reports that its measurements of work productivity before and after education show that the working group with supplemental education increased its productivity by 32 percent. The "EI" factory in Niš followed the progress of a group of five workers who assembled keyboards. Initially, when the workers were semiskilled, they were able to assemble 150 keyboards per shift, thus securing a starting base of 4.80 Dinars. The factory then spent 1,650 Dinars per person on evening classes, where the workers acquired skilled status. They increased their production to 280 keyboards per shift and raised their starting base to 5.95 Dinars. Thus a savings was achieved and cost price per worker decreased to 12,000 (1.45 Dinars to each Dinar invested in education).

8. UNESCO, *Statistical Data Bank.*—Trans.

9. Richta, *Civilization.*—Trans.

10. The system in the U.S.A. is different, and this figure includes part of the college education, but in any case participation is much higher.

11. Richta, *Civilization.*—Trans.

2. THE CRISIS OF THE TRADITIONAL UNIVERSITY

1. Zoran Vidaković, *Moderne proizvodne snage i revolucionarna praksa.*

2. See Rajko Tomović, "Kraj tehnološke ere," about the class character of technology and science, presented at the international conference "Socialism in the World."

3. Zoran Vidaković, *Moderne proizvodne snage;* Zvonko Damnjanović, *Diskusija o naučno-tehnološkoj revoluciji i samoupravljanju.*

4. Karl Marx, *The Eighteenth Brumaire of Louis Bonaparte,* p. 15.—Trans.

5. See "Budućnost 2000 godine," *Dedalus* (Časopis); i Richta, *Civilization at the Crossroads;* Milenko Nikolić, "Obrazovanje u uslovima zamene ljudskog rada mašinom."

6. Karl Marx, *The Grundrisse,* pp. 141-45.—Trans.

7. See Stevan Bezdanov, "Naučno-tehnološka revolucija i obrazovanje u razvoju socijalističkog samoupravnog društva," and other materials from the symposium, Naučno-tehnološka revolucija i obrazovanje u razvoju socijalističkog samoupravnog društva.

8. The intellectual equivalent of such trends is expressed by a powerful intellectual ethnocentrism, by the "Europe-centrism" of the intellectual content of the universities—the term used by the well-known sociologist in the West, Robert Nisbet. This trend has a long history.

From the beginning of its history in the twelfth and thirteenth centuries right down to the present moment, the university has been oriented intellectually toward the single, small, body of knowledge that first arose in that tiny part of the world we know as the Middle East; and, within this, chiefly from Israel and Greece. From Isaiah and Plato down to contemporary offerings in the humanities and also the social sciences is to be seen a line of history unwaveringly Western in emphasis.

Even when, in the late eighteenth and the nineteenth centuries, efforts began in the direction of comparative institutions, comparative history, comparative culture, these tended, as we know, to be profoundly Western in their precipitating motivations and values. The so-called comparative method—dear to the hearts of the founders of modern anthropology and sociology—was, in plain fact, a device for arraying the non-Western cultures of the world in such a way as to demonstrate the progressiveness of the West, to show that such countries as France and England formed a vanguard in the march of civilization. . . .

I am aware of the tokenisms in very recent decades—beginning just after World War II—by which tiny morsels of intellectual food from non-Western parts of the world were laid out on academic tables in this country. A course in Swahili here, in India's languages there; a survey of the history of Asia in one term here, an outline of African and Oceanic history there. . . . But one need only compare all that has been done in non-Western spheres with what remains in the curriculum that is solidly Western. Merely count courses in the catalogue: the number of courses in American, in English, in French or German literature, say, and those in the literatures of other whole civilizations. . . . Does rational judgment really support the existence of a year course on the minor poets of the English seventeenth century when perhaps no course at all is given in the university on the major poets of the entire history of the Asiatic continent? Plainly not. Dogma and faith are required. I prefer these words to say, "insularity" or "ethnocentrism."

Robert Nisbet, *The Degradation of the Academic Dogma,* pp. 36-40.

9. Helmut Schelsky, *Die Arbeit tun die Anderen.*—Trans.

10. But such an alliance presupposes a strong spiritual movement toward a new society, toward the formation of alternatives that will show to the technical intelli-

gentsia that by abolishing the bureaucratic division of labor they will gain more than they lose—as people and experts and as creators. Then the opposition to the irrational waste of the forces of production and management will not be expressed in an aspiration to regain the lost monopoly of power.

11. Samuel Bowles, *Contradictions in Higher Education.*

12. Bertrand Russell, *Education and the Social Order,* pp. 75-76.—Trans.

13. Schools for engineers should not be confused with the colleges of engineering that are the elite institutions for the education of the managing cadres. Here the schools for engineers are technical or vocational schools, where education is of shorter duration; a degree from these schools does not carry the prestige of a university degree. The programs for these schools are as a rule established by the associations of employers. Andre Gorz, *Tehnika, tehničari i klasna borba.*

14. Dragoljub Najman, *Visoko obrazovanje—čemu?*

15. Slobodan Ristanović, "Društvene nejednakosti i obrazovanje."—Trans.

16. *Komsomolskaya Pravda.*—Trans.

17. Paul Henderson, *Class Structure, and the Concept of Intelligence.*

18. Henderson, *Class Structure.*

19. Sir Francis Galton, *Hereditary Genius.*—Trans.

20. Charles Laveraux, *Dictionnaire synonymique de la langue francaise,* Paris, 1826.

21. See Edward O. Wilson, *Sociobiology;* and Robert Trivers, *Principles of Social Evolution.*—Trans.

22. See Zoran Vidaković, *Klase u savremenom društvu.*—Trans.

23. Kristen.—Trans.

24. Daniel Bell, *The Coming of Post-Industrial Society.*—Trans.

25. Bell, *The Coming of Post-Industrial Society.*—Trans.

26. Bell, *The Coming of Post-Industrial Society.*—Trans.

27. Vidaković, *Klase u savremenom društvu.*—Trans.

28. Karl Marx and Friedrich Engels, *Collected Works.*—Trans.

29. Nisbet, *The Degradation of the Academic Dogma,* pp. 72-73.—Trans.

30. Nisbet, *The Degradation of the Academic Dogma.*—Trans.

31. Alvin Toffler, *Future Shock.*—Trans.

32. Einstein was deeply concerned with the impact of science on society and with man's fate in general. Many of his rather interesting views can be found in his *Out of My Later Years.*

33. Andre Gorz, *Tehnika, tehničari i klasna borba.*—Trans.

34. Samuel Andrew Stouffer, *The American Soldier.*—Trans.

35. Nanter, *Students of Sociology and Psychology.*—Trans.

36. Max Horkheimer, *Critical Theory.*—Trans.

3. SOCIALISM AND EDUCATION

1. Fidel Castro, *Fidel Castro Speeches.*—Trans.

2. Nadezhda Krupskaya, *On Education.*—Trans.

3. Nadezhda Krupskaya, *On Education.*—Trans.

4. Mao Zedong, *Selected Works.*—Trans.

5. Mao Zedong, *Selected Works.*—Trans.

6. Albert Einstein, "Why Socialism?"—Trans.
7. Mahatma Gandhi, *Collected Works.*—Trans.
8.

The key link is in the goals of production. Production is based on the trinity: profit, power, prestige, and on the artificial stimulation of needs and the artificial obsolescence and accelerated replacement of products. This becomes one of the basic sources of the crisis. A component of this model of production and consumption (scientific reproduction) is the reigning pattern of culture—a psychology that maintains a social hierarchy and competition where each individual desires superiority. Its motto is: "If it is good for everyone, it is not valid; one will have prestige only if one has 'more than others.' " When goods, which were once possessed by the elite (various models of cars, types of houses, schools attended) become available to other classes, they are devalued. The threshold of poverty rises and new privileges unavailable to the masses are created. This modernization of poverty is one of the main sources of parasitic non-consumption and exploitation of natural resources. In essence, it is profit, power and prestige which prevents us from producing quality clothes, engines and cars, that will last longer, and organizing good and inexpensive public transportation, more collective services.

Gorz, *Tehnika, tehničari i klasna borba.*
9. Antonio Lettieri, *School and Factory.*

4. YUGOSLAV SOCIETY AND THE UNIVERSITY

1. The Socialist Autonomous Province of Vojvodina and the Socialist Autonomous Province of Kosovo and Metohija are both part of the Socialist Republic of Serbia. *Socialist Autonomous Province (socijalistička autonomna pokrajina)* denotes an autonomous socialist self-managing sociopolitical community making a constituent part of the Socialist Republic of Serbia. Its autonomous rights are defined by the SFRY Constitution and the Constitution of the Socialist Republic of Serbia. The socialist autonomous provinces have been formed for territories inhabited by a population of mixed ethnic composition (nations and nationalities).—Trans.

2. UNESCO, *Statistical Digest.*—Trans.

3. Data from the UNESCO Conference of the Ministers for Science and Technology of America and Europe, Belgrade, 1978.

4. Ivo L. Ribar, *Omladina i revolucija.*—Trans.

5. For Serbia, the review is offered by the following table:

	Institutions of Higher Education			Total Number of Students (In percentages)	
Occupation	*Schools of Higher Education*	*Colleges*	*Colleges of Art*	*Full-Time*	*Part-Time*
Agricultural workers	17.3	11.2	4.2	12.0	0.2
Industrial workers and workers in related fields	21.9	15.3	8.1	16.1	11.8
Transportation workers	4.6	3.3	1.7	3.4	1.1

Occupation	Institutions of Higher Education			Total Number of Students (In percentages)	
	Schools of Higher Education	Colleges	Colleges of Art	Full-Time	Part-Time
Workers in commerce	6.9	4.9	3.9	5.2	4.8
Workers in safety	3.0	4.3	3.8	4.1	1.8
Administrative and related personnel	6.7	9.6	7.7	9.1	11.8
Managing personnel	1.7	3.6	5.0	3.4	1.6
Experts and artists	9.0	18.8	26.7	17.5	28.9
Pensioners	17.1	20.4	26.4	20.0	20.1
Others	12.8	8.6	12.5	9.2	17.9
Total	100.0 (9.431)	100.0 (57.424)	100.0 (1.062)	100.0 (67.917)	100.0 (43.549)

6. Stipe Šuvar, *Saopštenje na godišnjem stručnom sastanku sociologa Jugoslavije.*

7. Sergej Flere, *Obrazovanje za sve.*—Trans.

8. Slobodan Ristanović, "Društvene nejednakosti i obrazovanje."

9. Materijal o socijalnom poreklu učenika i studenata S.R. Srbije (Republički sekretarijat za obrazovanje, Beograd).

10. *Bilten Saveznog zavoda za statistiku.*

11. Karl Marx. *The Eighteenth Brumaire of Louis Bonaparte,* p. 18.—Trans.

12. Giuseppe Tomasi di Lampedusa, *The Leopard.*—Trans.

13. See notes from the conference of the groups of technical, medical, natural-sciences and mathematical colleges, and the university institutes. See also notes from the conference of the delegates from the colleges and the university assembly concerning the main directions of the reform.

5. THE DEVELOPMENT OF EDUCATION AND SOCIAL NEEDS

1. Radomir Simić, "Osvrt na interesovanje mladih za pojedine fakultete Univerziteta u Beogradu na osnovu upisa u školskoj 1979/80 godini."

2. "The Results of the First Registration Term in the Third Grade of High School in Serbia."

3. Simić, "Osvrt na interesovanje mladih."

4. The data are for the University of Belgrade:

Number of Graduates	Graduated on Time	Graduated with a Delay		
		1-2 years	3-5 years	6+ years
6742	34.2%	37.4%	17.0%	11.4%

5. Republic Employment Office, 1970-1978.

6. Janez Jerovšek, "Ekspanzija slovenskega šolstva u luči krize ekspanzije visokega šolstva v industrijsko razvitih državah."

7. *Social compacts* (*društveni dogovori*) are self-management enactments adopted, on equal terms, by organizations of labor and their associations, self-managing interest communities and other self-managing organizations and communities, agencies of socio-political communities, trade unions, and other socio-political and social organizations, by which the parties thereto regulate socio-economic and other relations of common concern, as well as relations of general concern to the community. The purpose of social compacts is to replace the state's role in the resolution of social contradictions and to ensure cooperation and solidarity in the economic and other spheres of life. Social compacts are binding upon the parties that have concluded or acceded to them, and must be in conformity with the Constitution and statute.—Trans.

8. 1,300 billion old Dinars = 13 billion new Dinars = approximately $433,333,333.—Trans.

9. Krsta Avramović, vice president of RIV (*Republičko izvršno veće* [The Republic Executive Council]).—Trans.

10. *Associated labor* (*udruženi rad*) is a term used to denote all institutional forms of association of labor by workers who, organized on a self-management basis, perform with socially-owned resources economic and non-economic activities; the term also denotes all other forms of pooling of labor and resources by working people on these foundations.—Trans.

11. *Socio-political communities* (*društveno-političke zajednice*) are politico-territorial communities in which working people and citizens exercise the constitutionally-defined functions of power and management of other social affairs concerning their collective and/or general social interests, including the direction and coordination of social development (the Federation, republics, autonomous provinces, regional and municipal communities).—Trans.

12. Stipe Šuvar, *Tvornica i škola.*

13. *Self-management agreements* (*samoupravni sporazumi*) are self-management acts adopted, on equal terms, by workers in organizations of associated labor and by workers in work communities, communities of interest and other self-managing organizations, with a view to regulating and coordinating their interests for purposes of a more efficient specialization of production, the pooling of labor and resources, and the formation of work and other organizations of associated labor. In this way the regulative and intermediary role of the state concerning relations among working people is curtailed. A self-management agreement is only binding on those who have signed or acceded to it.—Trans.

14. These contracts could regulate these items: the right of employment of the establishment of a working relationship for an indefinite period of time; the right to

obtain a loan or scholarship under the conditions established by the general act of the organization of associated labor; the right to enter into a practicum in production; the right to participate in the distribution of income and to receive a salary proportionate to participation and results of work during the period of practice in production; the right for a traineeship; the right for further education alongside of and apart from work, and a commitment on the part of the students to graduate with good results and in a timely fashion; reimbursement of advance funding if the requirements of study are not met; a commitment to work in the organization of associated labor for a certain amount of time (including a period outside of one's locale as well as various other commitments) following the completion of professional education.

15. The results of the polling have shown that those who are more prepared for change in place of living are from these groups:

—persons from the underdeveloped regions (69.0 percent)

—persons without an income (69.0 percent)

—persons seeking employment for the first time (67.7 percent)

—unmarried persons (67.3 percent)

—persons who have waited for employment for up to one year (64.0 percent)

—persons with surplus professions (64.0 percent)

—persons up to 30 years of age (63.6 percent)

16. The *commune* (*opština*) is the basic self-managing socio-political community based on the power of, and self-management by, the working class and all working people, in which the working people realize and reconcile their interests and perform the functions of power and management of social affairs of common and general concern, with the exception of those functions which are under the Constitution vested in the broader socio-political communities—Trans.

17. *Školarina i njeno mesto u našem sistemu finansiranja vaspitanja i obrazovanja.*

18. The rudimentary beginnings of such practice exist, but they are limited. One poll shows that in 60 percent of all cases the work organizations have paid the expenses of education in the form of the tuition, and then only 50 to 85 percent of the full amount. A paid leave for examinations was given to the workers in 55 percent of the working organizations, and shortened work hours were allowed in 32 percent. But this was mainly the case when the workers were acquiring needed qualifications for the job that they already held. If the workers already had the necessary qualifications, they themselves paid for expenses of further education.

19. The Swedish experience should be further studied. It is possible that, starting in 1985, five years of work experience in a profession and a minimum age of twenty-five will entitle an individual to enroll at the university even without a high school education. (This takes into account certain abilities, pedagogical preparations, and individual initiative.)

6. THE UNIVERSITY, SCIENCE, AND THE DEVELOPMENT OF SOCIETY

1. Vojislav Petrović, "Izlaganje na savetovanju grupacija prirodnomatematičkih i biotehničkih nauka."

2. Maksim Todorović, "Izlaganje na savetovanju grupacija prirodnomatematičkih i biotehničkih nauka."

3. Vladimir Šolaja, "Izlaganje na savetovanju o glavnim pravcima reforme univerziteta."

4. Pavle Savić, the president of the Academy of Sciences and Arts, cautions about this dangerous trend in "Introductory Lecture at the International Seminar of the Universities of the United Nations and the University of Belgrade, October, 1979," an interview published in *NIN*.

5. Savić, "Introductory Lecture."—Trans.

6. Dušan Čalić, "Razvoj naučnoistraživačkog rada u SFRJ"; Vladimir Štambuk, "Naučno-tehnička revolucija i društvene promene."

7. OECD, *Review of National Science Policy: Yugoslavia.*

8. Zlatibor Petrović, "Izlaganje na savetovanju o glavnim pravcima reforme univerziteta."

9. In a discussion about the concepts of the reform of the university, Predrag Vranicki suggests one method of effecting this:

In all cases where the members of the institute could be used in teaching, the Community for Scientific Work would transfer the corresponding funds for the financing of these members to the Republic community for the financing of directed education. The Community for Scientific Work would separately finance only the real expenses of certain projects. In all those cases where the individuals would not, regardless of the reason, participate in teaching, their financing would be carried out through the project contract.

Marxsizam i socijalizam.

10. The introductory remarks of Milan Dragović, Miloš Sinađić, and Vlasta Novaković delivered at the conference of the College of Mechanical Engineering and the Economic Bureaus of Serbia.

11. Reports delivered at the conference of the deans of the colleges, by the President of the City Conference of the League of Communists of Belgrade Dušan-Saša Gligorijević and by the President of the Economic Bureau of Belgrade, Professor Milan Trajković.

12. Momčilo Dimitrijević, *Univerzitet i udruženi rad.*

13. Dimitrijević, *Univerzitet i udruženi rad.*

14. Predrag Radivojević, *O stanju kadrova u naučno-istraživačkim organizacijama.* See also the documentation, Part I and II of the Republic Community for Science and the Republic Secretariat for Education and Science, Beograd, 1979.

15. *Work organization* (*radna organizacija*) denotes a form of the pooling of labor and resources in which workers are linked by their common interests in work (in this case the work organization is composed of several basic organizations of associated labor); or are directly linked through the unity of the labor process (in this case the work organization has no basic organizations of associated labor). A work organization is an independent, self-managing organization of associated labor.—Trans.

16. *Social reproduction* (*društvena reprodukcija*) is a term used to denote the process of maintenance and development of society as a whole and covers both production and other activities aimed at the satisfaction of the interests and needs of working people, citizens, and the community as a whole, including educational, scientific, cultural, health, welfare and other activities carried out with a view to ensuring social development and advancing the living conditions of the people.

Social reproduction includes both the continuation of production on an unchanged scale (simple reproduction) and the continuous expansion of production in line with the rise in society's needs (expanded reproduction).—Trans.

7. THE ECONOMIC BASIS OF EDUCATION

1. Tihomir Vlaškalić, "Slobodna razmena rada kao uslov i osnova društveno-ekonomskih odnosa u oblasti visokoškolskog obrazovanja." *Self-managing interest communities (samoupravne interesne zajednice)* are associations formed by working people directly or through their self-managing organizations and communities, with a view to satisfying their personal and collective needs. Their aim is to link the interests of those who render specific public services with the interests of those who use such services. In self-managing interest communities, users and renderers of services freely exchange their labor (by means of money as the common medium of exchange) to satisfy their needs. According to the Constitution, the assemblies of self-managing interest communities in the spheres of education, science, culture, health, and welfare are authorized to decide, together and on equal terms with the assemblies of the competent socio-political communities (communes, provinces, republics), on all matters falling within these spheres. There are also self-managing interest communities in the fields of housing construction, power production, water resources management, transport, and so on.

2. Guidelines for the Community for the Directed Education for the Territory of the Republic in deciding on "The basic points of the self-managing agreement regarding the bases and criteria for the earning of income of the organizations of higher education through the *SIZ* of directed education."

3. At the colleges of social sciences, 16 percent of the total income comes from tuition.

8. SELF-MANAGEMENT AND THE NEW MONOPOLIES

1. The Associated Labor Act was passed on November 25, 1976, by the Assembly of the Socialist Federal Republic of Yugoslavia. It reflects the continuity of self-management.—Trans.

2. The conference was devoted to the participation of students in self-management—delegates from the University Assembly, student-assistant deans, and the President of the University Conference of the League of Socialist Youth of Belgrade took part in it.

3. This form exists at several universities. The colleges of the University of Belgrade have adopted it through the Self-Managing Agreement to associate within the University. The proposal, which was studied by the representatives of all colleges and institutes, was presented by a working group consisting of the deans of the colleges: Liberal Arts (Branko Gavela), Economics (Slobodan Unković), Mechanical Engineering (Vladimir Novaković), Medicine (Svetislav Kostić), Law (Pavle Ristić), Natural Sciences and Mathematics (Dr. Čeković), the President of the University Assembly (Jovan Veljković), Prorectors and Rectors of the university (U. Petrović, Mane Budisavljević, J. Jovičić, Mira Korugić, Miroslav Pečujlić), the Secretary of the University Committee of the League of Communists (Vaso Milinčević), the Presi-

dent of the University Conference of the League of the Socialist Youth of Serbia (B. Bugarčić), the President of the Trade Union of the Scientists and other scientific workers (P. Pravica), and Vlajko Brajić.

4. Basic self-managing organization or community (*osnovna samoupravna organizacija odnosno zajednica*) is a general term covering organization of associated labor, work communities, local communities, in which working people directly realize their socioeconomic and other self-managing rights and duties and on a self-management basis decide on questions concerning their socioeconomic status. —Trans.

5. A basic organization of associated labor (*osnovna organizacija udruženog rada*) is the fundamental form of association of labor in which workers directly and on equal terms realize their socio-economic and other self-management rights, and decide on other questions concerning their socio-economic status. A basic organization of associated labor is formed for each unit of a work organization which makes up a working whole (a plant, a technological unit, etc.) in which the results of joint labor can be expressed in terms of value on the market or within the work organization concerned.—Trans.

6. Some other more complex solutions are also possible, such as a college or several colleges and one or more similar work organizations becoming the basic self-managing interest community. Subsequently such a work organization is included in the city community.

9. A GREAT PEDAGOGICAL REFORM

1. Charles Darwin, *The Autobiography of Charles Darwin*, pp. 138-39.—Trans.

2. Radovan Richta, *Civilization at the Crossroads*.

3. This view seemingly contradicts the trend toward devaluation of working power and forces that limit the broad engagement of the educated work power. But this trend is actually connected to the "essentially limited scientific-technological revolution." Its goal is not the development of the potential powers that contemporary production forces carry within themselves, but rather technological growth that, above all, serves in the maximization of profit and the exploitation of cheap labor. A free and enthusiastic expansion of the forces of an authentic socialism that will break through the bourgeois and bureaucratic alternatives cannot be based on this perspective.

4. Prvoslav Ralić, *Politika*.

5. Milan Kučan, report at the conference printed in *Borba*.

6. Slobodanka Ast, "Malo do umereno usmereno." *NIN*, no. 1474 (8 April 1979).

7. Ast, "Malo do umereno usmereno."

8. Franc Šetinc, *O odnosu socijalizma i potrošačkog društva*.

9. Josip Broz, *O umetnosti, kulturi i nauci*.

10. Robert L. Hillard.

11. In Sweden, the candidates must pass examinations that are the equivalent of a high school education for those subjects that are relevant to their area of study.

12. See the works of Basil Bernstein.

13. Authoritarian pedagogy is particularly characteristic of the high school:

Research on the student-teacher relationship is giving some alarming results. Students have reported that insults, intimidation, belittling, and unjust grades are common at school. At the same time, the students were enthusiastic about the teachers who have combined a love for their profession with the friendly conduct. It is true (the students report) that we are not all the best students, but it should not be a reason for a teacher to call us an organized band of liars, a pack of donkeys for whom there is nothing in store but a pick and shovel.

Slavoljub Đukić, "Škola razumevanja."

14. Slavoljub Đukić, "Škola razumevanja."

15. A letter of the editorial board CIS *Student*.

16. Jovan Đorđević, "Naučno-tehnološka revolucija i savremeno opšte obrazovanje"—Trans.

17. Đorđević, "Naučno-tehnološka revolucija."

18. Popović, student-assistant dean, a report at the conference on the self-management transformation of higher education.

19. To this is closely connected the effort to publish contemporary, cheap textbooks and reference materials by using modern and cheaper technology. In this respect, we should initiate a social compact regarding cheap textbooks—a compact between the colleges and the publishers—that would set social norms for the publication of the textbooks.

20. One should see the write-up by the Danish students "For Socialist University," *Student*, March 1980, about the consequences of unhealthy competition.

BIBLIOGRAPHY

BOOKS

Aktuelna pitanja ostvarivanja srednjeg usmerenog obrazovanja u Beogradu. Beograd: Gradski komitet organizacije SK u Beogradu, 1979.

Analiza idejno-političkog rada i marksističkog obrazovanja u univerzitetskoj organizaciji SK Beograda. Univerzitetska konferencija organizacije SK Beograda—Komisija za idejnopolitički rad i marksističko obrazovanje, novembra 1976.

Anderson, Perry. *Considerations on Western Marxism.* Atlantic Highlands, N.J.: Humanities Press, 1976.

Apple, Michael W. "Commonsense Categories and Curriculum Thought." In *Schooling and Capitalism,* edited by Roger Dale, Geoff Esland, and Madeleine McDonald. Boston: Routledge and Kegan Paul, 1976.

Aronowitz, Stanley. "The Trap of Environmentalism." In *Schooling and Capitalism,* edited by Roger Dale, Geoff Esland, and Madeleine McDonald. Boston: Routledge and Kegan Paul, 1976.

Barbagli, Marzio, and Marcello Dei. "Power and Ideology in Education: Socialization into Apathy and Political Subordination." In *Schooling and Capitalism,* edited by Roger Dale, Geoff Esland, and Madeleine McDonald. Boston: Routledge and Kegan Paul, 1976.

Barnes, Barry. *Interests and the Growth of Knowledge.* Boston: Routledge and Kegan Paul, 1977.

Bastid, Marianne. "Economic Necessity and Political Ideals in Educational Reform during the Cultural Revolution." In *Power and Ideology in Education,* edited by Jerome Karabel and A. H. Halsey. New York: Oxford University Press, 1977.

Bell, Daniel. *The Coming of Post-Industrial Society: A Venture in Social Forecasting.* New York: Basic Books, 1976.

_____. *The Cultural Contradictions of Capitalism.* New York: Basic Books, 1976.

_____. "On Meritocracy and Equality." In *Power and Ideology in Education,* edited by Jerome Karabel and A. H. Halsey. New York: Oxford University Press, 1977.

Bernstein, Basil. Jezik i *društvene klase.* Beograd: BIGZ, 1979.

_____. "Class and Pedagogies: Visible and Invisible." In *Power and Ideology in Education,* edited by Jerome Karabel and A. H. Halsey. New York: Oxford University Press, 1977.

_____. "Social Class, Language and Socialisation." In *Power and Ideology in Education,* edited by Jerome Karabel and A. H. Halsey. New York: Oxford University Press, 1977.

Bluestone, Barry. "Economic Theory and the Fate of the Poor." In *Power and Ideology in Education,* edited by Jerome Karabel and A. H. Halsey. New York: Oxford University Press, 1977.

Boudon, Raymond. "Education and Social Mobility: A Structural Model." In *Power and Ideology in Education,* edited by Jerome Karabel and A. H. Halsey. New York: Oxford University Press, 1977.

Bourdieu, Pierre. "Cultural Reproduction and Social Reproduction." In *Power and Ideology in Education,* edited by Jerome Karabel and A. H. Halsey. New York: Oxford University Press, 1977.

_____. "The School as a Conservative Force: Scholastic and Cultural Inequalities." In *Schooling and Capitalism,* edited by Roger Dale, Geoff Esland, and Madeleine McDonald. Boston: Routledge and Kegan Paul, 1976.

_____. "Systems of Education and Systems of Thought." In *Schooling and Capitalism,* edited by Roger Dale, Geoff Esland, and Madeleine McDonald. Boston: Routledge and Kegan Paul, 1976.

Bourdieu, Pierre, and Jean-Claude Passeron. *Reproduction: In Education, Society, and Culture.* Beverly Hills, Calif.: Sage Publications, 1977.

Bowles, Samuel. *Contradictions in Higher Education.*

_____. "Unequal Education and the Reproduction of the Social Division of Labor. In *Schooling and Capitalism,* edited by Roger Dale, Geoff Esland, and Madeleine McDonald. Boston: Routledge and Kegan Paul, 1976.

Bowles, Samuel, and Herbert Gintis. *Schooling in Capitalist America: Educational Reform and the Contradictions of Economic Life.* New York: Basic Books, 1976.

_____. "I.Q. in the U.S. Class Structure." In *Power and Ideology in Education,* edited by Jerome Karabel and A. H. Halsey. New York: Oxford University Press, 1977.

Broz, Josip T. *O umetnosti, kulturi i nauci: izbor tekstova.* Priredio Miloš Nikolić, Subotica-Beograd, 1978.

Carnoy, Martin, and Jorge Werthein. "Socialist Ideology and the Transformation of Cuban Education." In *Power and Ideology in Education,* edited by Jerome Karabel and A. H. Halsey. New York: Oxford University Press, 1977.

Castles, Stephen, and Wiebke Wustenberg. *The Education of the Future: An Intro-duction to the Theory and Practice of Socialist Education.* New York: Pluto Press, Ltd., 1979.

Castro, Fidel. *Fidel Castro Speeches.* New York: Pathfinder, 1981.

Cicourel, Aaron V., and John I. Kitsuse. "The School as a Mechanism of Social Differentiation." In *Power and Ideology in Education*, edited by Jerome Karabel and A. H. Halsey. New York: Oxford University Press, 1977.

Cohen, David K., and Marvin Lazerson. "Education and the Corporate Order." In *Power and Ideology in Education*, edited by Jerome Karabel and A. H. Halsey. New York: Oxford University Press, 1977.

Damjanović, Zvonko. *Diskusija o naučno-tehnološkoj revoluciji i samoupravljanju.*

Darwin, Charles R. *The Autobiography of Charles Darwin.* Edited by Nora Barlow. New York: W. W. Norton, 1969.

Dawkins, Richard. *The Selfish Gene.* New York: Oxford University Press, 1976.

Denison, Edward F. *Accounting for United States Economic Growth, 1929-1969.* Washington, D.C.: Brookings, 1974.

Deželjin, Josip. *Naučno-tehnički progres i zaposlenost u SFR Jugoslaviji.* Rijeka: Marksistički centar—Biblioteka Znanje, 1977.

Differing Types of Higher Education, International Association of Universities. Papers—14. Paris, CEDEX, 1977.

Dimitrijević, Momčilo. *Univerzitet i udruženi rad.*

Djelpi, Etore. *Škola bez katedre.* Beograd: BIGZ, 1976.

Djukin, Zorka. *Efikasnost studija: Stanje i neki predlozi za pouzdanije praćenje i poboljšanje.* Novi Sad: Univerzitet, okt. 1976.

Dobrov, G. M. *Nauka o naukama.* Beograd: Uvod u opšte poznavanje naučnih delatnosti, zavod za izdavanje udžbenika S. R. Srbije.

Dobson, Richard B. "Social Status and Inequality of Access to Higher Education in the U.S.S.R." In *Power and Ideology in Education*, edited by Jerome Karabel and A. H. Halsey. New York: Oxford University Press, 1977.

Durkheim, Emil. "On Education and Society." In *Power and Ideology in Education*, edited by Jerome Karabel and A. H. Halsey. New York: Oxford University Press, 1977.

Einstein, Albert. *Out of My Later Years.* New York: Philosophical Library, 1950.

_____. "Why Socialism?" *Monthly Review*, May 1949, pp. 9-15.

Entwistle, Harold. *Class, Culture and Education.* New York: Methuen and Co. Ltd., 1978.

Flere, Sergej. *Obrazovanje za sve.* Beograd: Duga, 1973.

Freire, Paulo. *Pedagogy of the Oppressed.* Translated by Myra B. Ramos. New York: Continuum, 1970.

_____. *Education: The Practice of Freedom.* London: Writers and Readers Publishing Cooperative, 1976.

Galton, Sir Francis. *Hereditary Genius.* New York: Horizon Press, 1952.

Gandhi, Mahatma. *Collected Works.* New Delhi: Publications Division, Ministry of Information and Broadcasting, 1958.

Gintis, Herbert. "Towards a Political Economy of Education: A Radical Critique of Ivan Illich's Deschooling Society." In *Schooling and Captalism*, edited by Roger Dale, Geoff Esland, and Madeleine McDonald. Boston: Routledge and Kegan Paul, 1976.

Goody, Jack, and Ian Watt. "The Consequences of Literacy." In *Power and Ideology in Education*, edited by Jerome Karabel and A. H. Halsey. New York: Oxford University Press, 1977.

Gorz, Andre. *Tehnika, tehničari i klasna borba.*

Gramsci, Antonio. *Selections from Political Writings, 1910-1926.* Woodstock, N.Y.: Beekman Pubs., 1978.

_____. "The Intellectuals." In *Schooling and Capitalism*, edited by Roger Dale, Geoff Esland, and Madeleine McDonald. Boston: Routledge and Kegan Paul, 1976.

Granese, Alberto. *Dijalektika odgoja.* Zagreb: Školska knjiga, 1978.

Halsey, A. H. "Toward Meritocracy? The Case of Britain." In *Power and Ideology in Education*, edited by Jerome Karabel and A. H. Halsey. New York: Oxford University Press, 1977.

Henderson, Paul. "Class Structure and the Concept of Intelligence." In *Schooling and Capitalism*, edited by Roger Dale, Geoff Esland, and Madeleine McDonald. Boston: Routledge and Kegan Paul, 1976.

Horkheimer, Max. *Critical Theory.* Translated by Matthew J. O'Connell et al. New York: Continuum, 1972.

Ideology and Consciousness. London: Ideology & Consciousness, May 1977.

Inglesby, David. "The Psychology of Child Psychology." In *Schooling and Capitalism*, edited by Roger Dale, Geoff Esland, and Madeleine McDonald. Boston: Routledge and Kegan Paul, 1976.

International Association of Universities. *Problems of Integrated Higher Education: an International Case Study of the Gesamthochschule.* International Association of Universities, no. 11. Paris, 1972.

_____. *The Social Responsibility of the University in Asian Countries: Obligation and Opportunities.* International Association of Universities, no. 12. Paris, 1973.

Jelčić, Božidar. *Društveno-ekonomska osnova reforme visokog obrazovanja.* Zagreb: Centar za stručno usavršavanje i suradnju u udruženom radu, 1978.

Jerovšek, Janez. *Ekspanzija slovenskega šolstva u luči krize ekspanzije visokega šolstva v industrijsko razvitih državah.* Ljubljana: Centar za razvoj Univerze, 1977.

Jorgensen, Moše. *Škola koju su osnovali učenici*, BIGZ, 1977.

Kahn, Herman, William Brown, and Leon Martel. *The Next Two Hundred Years.* New York: Morrow, William, and Co., 1976.

Kanter, Rosabeth Moss. "The Organization Child: Experience Management in a Nursery School." In *Power and Ideology in Education*, edited by Jerome Karabel and A. H. Halsey. New York: Oxford University Press, 1977.

Karabel, Jerome. "Community Colleges and Social Stratification: Submerged Class Conflict in American Higher Education." In *Power and Ideology in Education*, edited by Jerome Karabel and A. H. Halsey. New York: Oxford University Press, 1977.

Karabel, Jerome, and A. H. Halsey. "Educational Research. A Review and An Interpretation." In *Power and Ideology in Education*, edited by Jerome Karabel and A. H. Halsey. New York: Oxford University Press, 1977.

Kardelj, E. *Omladina u samoupravljanju.*

Katz, Michael B. "From Voluntarism to Bureaucracy in American Education." In *Power and Ideology in Education*, edited by Jerome Karabel and A. H. Halsey. New York: Oxford University Press, 1977.

Knoll, Joachim H. *The University in West Germany: The Education of the Future.*

Kogan, Maurice. *The Politics of Educational Change.* New York: Praeger, 1978.

Krupskaya, Nadezhda Konstantinova. *On Education.* Moscow: Foreign Languages Publishing House, 1957.

Langran, Pol. *Uvod u permanentno obrazovanje.* Drugo, prošireno izdanje, BIGZ 1976.

Levitas, Maurice. *Marxist Perspectives in the Sociology of Education.* Boston: Routledge and Kegan Paul, 1974.

Lilge, Frederick. "Lenin and the Politics of Education." In *Power and Ideology in Education*, edited by Jerome Karabel and A. H. Halsey. New York: Oxford University Press, 1977.

Lobro, Misel. *Obrazovanje pre svega.* Beograd: BIGZ, 1979.

Lucien, Seve. *Man in Marxist Theory and the Psychology of the Personality.* Atlantic Highlands, N.J.: Humanities Press, 1978.

Mađenović, Milorad. *Univerzitet i reforma: iskustva u radu na reformi univerziteta u nekim zemljama.* Sarajevo: Svjetlost, 1977.

Mao Zedong. *Selected Works of Mao Zedong*, 5 vols. Peking: Foreign Languages Press, 1961-1977.

Marx, Karl. *The Eighteenth Brumaire of Louis Bonaparte.* New York: International Publishers, 1963.

_____. *The Grundrisse.* Edited and translated by David McLellan. New York: Harper & Row, 1971.

Marx, Karl, and Friedrich Engels. *Collected Works.* New York: International Publishers, 1975.

Miles, Michael W. "The Student Movement and the Industrialization of Higher Education." In *Power and Ideology in Education*, edited by Jerome Karabel and A. H. Halsey. New York: Oxford University Press, 1977.

Najman, Dragoljub. *Visoko obrazovanje—čemu?* Beograd: Jugoslovensko udruženje "Nauka i društvo," 1976.

Naučnoistraživačke institucije zemalja u razvoju, I i II deo. Beograd: Savezni zavod za međunarodnu naučnu, prosvetnokulturnu i tehničku saradnju, 1975.

Nesazal, Karel, ed. *Planning and Social Forecasting: Social Processes.* Praha; Academic, 1978.

Nisbet, Robert. *The Degradation of the Academic Dogma: The University in America, 1945-1970.* New York: Basic Books, 1971.

Organization for Economic Cooperation and Development. *Reviews of National Science Policy:Yugoslavia.* Paris: OECD, 1976.

Paci, Massino. "Education and the Capitalist Labor Market." In *Power and Ideology in Education*, edited by Jerome Karabel and A. H. Halsey. New York: Oxford University Press, 1977.

Pečujlić, Miroslav. *Budućnost koja je počela, naučno-tehnološka revolucija i samoupravljanje.* Beograd: Institut za političke studije Fakulteta političkih nauka, 1976.

Ponzio, Augusto. *Jezična proizvodnja i društvena ideologija.* Zagreb: Školska knjiga, 1978.

Radivojevíc, Predrag. *O stanju kadrova u naučno-istraživačkim organizacijama.* Beograd, 1979.

Ralić, Prvoslav. *Savremeni problemi razvoja marksističke misli.* Beograd: Politička uprava SSNO, 1976.

Ribar, Ivo L. *Omladina i revolucija.* Beograd: Mladost, 1976.

Richta, Radovan. *Civilization at the Crossroads: Social and Human Implications of the Scientific and Technological Revolution.* Translated by Marian Šlingóva. 3d ed., rev. and enl. White Plains, N.Y.: International Arts and Sciences Inc., 1969.

Riesman, David. *Ten Years of Higher Learning in America Since the Event of 1968.*

Ringer, Fritz K. "Cultural Transmission in German Higher Education." In *Power and Ideology in Education,* edited by Jerome Karabel and A. H. Halsey. New York: Oxford University Press, 1977.

Rose, Steven, and Hilary Rose. "The Politics of Neurobiology: Biologism in the Service of the State." In *Schooling and Capitalism,* edited by Roger Dale, Geoff Esland, and Madeleine McDonald. Boston: Routledge and Kegan Paul, 1976.

Rossanda, Rossana, L. Berlinguer, and M. Cini. "Theses on Education: A Marxist View." In *Power and Ideology in Education,* edited by Jerome Karabel and A. H. Halsey. New York: Oxford University Press, 1977.

Russell, Bertrand. *Education and the Social Order.* London: Allen Unwin Books, 1932.

Samoupravni preobražaj i reforma visokog školstva Beograda. Beograd: UK organizacije SK Beograda, Komisija za samoupravljanje, reformu i razvoj visokoškolskog obrazovanja i naučni rad., oktobra 1978.

Sarup, Madan. *Marxism and Education.* Boston: Routledge and Kegan Paul, 1978.

Savić, Pavle. *Nauka i društvo.* Beograd: Srpska Književna zadruga, 1978.

Savičević, Dušan M. *Povratno obrazovanje.* Beograd: BIGZ, 1975.

Schelsky, Helmut. *Die Arbeit tun die Anderen,* 1979.

Schuller, Tom, and Jarl Bengtsson. "A Strategy for Equity: Recurrent Education and Industrial Democracy." In *Power and Ideology in Education,* edited by Jerome Karabel and A. H. Halsey. New York: Oxford University Press, 1977.

Schultz, Theodore W. *Investment in Human Capital.* New York: Free Press, 1970.

Scott, Geoffrey. *The Architecture of Humanism: A Study in the History of Taste.* New York: W. W. Norton & Co., Inc., 1974.

Sergejev, Dimitrije. *Za novi univerzitet.* Beograd: BIGZ, 1977.

Šetinc, Franc. *O odnosu socijalizma i potrošačkog društva.*

Sewell, William H., and Vimal P. Shah. "Socio-economic Status: Intelligence and the Attainment of Higher Education." In *Power and Ideology in Education,* edited by Jerome Karabel and A. H. Halsey. New York: Oxford University Press, 1977.

Sinđić, Miloš. *Naučno-tehnički progres i mašinogradnja.* Beograd: juna 1978.

Sklair, Leslie. *Organized Knowledge: A Sociological View of Science and Technology.* New York: International Pubns. Service, 1974.

Školarina i njeno mjesto u našem sistemu finansiranja vaspitanja i razvoj obrazovanja, 1972.

Sohn-Rethel, Alfred. *Intellectual and Manual Labour: A Critique of Epistemology.* Atlantic Highlands, N.J.: Humanities Press, 1978.

Spearman, Charles Edward. *The Abilities of Man: Their Nature, and Measurement.*
New York: Macmillan, 1927.

Šta, kuda i kako posle osnovne škole. Srednje usmereno obrazovanje i vaspitanje
u S.R. Srbiji, BIGZ.

Stojanović, Vojislav K. *Mesto i uloga udruženja univerzitetskih nastavnika i drugih
naučnih radnika u visokoškolskoj nastavi i nauci?* Beograd: Udruženje
univerzitetskih nastavnika i drugih naučnih radnika S.R. Srbije, 1978.

Stouffer, Samuel Andrew. *The American Soldier.* Princeton: Princeton University
Press, 1949.

Study of the I.Q. Controversy: Critical Readings. London: Quartet Books.

Suhodolski, Bogdan. *Tri pedagogije.* NIP DUGA, 1974.

Šuvar, Stipe. *Saopštenje na godišnjem stručnom sastanku sociologa Jugoslavije.*
Dubrovnik, 1971.

_____. *Tvornica i škola.*

_____. *U susret reformi odgoja i obrazovanja.* Zagreb, 1977.

The Radicalisation of Science, Critical Social Studies. London: Macmillan, 1976.

The Year 2017: Past, Present, and Future. Novosti Press Agency, 1968.

Thurow, Lester C. "Education and Economic Equality." In *Power and Ideology
in Education,* edited by Jerome Karabel and A. H. Halsey. New York: Oxford
University Press, 1977.

Toffler, Alvin. *Future Shock.* New York: Bantam Books, 1971.

Toffler, Alvin, ed. *Learning for Tomorrow: The Role of the Future in Education.*
New York: Vintage Books, 1974.

Tomasi di Lampedusa, Giuseppe. *The Leopard.* New York: Pantheon, 1960.

Touraine, Alain. *The Post-Industrial Society: Tomorrow's Social History: Classes,
Conflicts, and Culture in the Programmed Society.* London: Wildwood
House.

Trow, Martin. "The Second Transformation of American Secondary Education." In
Power and Ideology in Education, edited by Jerome Karabel and A. H.
Halsey. New York: Oxford University Press, 1977.

UNESCO. *Thinking Ahead: UNESCO and the Challenges of Today and Tomorrow.*
Paris: UNESCO, 1977.

_____. *Statistical Digest.* Paris: UNESCO, 1981.

Univerzitet i privreda. Republičko savetovanje u Nišu 26.06.1 Niš, Univerzitet, 1973.

Vidaković, Zoran. *Društvena moć i radnička klasa.* Beograd: Rad, 1970.

_____. *Klase u savremenom društvu.*

_____. *Kovači lažnog progresa.*

_____. *Moderne proizvodne snage i revolucionarna praksa.* Beograd: Izdanje
Fakulteta političkih nauka, 1969.

Vranicki, Predrag. *Marksizam i socijalizam.* Zagreb: Liber, 1979.

Willis, Paul. "The Class Significance of School Counter-culture." In *Schooling and
Capitalism,* edited by Roger Dale, Geoff Esland, and Madeleine McDonald.
Boston: Routledge and Kegan Paul, 1976.

Wilson, Edward O. *Sociobiology: The New Synthesis.* Cambridge: Harvard University Press, 1975.

World Bank Staff. *World Development Report.* Washington, D.C.: World Bank,
August 1978.

Young, Michael. *Knowledge and Control: New Directions for the Sociology of*

Education. New York: Collier Books, 1978.

————. *The Rise of the Meritocracy.* New York: Penguin Books, 1961.

Zakić, Milorad D. *Obrazovanje u SAD, SSSR i zapadnoj Evropi.* Beograd: Grafos, 1970.

Zdravković, Silvia. *Univerzitetski nastavnici u savremenom jugoslovenskom društvu.* Beograd: Savremena administracija, 1977.

ARTICLES, ANALYSES, AND DOCUMENTS

The symposium, Naučno-tehnološka revolucija i obrazovanje u razvoju socijalističkog samoupravnog društva, has been abbreviated as NTR.

"Aktuelni problemi studentskog standarda kroz analizu ostvarivanja društvenog dogovora o učeničkom i studentskom standardu." *Univerzitet danas - Časopis Zajednice univerziteta Jugoslavije, Beograd,* 1973, 3-4.

"Aktuelnosti u vaspitanju i obrazovanju." Republički zavod za unapređivanje vaspitanja i obrazovanja, Beograd, 1978, br. 5.

Andrejević, Miloje. "Samoupravno povezivanje nauke i privredne prakse." *Ekonomika* 1 (1979).

Anić, Petar. "Aktuelni problemi visokoškolskog obrazovanja," *Ekonomika* 1 (1979).

Apostolski, Mihailo. "Naukata se poznačaen nositel na progresot." *Nova Makedonija* 23, no. 9 (1978).

Association Internationale des Universités International (Association of Universities). *Bulletin* (Paris) 25, no. 3 (1977); 26, no. 4 (1978); 27, no. 4 (1979).

Ast, Slobodanka. "Napisi o reformi visokog školstva u listu." *Nedeljne informativne novine.* 1978: brojevi 1417, 1418, 1421, 1423, 1424, 1447, 1455; 1979: br. 1474, 1479, 1486, 1487, 1490, 1501, 1503; 1980: 1515.

Berberović, Ljubomir. "Naučnoistraživački rad studenata—bitna komponenta visokog obrazovanja." *Univerzitet danas* 3-4 (1978).

Bertolino, Milorad. "Svestrano razvijena ličnost i problemi deprofesionalizacije." Simpozijum NTR, Novi Sad, 1980.

————. "O zameni učenja studiranjem." *Univerzitet danas* 1-2 (1979).

Bezdanov, Stevan. "Naučno-tehnološka revolucija i obrazovanje u razvoju socijalističkog samoupravnog društva." Simpozijum NRT, Uvodno izlaganje, Novi Sad, 1980.

Bilten gradske samoupravne interesne zajednice zapošljavanja Beograd. Beograd, 1978, br. 33.

Bilten Saveznog zavoda za statistiku. br. 1066, 1975.

Blagojević, Borislav. "Neka pitanja reforme visokog školstva i neposdredni politički zadaci na pravnom fakultetu u Beogradu."*Univerzitet danas* 4 (1969).

Blagojević, Stevan. "Prioritetni pravci tehnoloških i ekonomskih istraživanja u naučnoj politici Jugoslavije." *Direktor* 12 (1977).

————. "Udruženi rad, naučna politika i privredni razvoj." *Jugoslovensko bankarstvo* 3-4 (1978).

Bogavac, Tomislav. "Suština i sadržaj samoupravnog socijalističkog preobražaja obrazovanja i nauke." *Marksističko obrazovanje,* 1978.

Borčić, Branko. "Reforma univerziteta u Jugoslovenskoj samoupravnoj zajednici." *Univerzitet danas* 1-2 (1973).

Brodogvari, Ferenc. "Opaske o smislu funkcije nauke." *Savremenost* 4-5 (1979).

Broz, J. T. "Reč profesorima i studentima Beogradskog univerziteta povodom promocije za počasnog doktora nauka univerziteta u Beogradu, *Univerzitet danas* 5-6 (1972).

Budin, Ivan. "Reforma i obrazovanje uz rad." *Obrazovanje i rad* 5 (1977/1978).

"Budućnost 2000 Godine." *Dedalus* (Časopis).

Čalic, Dušan. "Razvoj naučnoistraživačkog rada u SFRJ, Kritički osvrt." *Organizacija i kadrovi* 7-8 (1978).

_____. "Razvoj naučnoistraživačkog rada u SFRJ." Simpozijum NTR i obrazovanje u razvoju socijalističkog samoupravnog društva, 1980.

Čelenković, Teodosije. "Podruštvljavanje politike obrazovanja - imperativ vremena." *Samoupravljanje* 4 (1979).

Ćimić, Esad. "Kako predavati/proučavati marksizam?" *Argumenti*, Rijeka.

Čobeljić, Nikola. "Privredni razvoj i zaposlenost." *Glas SANU* (Beograd) Odeljenje društvenih nauka, 1978 (knj. XX).

Damjanović, Z. i D.HAK. "Interdisciplinarne studije." XVIII zasedanje Međunarodnog seminara Univerzitet danas, Dubrovnik: septembar 1973.

Damjanovski, Anatoli. "Reforma nastavnog procesa na univerzitetu u skladu sa usmerenim obrazovanjem." *Univerzitet danas* 1-2 (1978).

Devetaković, Stevan. "Naučno-tehnički progres kao faktor privrednog razvoja Jugoslavije." *Marksistička misao* 1 (1978).

"Dikusija za okruglim stolom . . . put do samoupravne škole." *Pedagogija* (Časopis) 3 (1978).

Dimitrijević, Momčilo. "Univerzitet i privreda"; Referat na Savetovanju posvećenom slobodnoj razmeni rada; Referat o naučnoistraživačkom radu - Skupština Zajednice univerziteta Jugoslavije; Referat o nauci i udruženom radu -Savetovanje u Nišu.

Đokić, A. "Izlaganje na savetovanju sa grupacijama fakulteta i savetovanje sa delegatima skupštine univerziteta o pravcima reforme univerziteta."

Đorđević, Božidar. "Univerzitet i privreda." *Univerzitet danas* 1 (1967).

Đorđević, Jovan. "Naučno-tehnološka revolucija i savremeno opšte obrazovanje." Simpozijum NTR, Novi Sad, 1980.

Đorđević, Miroslav. "Izlaganje na konferenciji SK o samoupravnom preobražaju visokog školstva."

Dragišić, Dragoljub. "Visokoškolsko obrazovanje kao integralni deo samoupravnog društva." *Univerzitet danas* 3-4 (1978).

Dragović, Milan. Uvodno izlaganje na Savetovanju dekana i direktora viših škola o srednjoročnom planu razvoja obrazovanja: "Društveni dogovor o zapošljavanju u SR Srbiji van teritorija socijalističkih autonomnih pokrajina." Beograd, jula 1978.

Dukić, Slavoljub. "Škola razumevanja." *Politika*, March 1979.

Flere, Sergej. "Antinomije savremenog univerziteta." *Argumenti* 1 (1980).

_____. Savremeni sociološki pesimizam prema društvenom značaju obrazovanja." *Naše teme* 12 (1978).

Gligorijević, Jovan. "Naučni rad - osnova i sadržaj savremene univerzitetske nastave." *Univerzitet danas* 3-4 (1978).

Golubović, Marko. "Osnovni faktori od uticaja na brzi porast produktivnog zapošljavanja i politiku zaposlenosti u SR Srbiji." *Samoupravljanje* 5 (1979).

_____. "Problemi zaposlenosti u SR Srbiji." *Marksistička misao* 3 (1979).

Hadžiomerović, Hasan. "Ekspanzija visokog obrazovanja u savremenom društvu." *Bilten Univerziteta u Sarajevu* 52 (1972).

Hodža, Hajredin. "Integracija i samoupravna transformacija prištinskog univerziteta." *Univerzitet danas* 5-6 (1978).

"Idejno-politička pitanja planiranja razvoja naučnoistraživačkog rada." Beograd, Komisija Predsedništva SK SKS za idejno delovanje SK u obrazovanju i nauci i Sekcija Republičke konferencije SSRN Srbije za nauku, decembar, 1979.

"Informacija o prostornim kapacitetima univerziteta u Beogradu i potrebama fakulteta za prostorom." Sektor za održavanje i izgradnju univerzitetskih objekata, interni materijal.

"Informacije o zapošljavanju." Republička zajednica za zapošljavanje, Beograd, novembra 1977.

Ivanović, Branko. "Visoko školstvo - reforma i mogućnosti." *Pobjeda* 10 (1978).

Ivanović, Dragiša. "O nekim praktičnim pitanjima reforme univerziteta." *Univerzitet danas* 9-10 (1969).

_____. "Društvena uloga univerziteta." *Univerzitet danas* 5 (1968).

"Izveštaj o radu republičke zajednice za zapošljavanje u privredi 1975-1978." Republička zajednica za zapošljavanje, Beograd.

"Izveštaj o rezultatima istraživanja 'naučno-nastavno osoblje Univerziteta u Beogradu.' " Beograd, Univerzitet, juni 1977.

Janković, Dragoslav. "L'Universite de Beograd dans la societe Yougoslave contemporaine." Socialisme dans la theorie et la pratique yougoslave, 1977.

Jelčić, Barbara i Božidar Jelčić. "Sveučilište i potrebe suvremenog društva." *Univerzitet danas* 3-4 (1978).

Jelčić, Božidar. "Reforma visokoškolskog obrazovanja." *Univerzitet danas* 5-6 (1978).

Jerovšek, Janez. "Ekspanzija slovenskega šolstva u luči krize ekspanzije visokega šolstva v industrijsko razvitih državah." Centar za razvoj univerze, Ljubljana, 1977.

Jovanov, Neca. "Pretpostavke ostvarivanja veće uloge i odgovornosti nauke za razvoj društva." *Socijalizam* 3 (1979).

Kardelj, Edvard. "Demokratija u politici i sloboda u nauci." *Oslobodenje* 12-02-1979.

_____. "Nauka i stručne službe u političkom sistemu." *Putevi* 1 (1979).

_____. "Samo konzervativnom empirizmu nauka nije potrebna." *Vaspitanje i obrazovanje* 1 (1979).

_____. "Samoupravljanje, nauka i uloga univerziteta." Socijalizam u svetu (reč prilikom proglašenja za počasnog doktora Univerziteta "Džemal Bijedić," 1979.)

Kirn, Andrej. "Nauka kao društvena revolucionarna i konzervativna snaga." *Teorija in praksa* 12 (1976).

Kompanjot, Zoran. "Osnovni reformski procesi na sveučilištu u Rijeci." Rijeka, Sveučilište, 1978.

"Kompleksna istraživanja efikasnosti studiranja na visokoškolskim ustanovama Bosne i Hercegovine, pedagoški standardi, nastavni rad." (Naučni projekat), Univerzitet u Sarajevu, 1976.

Kovačević, Bogosav. "Analiza upisa studenata u prvu godinu 1978/79," *Argumenti* 1 (1980).

_____. "Nastava kao radni proces." Naučni skup Didaktički problemi u procesu visokoškolske nastave Beograd, Viša škola, oktobar 1977.

Kovačević, Milivoj. "Pravni institut društvenog uticaja na delatnost visokoškolskih organizacija." *Univerzitet danas* 3-4 (1978).

Kozić, Petar. "Naučno-tehnološka revolucija, obrazovanje, socijalističko samoupravljanje." Simpozijum NTR, Novi Sad, 1980.

Kožul, Franjo. "Socijalni smisao obrazovanja i reforma univerziteta." *Univerzitet danas* 3-4 (1978).

Krajnc, Ana. "Položaj in vloga znanosti na univerzi." *Komunist* (S1.), 11-05-1979.

Letica, Slaven. "Reforma obrazovanja i politika zapošljavanja." *Ekonomska politika* 27-11-1978.

_____. "Zaposlenost u Jugoslaviji pokraj 1978. Godine." *Zapošljavanje i udruženi rad* 3-4 (1978).

Magazinović, Vojislav. "Prednosti i problemi ekspanzije visokog školstva u SR BiH." *Bilten Univerziteta u Sarajevu* 52 (1977).

Mandić, Ivan. "Teorijski pristup problemu zapošljavanja." *Privreda* 1 (1979).

Marinković, Josip. *Argumenti* (Rijeka) (1980).

Marjanović, Miloš. "Doktorske disertacije na Beogradskom Univerzitetu." Zbornik Matrice srpske za društvene nauke 63 (1977).

Marjanović, Slavko. "Student kao organizator sopstvenog rada - intelektualna obrada informacija." *Tehnika* 4 (1978).

Marković, Danilo. "Tito o ulozi nauke u izgradnji socijalističkog društva." *Marksističke teme* 2 (1977).

_____. "Značaj naučnoistraživačkog rada nastavnika visokih škola za osavremenjavanje visokoškolskog obrazovanja." *Univerzitet danas* 3-4 (1978).

Marković, Radosav. "Društveni dogovor u oblasti zapošljavanja i problemi njihove praktične primene." *Pravni život* 5 (1979).

Marksistički Centar Univerziteta. Savetovanje o dostignućima u savremenoj biologiji i medicini i njihovim društvenim implikacijama: marksizam u srednjem usmerenom obrazovanju i nastava marksizma na univerzitetu posle 1981. godine; društvo i razvoj gradova.

Marksizam u svetu, BIGZ, broj. 3 (mart 1974); broj. 1 (januar 1975); broj. 2 (februar 1977).

Matić, Filip. "Temeljna promena društveno-ekonomskog položaja vaspitanja i obrazovanja treba i mnogo truda i vremena, uz dobru društvenu akciju, obaveštenost i svestranu organizovanost." *Borba* 02-03-1979. (Razgovor sa saradnikom lista.)

Meadows, Dennis, and Lewis J. Perelman. "Granice rasta izazov visokom obrazovanju." *Bulletin Yugoslav Commission for UNESCO* br. 4 (1977).

Mijanović, Miloš. "Osnovne pretpostavke za dugoročno planiranje stručnih kadrova u organizacijama udruženog rada."

Mijatović, Jugoslav. "Elementi ciljne politike u zapošljavanju." *Poslovna politika* 12 (1977).

Milačić, Vladimir and Radomir Simić. "Slobodna razmena rada kao deo jedinstvenog dohodovnog sistema i prikaz nekih rešenja na mašinskom i rudarsko-geološkom fakultetu univerziteta u Beogradu." Beograd, Univerzitet.

Milanović, Vladimir. "Udruživanje rada ili najamni odnosi u sferi naučnih istraživanja." *Marksistička misao* 1 (1979).

Milinčević, Vaso. "Referat na konferenciji SK univerziteta o samoupravnom preobražaju visokog školstva."

―――――. "Uvodno izlaganje na savetovanju sa grupacijama fakulteta."

Milutinov, Milan. "Uvodno izlaganje sa sednice komisije skupštine SRS o reformi obrazovanja." 1979.

Mitić, Vojislav. "Reforma obrazovanja i vaspitanja u SR Srbiji" (dokumenti), Beograd, Republički sekretarijat za informacije, 1978.

Mladenović, Milorad. "Multidisciplinarni institut kao obrazovna institucija." Univerzitet danas 3-4 (1978).

Mladi istraživači Srbije. "Ideja - Akcija - Pokret - organizacija omladinskog naučnoistraživačkog stvaralaštva." Beograd, aprila 1979 (interni materijal).

Možina, Stane. "Nacrtovanje in izobrazevanje kadrov v združenem delu." Simpozijum NTR, Novi Sad, 1980.

Naše teme. Časopis za društvena pitanja, Zagreb, 1979, br. 1.

"Naučnoistraživački rad u privredi Beograda i saradnja privrednih i naučnoistraživačkih organizacija." Beograd, Privredna komora Beograda, novembar 1979.

"Neki osnovni pokazatelji o fakultetima i institutima udruženim u Univerzitet u Beogradu." Beograd, Univerzitet, August 1979.

Nenadović, Tomislav, and Predrag Radivojević. "Položaj i problemi daljeg razvoja instituta u oblasti prirodnih i tehničkih nauka." Beograd, Marksistički centar CK SK Srbije, marta 1978.

"Neposredni zadaci i osnovna opredeljenja o pravcima reforme visokoškolskog obrazovanja." Univerzitet u Beogradu, Univerzitet umetnosti u Beogradu, Zajednica viših škola SR Srbije, Gradski komitet SK Beograda, Univerzitetski komitet SK Beograda. Univerzitet danas 3-4 (1976),

Nikolić, Milenko. "Obrazovanje u uslovima zamene ljudskog rada mašinom." Simpozijum NTR, Novi Sad, 1980.

Nikolić, Miloš. "Teorijsko-metodološki problemi izučavanja osnova marksizma." Beograd, Marksistički centar CK SKS, oktobra, 1975.

Nikolić, M., M. Dimitrijević, M. Trkulja, M. Andrejević. "Položaj i mogućnosti naučnoistraživačkog rada na univerzitetu." Marksističke teme 3-4 (1978).

Novosti u vaspitanju i obrazovanju. Beograd, Republički zavod za unapređivanje vaspitanja i obrazovanja, Beograd, nov. 1977, br. 8, br. 9.

"O idejno-političkim pitanjima u vaspitno-obrazovnoj delatnosti." Sa uvodnim izlaganjima Milomira Petrovića, Mirka Mirkovića, Beograd, 1979.

Oreb, Milivoj. "Tito i nauka." Vojnoistorijski glasnik 2-3 (1977).

"Osnovne promene u srednjem usmerenom obrazovanju i vaspitanju." Beograd, Republički zavod za unapređivanje vaspitanja i obrazovanja, aprila 1978.

"Osnovno i usmereno obrazovanje radnika i zadaci sindikata." Beograd, Gradsko veće Saveza sindikata Beograda, Informacije br. 14, 1978.

Papers Presented at the "First International Seminar on Science and Technology in the Transformation of the World." Beograd, Univerzitet, 1979.

Papić, Žarko. "Problemi formiranja i razvoja naučnoistraživačkog podmlatka." Ideje 5 (1979).

―――――. "Samoupravno interesno organizovanje u nauci." Komunist 23-03-1979.

Pašić, Najdan. "Univerzitet i društvo." Univerzitet danas 1-2 (1976).

Pavičević, Branko. "Trenutak akademija." Ovdje 105 (1978).

Petrović, Milenko. "Naučna svest i stav rezerve." *Savremenost* 4-5 (1979).

Petrović, Vojislav. "Izlaganje na savetovanju grupacija prirodnomatematičkih i biotehničkih nauka."

Petrović, Zlatibor. "Izlaganje na savetovanju o glavnim pravcima reforme univerziteta." Beograd, januar 1979.

Pišćević, A. "Izlaganje na plenumu nastavno-naučnih veća beogradskog univerziteta."

Pjanić, Zoran. "Univerzitet nekad i sad." *Univerzitet danas* 9-10 (1969).

Pogačnik, Jože. "Nekaj iskušenj iz dela za visokoškolsko reformo." *Naši razgledi* 1 (1979).

"Polazne osnove samoupravnog sporazuma o osnovama i merilima sticanja dohotka visokoškolskih organizacija preko SIZ usmerenog obrazovanja." Beograd, Zajednica usmerenog obrazovanja za teritoriju Republike, 1979.

"Politika i rezultati upisa studenata u prvu godinu studija školske 1979/80." *Godine u Beogradu*. Beograd, Gradski komitet za obrazovanje i nauku, decembra 1979.

"Položaj studenata u upravljanju visokoškolskim organizacijama." Beograd, august 1978.

Popović, Dragutin. "Organizovana naučnoistraživačka delatnost fakulteta preduslov za viši nivo funkcije obrazovanja i usavršavanja visokoškolskih kadrova." *Univerzitet danas* 3-4 (1978).

"Postdiplomski studij iz marksizma na Univerzitetu u Beogradu, nacrt."

Potkonjak, Nikola. "Naučno-tehnološka revolucija i socijalističko samoupravljanje, osnove marksističke koncepcije radnog i politehničkog obrazovanja i vaspitanja." Simpozijum, NTR, Novi Sad, 1980.

"Predlog kadrova deficitarnih i suficitarnih zanimanja u 1978. godini po zajednicama." SR Srbija van socijalističkih autonomnih pokrajina, Beograd, Republička samoupravna interesna zajednica zapošljavanja, Sept. 1978.

"Predlog osnovnog programa istraživanja instituta za razvoj univerziteta" (Idejna skica istraživačkih projekata), (Načelno obrazloženje). Beograd, Univerzitet, 1979.

"Predlog zaključaka o zadacima saveza komunista u ostvarivanju opštenarodne odbrane i društvene samozaštite u visokom školstvu Beograda." V sednica Univerzitetske konferencije organizacije SK Beograda, Beograd, 9-01-1979.

"Pregled Mogućnosti zapošljavanja u periodu 1976-1980. god." Teritorija Republike van Pokrajina, Beograd, Republička zajednica za zapošljavanje, oktobar 1977.

"Preobražaj obrazovanja i vaspitanja." Beograd, 20, marta 1979.

"Problemi zapošljavanja kadrova sa visokom školskom spremom." Beograd, Republička zajednica za zapošljavanje, decembar, 1977.

"Program aktivnosti o sprovođenju zaključaka o nekim aktuelnim pitanjima kadrovske politike u privredi." Beograd, Privredna komora Srbije, novembar 1978.

Projekat. "Strategija permanentnog obrazovanja i sistema periodičnih inovacija znanja poslovnih kadrova u samoupravnoj privredi." Naša i inostrana iskustva, sveska II, Beograd, Zavod za ekonomske ekspertize, maj 1975.

Prpić, Katarina, and Slaven Letica. "Aktivna politika zapošljavanja u 1979. godini." *Zapošljavanje i udruženi rad* 4-6 (1978).

Rajković, Jugoslav. "Planiranje kadrova i prijem studenata - osnova saradnje univerziteta i srednjih škola." *Univerzitet danas* 3-4 (1973).

Rajković, J., and Z. Đuričić. "Činioci usmeravanja kandidata ka studijama." *Univerzitet danas* 3-4 (1973).

Ralić, Prvoslav. *Politika*, mart 1980.

"Reforma obrazovanja: Organizacija odgojno - obrazovnog procesa u završnom stupnju srednjeg obrazovanja." Zavod za prosvjetno-pedagošku službu SR Hrvatske, Zagreb, 1977.

"Reforma obrazovanja i vaspitanja u SR Srbiji." Beograd, Dokumenti i uputstva, Republički sekretarijat za obrazovanje i nauku i Republički zavod za unapređivanje vaspitanja i obrazovanja, 1978.

"Reforma obrazovanja i vaspitanja u SR Srbiji." Dokumenti - Beograd, Republički sekretarijat za informacije, 1978.

"Rezultati ankete o uslovima studiranja." Novi Sad, Univerzitet, 1977.

Ristanović, Slobodan. "Društvene nejednakosti i obrazovanje." Beograd, Republički zavod za unapređivanje vaspitanja i obrazovanja, 1979.

Rodin, Davor. "Reforma visokog školstva kao proces njegova odumiranja," *Univerzitet danas* 3-4 (1978).

Saopćenja (Zagreb) 13-15 (1979).

"Savetovanje o planiranju kadrova u obrazovanju." Beograd, Privredna komora Srbije, 1978.

"Savetovanje o planiranju razvoja obrazovanja i usavršavanja visokostručnih kadrova mašinske struke." Beograd, Mašinski fakultet u Beogradu, Kragujevcu i Nišu, Fakultet tehničkih nauka u Novom Sadu, Tehnički fakultet u Prištini, Privredna komora SR Srbije, Poslovna zajednica mašinogradnje i elektomašinogradnje, juli 1978.

Savić, Pavle. "Introductory Lecture at the International Seminar of the Universities of the United Nations and the University of Belgrade." *NIN*, October 1979.

———. "O stanju nauke u nas, mestu i ulozi Srpske akademije nauka i umetnosti." *Politika* 01-07-1978.

Seger, Berislav. "Neophodna je sprega politike i nauke," *Borba*, 03-07-1978. (intervju Tanjugu).

Šetinc, Franc. Jesmo li potrošačko društvo, Beograd, 1979.

Simić, Radomir. "Osvrt na interesovanje mladih za pojedine fakultete Univerziteta u Beogradu na osnovu upisa u školskoj 1979/80. godini."

"Sistem i pravci promena u obrazovanju i usavršavanju nastavnika u republikama i pokrajinama." Simpozijum Savremene koncepcije i perspektive obrazovanja nastavnika, Sombor, 1978.

Šolaja, Vladimir. "Materijalni i kadrovski uslovi naučnoistraživačkog rada," *Marksistička misao*, 1979, 1.

———. "Neka praktična gledanja na slobodnu razmenu rada u naučnoistraživačkim intervencijama za privredu," *Samoupravljanje*, 1979, 4.

Šoljan, Nikša Nikola. "Za jedinstvenu reformu obrazovanja," *Naše teme*, 1979, 1.

Stambolić, Ivan. Razgovor sa rektorskim kolegijumom u 1979.

Štambuk, Vladimir. "Naučno-tehnička revolucija i društvene promene."

Stanje i problemi naučnoistraživačkog rada u organizacijama udruženog rada u Srbiji."

"Stanje kadra u naučnoistraživačkim organizacijama, sa predlogom mera." Beograd,

Republička zajednica nauke, Republički sekretarijat za obrazovanje i nauku, Sept. 1979, AS br. 275.

Stanković, Bogoljub. "Ostvarivanje socijalističkog samoupravnog preobražaja univerzieteta u Novom Sadu." *Univerzitet danas* 1-2 (1979).

"Stavovi predsedništva saveza studenata Jugoslavije o reformi univerziteta." *Univerzitet danas* 1 (1969).

"Stenografske beleške sa savetovanja o planiranju kadrova i obrazovanja." Beograd, Privredna komora Srbije, mart 1978.

"Stenografske beleške sa savetovanja o reformi visokog obrazovanja i univerziteta." održanog u Beogradu 10-01-1979.

Stojadinović, Dragić. "Shvatanja klasika marksizma-lenjinizma o uticaju naučno-tehničkog progresa na zaposlenost." *Ekonomija* 3, (1979).

Stojanović, Vojislav. "Perspektive u razvoju visokoškolskog obrazovanja i nauke." *Univerzitet danas* 1-2 (1974).

Stošić, Tomislav. "Kibernetski pristup utvrđivanju promena u strukturi znanja." *Poslovna politika* 3 (1979).

Todorović, Maksim. "Izlaganje na savetovanju o grupacija prirodnomatematičkih i biotehničkih nauka."

_____. "Izlaganje na savetovanju sa grupacijama fakulteta."

_____. "Savetovanje sa dekanima po problematiči upisa."

Todorović, Mijalko. "O reformi univerziteta." *Socijalizam* 1 (1970).

Tomović, Rajko. "Kraj tehnološke ere." Communication presented at the symposium, "Socialism in the World."

Turza, Karel. "Diskusija o marksizmu." *Omladinske novine*, mart 1980.

Unković, Slobodan. "Izlaganje na savetovanju o glavnim pravcima reforme univerziteta."

_____. "Izlaganje na savetovanju sa grupacijama fakulteta."

Vlaškalić, Tihomir. "Slobodna razmena rada kao uslov i osnova društveno-ekonomskih odnosa u oblasti visokoškolskog obrazovanja."

Vranić, Dušan. "Zašto je bauk." *Borba*, 07-03-1980.

INDEX

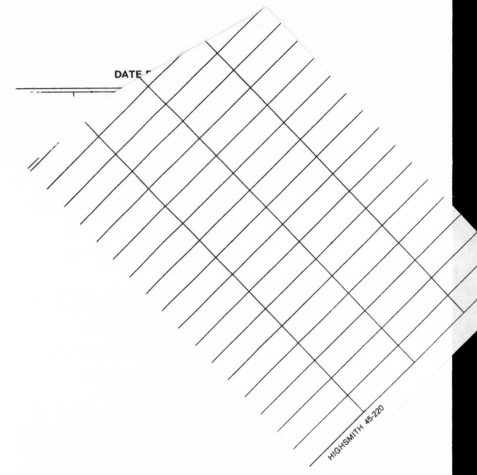

DATE

HIGHSMITH 45-220